"*11,000 Days at School* is an insightful, honest and fascinating must-read . . . especially for anyone who has gone to school, dreamed of school, dreaded school, worked at school, had kids, relatives or friends in school . . . basically all of us! Greer has captured the good and not-so-good times of everyday life in the public school system while wearing a multitude of "hats" over the years. Throughout the book, we are so very much reminded how life at school is simply a microcosm of what awaits outside the doors . . . and how it takes special people to prepare our future generations."

— Larry Hayes
Trustee, Burnaby Board of Education SD41
graduate of the Burnaby Public School System

"From 11,000 days spent in schools as a student, teacher and administrator, Hugh Greer gathers an assortment of anecdotes and vignettes guaranteed to entertain. With self-effacing humour developed early as a young class clown growing up in Burnaby, BC, Greer captures each moment with straightforward ease reminiscent of the late Stuart McLean. You don't have to be a teacher or even a vice-principal to appreciate what Greer brings to life. You just have to have spent time in school."

— Gary Little
Associate Superintendent (Retired), Vancouver School Board
author of *To Hell and Back*

"This story of [Greer's] journey from elementary school clown to respected secondary vice-principal is told with humour, compassion and the wisdom gleaned from those 11,000 days in the classroom. He shares a rare and compelling insight into the world of education, and his anecdotes often had me chuckling or laughing out loud, bringing back memories of my own journey through the Burnaby school system. This book reinforces my long-held view that teachers are the unsung heroes of our communities. Bravo, Mr. Greer!"

— Svend Robinson
former Member of Parliament (1979–2004)
J.S. Woodsworth Resident Scholar (2020–2021)
Simon Fraser University

From his early days as a child in the classroom to his later years as a vice-principal, Mr. Greer chronicles his time at various schools with memorable and amusing anecdotes. His self-deprecating humour and engaging storytelling style, not to mention his desire to upset his parents with his career choice, hooked me from the beginning. While many of the stories had me laughing out loud, others had a more sobering effect. Mr. Greer's 11,000 day journey through the school system highlights the real, meaningful and lasting difference teachers and other school staff can make in the lives of their students. Thank you, Mr. Greer!

— Manjeet K. Chana, LLB
former student of Hugh Greer

11,000 Days at School

11,000 DAYS
at School

**From Class Clown to
High School Vice-Principal**

Hugh Greer

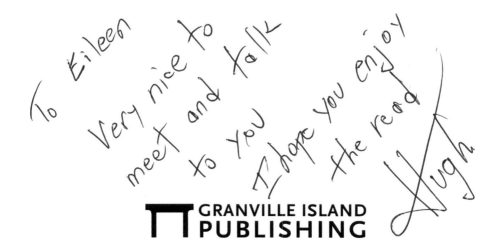

To Eileen
Very nice to
meet and talk
to you
I hope you enjoy
the read
Hugh

**GRANVILLE ISLAND
PUBLISHING**

ISBN: 978-1-989467-54-1 (paperback)
ISBN: 978-1-989467-55-8 (ebook)

Editor: Edward Zegarra
Copy editor: Marianne Ward
Designer: Paul DuVernet Mica Design
Cover Artist: Linda Jones

Granville Island Publishing Ltd.
105 – 1496 Cartwright St.
#14354, Granville Island
Vancouver, BC, V6H 3Y0
Tel: 604-688-0320
Toll free: 1-877-688-0320
jo@granvilleislandpublishing.com
www.granvilleislandpublishing.com

Printed in Canada

This book is dedicated to Jenson, Ivo and Monty, my three amazing grandsons. This is your grandpa, boys. Sorry about that.

Contents

Author's Note

Upsetting my parents was not the only reason I chose to become a teacher, but it was a significant contributing factor. For the first twelve years of my life, I was my parents' only offspring and was the recipient of all the anxiety that went with raising a child. I know it concerned them that I was average, or slightly below average, at most things. I was not a great athlete, nor did I display signs of academic aptitude. My social skills were less than refined. I think it worried them that they were raising a very ordinary child.

Our small, 950-square-foot home was located in a remote, secluded area in North Burnaby. The atmosphere inside was calm and peaceful most of the time. On one occasion I remember my mother and father having a heated conversation about the fact that all I ever seemed to want to do was kick, catch or throw a ball. My mother was concerned that my interests were too limited and thought it would be a good idea if I learned to play a musical instrument. I was not enthusiastic about this idea but felt relieved when I was asked what instrument I would like to learn. The truthful answer would have been "No instrument," but I knew my fate was cast, so I chose what I thought would be a 'cool' instrument and one that would impress my friends. The trumpet seemed to fit this bill and appeared easy to play. It only had three little buttons to worry about, and I had lots of hot air to blow into it.

A couple of weeks later, I returned home and was informed that my musical instrument was on the dining room table. I was confused when I saw the container my trumpet was in. It looked more like a suitcase than a trumpet case. My confusion turned to outrage when I opened the case to discover not my 'trumpet of coolness' but my new 'accordion of squareness', the least cool instrument a twelve-year-old boy could play. One hundred and twenty buttons of horror!

A subtle power struggle would exist between my parents and me throughout the rest of my childhood and continue well into my adulthood.

I grew up in a home where my parents spent most of their waking hours criticizing teachers. Most evenings at the dinner table, I would hear how useless and incompetent they were. I heard about how teachers couldn't spell and at the end of the day left their classrooms filthy and in disarray. I heard about how overpaid they were and how they had far too many holidays. The problem was that for many years, both my mom and my dad worked all day with teachers. Ironically, and in spite of their negative musings about them, many of my parents' closest friends were teachers, and when my mom and dad socialized with them it always seemed to be very pleasant. After years of working in close proximity with teachers, both my parents became quite jaded toward many of them.

I am sure my decision to become a teacher was not solely based on my desire to upset them, but also on some altruistic motivation about helping young people and making a difference. In elementary school I briefly toyed with the idea of becoming a teacher, but my decision was firmly forged shortly after I began my grade-eight year, when I decided that I wanted to have the same job as my physical education (PE) teacher. Who wouldn't? The guy ran around outside all day long in the sunshine and fresh air, playing games and having fun. And for this he got paid a lot of money and got two weeks off every Christmas and a week in the spring, plus two months off in the summer.

When I look back at my childhood and remember the times I was at odds with my parents, I realize it must have seemed like a great idea to tell them I was going to become 'one of them' just to upset them one more time.

Just to clarify, my dad was a great father. He patiently explained things to me, he took me to soccer games, where he constantly reminded me what a great player he had been in his day. He loved taking me fishing and showing me, with his arms as wide as he could stretch them, the size of the fish he had caught on his last fishing trip. His dad died when my dad was ten years old, and the evening of the funeral, my dad's mother told him that the family could no longer afford to have him continue at school and that she had arranged for him to begin full-time work, delivering meat on his bicycle in Burnaby Heights for Rocky the butcher. My father's one and only school was Gilmore Elementary. Dad thought he got credit for grade five, but he wasn't sure.

Knowing that most people were aware of the fact he did not have a great deal of formal education gave my father tremendous pride that he was able to provide as well as he did for our family. If I heard it once, I heard it a thousand times: "I didn't finish high school and I didn't go to university, and I turned out all right. What's the big deal about going to university?" For me, this became just one more reason why I wanted to go.

Most of his working life, my dad was a high school janitor with the Burnaby School District. As with most things associated with schools, his title changed over his career. He started as a cleaner, then a sweeper, then a janitor, then a custodian, for a while a foreman and finally, when he retired, a building engineer. He was never happier than when he was telling people that he made more money than half of "those university-educated teachers" at 'his' school. In his mind, it was 'his' school. He cleaned it, but he also organized and ran it. The students came and went, as did the teachers and administrators, but 'Big Jim' was the constant. He was never shy about expressing his opinion about how the teachers at 'his' school should do their job. He was equally outspoken about how the administrators should do theirs. One of his more memorable rants took place at dinner the day he had received a note from a teacher asking him to wire closed all the windows in the teacher's classroom because the students kept throwing things out of them. My dad was livid. "He wants me to wire the windows shut. The fire marshal would love that. How stupid can you be? Why doesn't he just do his job and control his students? It's not that hard." I realize he had a point, but his indignation was overwhelming.

I was also lucky to have the mother I had. She was supportive of me and worried herself sick about what would become of the only child she had for the twelve years before my sister was born. I often gave her cause for this. Unlike my father, she recognized the value of education and, even though there were times she thought it unlikely, hoped I would be the first person in our family to attend university. She was an intelligent woman, who, because of circumstances, did not have the opportunity to complete any post-secondary education after graduating from high school. A couple of things got in her way.

She served in the Second World War in the Women's Royal Canadian Naval Service (the Wrens) and shortly after had a baby, derailing her educational dreams. She would have done very well at university as she was a quick learner and excellent thinker. She was also an outstanding writer and had several of her pieces published, including a novel titled *The Girls of the King's Navy*, which documents her naval service during the war. I believe she was much smarter than many of the teachers and administrators she worked with as an elementary school secretary. I am sure she realized this as well, but it did not interfere with her work. At work she was professional and polite. At home, she, like my dad, could not believe how some of the teachers at 'her' school had completed a university education. "Their grammar is appalling. They can't spell the simplest words. How did they ever graduate from university?" In some ways this may have given her hope for me. If those 'dummies' could go to university, perhaps her own 'dummy' son could as well.

So, with all this negativity about teachers constantly spewing from my parents, and the constant struggle for power and control between us, what choice did I have but to become one? I was, after all, their first-born child, and it was my duty to drive them to delirium.

There were a few details I had to take care of before I was able to fulfill my dream, however. I needed to complete some education of my own before I would be allowed to instill education into others. My first hurdle was kindergarten, followed by a few much more difficult obstacles, like elementary, junior high and senior high school. The prospect of graduating from university was daunting, but if I was to fulfill my dream, these not-so-small hurdles would also have to be conquered.

The likelihood of completing all these requisites, minuscule; the result, priceless.

Preface

Are you kidding me? This can't be right. I counted again. Yes, over eleven thousand. I have spent over eleven thousand days of my life in a school. No matter how many times I counted, the numbers still added up to just over eleven thousand days that I have spent in some type of school setting. A year in kindergarten, twelve years of public school, five in university completing my undergraduate degree, the equivalent of two more years, which actually took six years of part-time study, to finish my master's degree and then a combined thirty-five years working as a high school teacher, counsellor and administrator. Yup, just over eleven thousand days.

In many ways, teaching is a unique career, but one particular aspect of it makes it very different from other careers. Everyone you talk to has an opinion about it, and most individuals believe they are an expert when it comes to teaching and running a school. This is because almost everyone has spent years in a classroom, and they think this entitles them to be a critic. Parents, family members, people who live close to a school, virtually everyone has an opinion.

You don't often find this attitude about other careers. I assume you have never heard a passenger on any flight you have ever taken say, "You know, I don't think the pilot is flying this plane properly."

This is because most of the passengers on the flight have never flown an airplane and have no idea how to do it.

When you are sitting at your table enjoying a steak dinner with friends, I doubt that anyone has said, "I'm thinking the farmer that raised this cow didn't know what they were doing." Most people have no idea how to properly feed and raise a cow to become a good steak dinner.

But almost all people have spent at least twelve years in school, many much more time than that, and as a result, believe they know exactly how things should be done. Everyone has an opinion and everyone is an expert. This adds a factor of difficulty to the job that most other careers don't have. It does not, however, take away from the fact that teaching is the most rewarding and enjoyable career imaginable.

I place a great value on the educational process and am proud of the education British Columbian students receive. I also appreciate the seriousness and difficulty that encompasses the art of teaching. The educational experiences provided to us by our teachers have helped mould us into the successful people we are today and have contributed enormously to the quality of life we now enjoy. However, after spending more than eleven thousand days at school, I have come to the conclusion that 'education' is much more than classroom teaching and classroom learning. It is a microcosm of life, with all the highs and lows and ups and downs that life delivers. During my eleven thousand days, I have witnessed inexplicable behaviour from students as well as adults. I have watched as the serious morphed into the bizarre. I have observed the most hilarious situations imaginable and have been devastated by the worst sadness and grief possible. This book is an account of some of the more memorable moments I witnessed during my more than eleven thousand days in school. You may recall your own school memories and how absurd, funny and/or difficult they were. We all have them, whether we have spent only a few years in school or several, but those with many more years as a member of a school staff will undoubtedly have the most.

It is difficult for me to label what I have written here. I suppose it could be called a memoir but perhaps more accurately be described as an autobiographical work of fiction. Given that some of the stories are over sixty years old, I cannot guarantee they are all 100 percent accurate. I may have filled in some of the details, but I believe this is forgivable under the guise of 'literary licence'. The recollections are as accurate as I can make them. Much of the detail in the early stories can be credited to my parents, who, for years and on multiple occasions, kept the stories alive by retelling them at family and social gatherings. This is an unfortunate, or perhaps in hindsight fortunate, by-product of having my parents in the building with me for nine out of ten of my first years in school.

None of the stories are meant in any way to offend or embarrass anyone, and if they do, I unreservedly and sincerely apologize.

Mark Twain is quoted as saying, "I never let my schooling interfere with my education." What a crock; I could not disagree more.

Part 1

The Student Years

Tinkerbell Cooperative Kindergarten

- 1 year -

Ellesmere United Church was built in 1930 and, in 1955, had a congregation of several hundred worshippers. Sunday services were held there, and it was where I attended Sunday school and memorized my catechism. It was also the location where my parents very occasionally worshipped and where I attended my first day of school, then called kindergarten. Today on this site, there are thirty-two strata townhomes, and there is no evidence of Ellesmere United Church or the Tinkerbell Cooperative Kindergarten (TCK). In 2007, the building was razed and the church relocated to the top of Burnaby Mountain, where it is now referred to as a 'loft church', whatever that is.

My mother was one of the founding parents of the kindergarten, and I was a member of its inaugural class. In 1955, kindergarten 'education' was not part of the public school system in British Columbia. A group of parents who lived in the Capitol Hill neighbourhood of North Burnaby decided there was a need for a kindergarten in the area, so they started a fundraising campaign and in one year raised $142. This, apparently, was enough money to begin a school. The TCK permanently closed its doors in 1968, but not before its students gained some lifelong memories and valuable learning experiences. My kindergarten education took place each morning, five days per week. My teacher, Mrs. Brown, was a kind-hearted, sweet, portly woman. At the time, she seemed about ninety years old to me, but as I journey toward that age myself, I imagine she was much younger. More likely she was in her mid-forties. She wore loose-fitting floral-print dresses and gave wonderful, comforting hugs. Best practice for teachers during my kindergarten year is not considered best practice now.

Storytime with Mrs. Brown at TCK c. 1955

My role as class clown began the first day I walked into my kindergarten class. I enjoyed nothing more than making my classmates laugh—a skill, or perhaps flaw, that stayed with me over the next sixty years.

The goal of kindergarten in 1955 was to support children with socializing, cooperating and following directions. There was no learning, just fun. Today, learning takes a different trajectory. My three-year-old grandson has just completed his first year of education at a Montessori preschool. He is able to recognize all his numbers, name his colours, and count to thirty. Last week he explained, in great detail, how the *Falcon 9* first-stage rocket boosters detach and then went on to inform me that after that, the second-stage engine ignition takes place. He also informed me that the *Falcon 9* was going to land at the International Space Station and asked me if I knew what that was. Congratulations, Jenson, on all your early learning. Big deal. I may not have learned all that much in kindergarten, but I bet I had a lot more fun than today's 'kindergarteners'.

The Sex Talk

In spite of the 'no learning' practice of the 1955 kindergarten classroom, I did manage to learn a great deal. One day, my friend Ricky took me aside and gave me a comprehensive lecture on 'the birds and the bees'. Ricky was a fountain of knowledge. I cannot imagine where he learned all this. It certainly was not from our teacher, and—assuming his home was similar to mine—it was not from either of his parents as this topic was the most taboo topic in most 1950s homes.

After school that day, as I walked home with my mother, I announced that I had learned where babies come from. In great detail, I shared with my mom all of my newfound knowledge, almost as if I didn't think she knew anything about the topic. She was very calm and did a wonderful job listening to me until I was done, and then I decided, rather than continuing to enrich her knowledge about sex, it would be more fun to watch *Howdy Doody* on TV. Her only response to my lecture was to calmly say, "I see."

Later in the afternoon, my dad was working on some project in our basement, and I had joined him, no doubt to provide him with moral support and some instruction. After losing interest, I decided it was time to go upstairs. As I reached the halfway point of the stairs, my father called out to me.

"I hear that today at school you learned from one of your friends where babies come from."

"Yes, I did."

"You think that when a woman wants a baby she goes to her doctor, and the doctor gives her a shot in the arm."

"That's right."

"And then a baby grows in her stomach. Have I got it right?"

"Yes."

"And when the baby is ready to be born, it comes out the mom's belly button. Have I got this right?"

"Yes."

"Well, that's not the way it happens. Now go upstairs and get ready for supper." It is a good thing that eventually I learned the 'how it's done' thing correctly, as for some years during my career, I taught this information to high school students. Thank goodness for the Boy Scouts of Canada and the opportunity they provided me to learn about these things from my friends during our camping trips.

The Butt Sliver

The students in my classroom, a.k.a. church hall, were blessed with a lovely miniature log cabin that, with great enthusiasm, we would regularly assemble and disassemble. One morning, after the cabin had been constructed and we were expected to be cooperatively playing 'mommies and daddies', I decided it would be much more fun for me, and much more entertaining for my classmates, if I climbed up to the peak of the cabin, straddled it and pretended to ride it like a horse. As with most of my creative attempts to entertain my classmates, my friends thought I was hilarious; my teacher, not so much. I am not sure that Mrs. Brown actually said anything to me, or if I correctly interpreted her glare, but clearly she communicated to me that I was to immediately dismount from my stallion and regain my position on the floor with the rest of my classmates.

The dismount proved to be more difficult than the mount, and as I slid down the cedar structure, which I referred to as my horse Silver (after all, this was 1955 and *The Lone Ranger* was very big on one of the two television stations our black-and-white TV could

5

receive), I felt a sharp pain in my right butt cheek. Unlike the perfect manoeuvre I imagined, stylishly dismounting from my leather saddle like the great Kemo Sabe himself, I managed to find the only protruding sliver in the cabin roof and embedded it firmly in my tender young backside. At the time, I was convinced the intrusion that had been thrust into me was the size of a two-by-four, but now, in my more mature years, I must admit it was more likely a rather small, insignificant sliver. However, at age five, it became the most traumatic event of my short, uneventful life, and I proceeded to wail like a racoon caught in a leghold trap.

A startled, fear-ridden Mrs. Brown arrived without haste and gave me one of her aforementioned comforting hugs. Of course, there was no first-aid-trained person on site as there is now mandated at each school, so the 'removal job' became the responsibility of poor Mrs. Brown. Without hesitation, off Mrs. B. and I went to locate the seldom used first aid kit. Then out of the kindergarten area we walked and into the church proper. We ventured into what seemed to this five-year-old a large, mysterious dark cavern of formality and foreboding. Mrs. Brown knew her responsibilities and escorted me to the very darkest, most private sanctum of the church, where only the great man himself, the church minister, was permitted.

With great skill and confidence, Mrs. Brown withdrew the necessary medical instruments from the first aid kit and pre-pared herself for my impending surgery. Needle in hand and mercurochrome, which, according to Google, is no longer sold in many countries because of its high mercury content, were awaiting introduction to my backside.

"Pull down your pants, Hughie."

Without hesitation, I dropped my trousers.

"And your underpants. Now bend over."

So there I stood, pants and undies at my ankles, with my naked butt sticking out in the remotest part of the church as a female teach-er examined my naked bottom. Today, well, let's just say, "not hap-pening." In 1955, it was nothing but a kind and innocent moment, until Mrs. Brown started to extricate the two-by-four from its place of embedment. The pain was unbearable, the screaming enough to awaken the dead. Finally, the torture ended and the Band-Aid was applied. I heard from behind me, "You were very brave, Hughie. Now let's go back to class."

Never again was this event spoken of. As I age, I am trying not to become one of those 'I hate change' people, but when I think back to this, the first but certainly not the last traumatic day of my eleven thousand in school, I lament how many things in schools have changed. No judgment, just a little sadness, that today the removal of a 'butt sliver' would require multiple copies of documentation, as well as a male witness and an explanation of how the situation was handled and, undoubtedly, parental notification. And if the situation was to be handled the same way today, perhaps criminal charges.

For me, it was much better to follow the 'never spoken of again' model. At the time, I felt like it was just another day at school, but I also did not want anyone other than Mrs. Brown to know what had taken place in the back of the church that day. What five-year-old wants their classmates, their mom and dad and probably a dozen or so friends and neighbours knowing that their teacher had seen their naked butt? The sliver may not have left a permanent scar, but the world knowing about this may very well have left a lifelong psychological scar.

After a year of half-day attendance at kindergarten and a significantly delayed academic and social skill set, without any ability whatsoever to read, write or count, I was, apparently, ready for 'real' school.

Capitol Hill Elementary School

- 6 years -

In 1956, Capitol Hill Elementary School was one of the largest elementary schools in the province. The year I entered grade one, it had a population of approximately 500 students. When I look at my grade-one class picture, one feature stands out. We all look the same. There are thirty-one of us, and there is not one student of colour. We are all white, we all look happy, well groomed and well fed. Of the 197 students pictured in my six Capitol Hill class photos, there is one Asian student and one South Asian student. Both are in my grade-five class. The other 195 are white. It saddens me that I never had the opportunity to spend time with classmates who had come from other cultures.

This was a time before the city of Burnaby, and the Lower Mainland of British Columbia generally, were 'discovered' and considered to be a safe and prosperous place to live. It was not until the decade following Expo '86 that Burnaby became well known overseas and began its growth into a multicultural community. I consider the homogeneity of my school at the time to be a gap in my childhood education. I am grateful that my own children were able to attend schools with students from many different cultural backgrounds, because it enriched them by providing them with an awareness of the cultural diversity of the world they inhabit.

I make another observation when I look at my grade-one photo. This observation dismays me a great deal. Of the seventeen boys in my grade-one class, I am the only one wearing a bow tie. Thanks, Mom!

Today, Capitol Hill registers approximately 375 students. Over half of them have English as their second language. The school offers a MACC (multi-age cluster class), a French immersion program and is home to one of the district's special education classes. In 1956, we were offered the one-size-fits-all education program. The take-it-or-leave-it philosophy of learning. The gifted students were restricted to working at an average pace and were not given the opportunity of an enriched education. Sadder than that, many of the special needs students were banished to their own segregated schools.

The Pencil

Similar to my kindergarten teacher, Mrs. Brown, my grade-one teacher, Mrs. Barwell, was kind and gentle. Every school day, she wore a skirt and blazer and was impeccably groomed. Mrs. Barwell was a bit younger than Mrs. Brown, and although she was kind, she was very stern. She was serious about our learning, and her classroom was humour-free. I credit her with helping to convince my parents that I was not stupid. Before entering grade one, I showed signs of limited ability. When I was much older, my mother shared with me how concerned my father was about me. In his usual tactful manner, he questioned my academic future by asking my mother one day, "What's wrong with that dummy?" Mrs. Barwell, on the other hand, was more into diagnosing my learning struggles and noticed that I couldn't see a thing she wrote on the chalkboard and suggested to my parents they take me for an eye examination. To my father's great relief, the optometrist diagnosed me with quite severe astigmatism. What a relief to us all when, after I began to wear my glasses, I began to answer the odd question from the board as a result of being able to see the words written there.

Grade-one class photo with author in the front row (second from the right) proudly wearing his bow tie

Mrs. Barwell often spoke to our class, with great pride, about her daughter. Miss Barwell was in her early twenties and had decided to follow in her mom's footsteps and become an elementary school teacher. At the time of my grade-one experience, she was just beginning her teacher education program at the University of British Columbia and, having completed several academic courses, was enthusiastic about some practical experience. After discussing the possibility with the school's principal, Mrs. Barwell and her daughter decided it would be acceptable for Miss Barwell to do some practice teaching with our class. As I recall, Miss Barwell was kind, young and pretty. All the attributes that a grade-one student thought desirable in a teacher. I decided she was suitable for a career in teaching. At age six, I was evaluating teachers.

During the first several classes that Miss Barwell 'taught', her mom worked alongside her—my first exposure to the team-teaching model. As time went by, mom gradually let daughter take more and more ownership of the lessons and sat in the back of the classroom as teachers do when they are observing a student teacher.

I assume after more time and more success, mom was confident that her daughter could handle our class without mom being in the room and decided to let daughter perform her magic, solo. As a result, one day after lunch, we returned to our classroom and found no trace of Mrs. Barwell. It was Miss Barwell's time to 'be a teacher'. It was 1957 and none of us were going to misbehave and risk being sent to the office or more frighteningly, having our parents informed that we had been rude to our teacher's daughter. Without a doubt, this was going to be a relaxing and confidence-building experience for Miss Barwell. That is, until Ronnie started fooling around and fell out of his desk and firmly inserted his pencil into his left hip.

Ronnie was my good friend. He was fun, kind and the biggest kid in grade one. At the time I thought he was some kind of giant, but in reality, he was probably slightly bigger than me and slightly bigger than the average grade-one male student.

It wasn't the first time I had seen someone fall out of their desk at school. It had happened a couple of other times when students poorly negotiated exiting their desk or too enthusiastically attempted to enter. It was, however, the first time I had seen a desk-clutching giant fall out of a desk.

At first, Ronnie just lay there, motionless. None of my classmates made a sound, except I seem to remember hearing a couple of giggles. We all just stared down at Ronnie and waited for him to regain his normal position of sitting in his desk. For the longest time, nothing. No movement. No sound. And then, this horrible, guttural moaning. It was terrible. Ronnie the giant was in agony.

What seemed a long time later, a startled Miss B. managed a very weak, "Ronnie, are you okay?"

I guess it was a reasonable thing to ask given the situation, but to be honest, every one of the thirty-one of us five- and six-year-olds knew Ronnie was not okay.

I had the best view in the room. There he was, lying right in front of me. What a lucky day for me. What a great story I was going to be able to tell my friends at recess, my soccer teammates at practice, my parents and especially my grandma, who picked me up every day after school and clung to my every word.

What happened next is a bit of a blur, but like some kind of magic, Mrs. Barwell appeared and told us all to stand up and move to the back of the room. Thirty of us, not Ronnie of course, obediently shuffled in silence to the back of the room and stared in horror. Our principal, Mr. James, arrived, which terrified us more than Ronnie's predicament. What I remember about the next several minutes is that not a single one of us uttered a word. The ambulance men arrived; there was no such thing as a paramedic or EMT in 1957. I heard a comment from one of the adults in the room about lead poisoning, and shortly after, it was decided not to remove the pencil from Ronnie's hip, but to leave it there until it could be safely removed at the hospital.

So Ronnie and his new friend HB were gently loaded onto a stretcher and removed from our classroom. Mrs. Barwell took back control of our room, and we never saw Miss Barwell again. After her traumatic introduction to teaching, I assumed that was that for her, and she would most likely decide teaching was not going to be her thing. However, years later my mother informed me that in spite of this most unnerving of days, Miss Barwell did complete her degree and teacher training requirements and became an elementary school teacher. Good for her. After a day like that, it would have been understandable if she had decided to choose a less traumatic career.

The Walrus

The fact that my mother was the head secretary at my elementary school was, in itself, not a problem. She was a nice lady. She was popular with the staff and the students, and I was happy to have her at school with me. My issue was her personal relationship with my teachers and how every other kid in the school got away with stuff I never did. My mother always knew the results of my tests before I did. She always knew what I had said or done in class. If my friends failed tests, talked too much or acted stupid, their mothers seldom knew. Admittedly, this problem could have been alleviated if I hadn't failed so many tests and talked too much and acted stupid on a regular basis. I had decided early in my educational career, actually in kindergarten, that I enjoyed being the class idiot. I guess this was my penance.

My modus operandi, which had begun in kindergarten, continued in elementary school as nothing made me happier than cracking up my classmates. It became, and remained for many years, my main goal in attending school. It was the number one reason that in twelve years of public school, I never once skipped a class. I never understood skipping school. It seemed the most boring of ideas. How can you make people laugh if all the people are at school and you're hiding in some bathroom or vacant lot? Just one of the many reasons I never skipped a class. Not because I was a 'suck-up' but because I didn't want to miss an opportunity to entertain my classmates. I also had no imagination about where I would go or what I would do if I did skip. Of course, another reason I never skipped a class in school was that I was not at all interested in being on the receiving end of my father's tirade if I had been caught, and I would most assuredly have been caught.

My TV heroes were Red Skelton, Jackie Gleason and, of course, the brilliant Three Stooges. I wanted to be just like them. Creative, brilliant and, most of all, popular. What better stage for me than an elementary classroom with thirty-five or so captive members of an audience thirsting for my groundbreaking, intelligent humour. Even Miss Welcher, my grade-three teacher, thought I was witty and amusing. Or so I thought. What I failed to realize was that every one of my little pranks and witticisms was being reported each lunch hour, not only to my mother, but to every other teacher who happened to be in the staff room at the time.

My mother was very selective about sharing the information she received about me. She often kept it to herself because, I believe, she was nervous about how my father would react to some of my good-natured classroom entertainment. Every so often my creativity was too good for her to ignore, however. For instance, did you know that if you carefully insert a pencil up each nostril, stick out your front teeth and clap your hands in front of you, you will look exactly like a walrus? I do. And this is what I did during our lesson on walruses. I sure was one clever and imaginative kid. Best of all, Miss Welcher was so impressed, she called up to the office and invited my mother to come to our classroom and take a look.

I have no idea how long she was looking through the window of the door to our classroom, but eventually I saw her. Her face did not reveal anger, just sadness. I believe her face was saying, "There are thirty-five grade-three students in that class. Why does it have to be my son, my only child, who is playing the idiot clown?"

At dinner that evening my father started the conversation with, "I understand you do a really good walrus imitation." Of course, I agreed with him and asked him if he would like to see it.

"I sure the bloody hell don't want to see it. And neither does Miss Welcher!" I was so confused. I was sure that when I had the pencils up my nose and was doing my walrus imitation, I looked exactly like a walrus. How could he not want to see it? How could Miss Welcher not appreciate it? It was brilliant.

In fairness to my father, it was not only these reports from my mother, via my teachers, that upset him. My term report card comments were often not flattering and frequently upset him.

From my grade-two, third-term report card: "He has difficulty with his writing and art due to lack of co-ordination of his fingers."

From my grade-three, first-term report card: "His enthusiastic manner often leads to mischievous behaviour." Sorry, Dad.

As was explained to me during dinner, after dinner, before bed that night, again in the morning before I departed for another day of school and multiple times after that, it was not okay for me to entertain my classmates during lessons. Apparently, entertaining my friends was restricted to outside of school time. Yeah, right. Good

> REMARKS*
>
> **Third Report:** *Hughie is making a special effort to complete his work. He has difficulty with his writing and art due to lack of co-ordination of his fingers.*
>
> **Fourth Report:** *I wish you success in grade three, Hughie.*

Grade-two report card comment indicating my lack of coordination and 'predicting' my future as a PE teacher

luck with that, Dad. I had found something I was good at, and I was determined to keep it going, to expand my repertoire and be the best class clown I could be. A lofty goal that I worked to perfect for my remaining eight years in public school and, perhaps more than I should have, during my teaching career.

The Death

As I look back upon my years in elementary school, I have no memory of there being any counselling support for students. I believe that is because there was none. There certainly was no support for students who experienced a sudden death, either in their family or at school. Trauma teams and emotional support services were unheard of.

My first memory of being exposed to a sudden death happened during my grade-five year. One Monday morning, we were informed by our teacher, Mrs. Alder, that over the weekend, the brother of one of our classmates had been hit by a train and had died. We were told to act as if nothing had happened and everything was normal. We were instructed not to discuss this incident with our classmate and in essence pretend it hadn't happened. What made the death of her brother even more devastating was that she had actually

15

been with him at the time of his death and had witnessed the entire tragedy. I am sure this was the worst experience in my classmate's life, and it may still be, to this day, the worst experience she has ever endured, but it was also horrible for us in the class. Our classroom teacher was a kind and caring person but had no training in how to support a class of grieving and confused ten-year-olds. We were left on our own to figure out how to deal with the emotions this event caused us. For many of us, this was our first exposure to death. We had no idea what we should do. Look at our classmate or don't look at her? Talk to her or ignore her? The weeks that followed were horrible, but somehow, we got through them. This was not at all an appropriate or empathic way to handle what for many of us was our first exposure to death.

Today, when a school experiences a traumatic event such as a sudden death, students are fortunate to have a great deal of support available to them. There are formal and written procedures for the school to follow, and through these protocols, students receive the guidance and compassion they require and deserve. Every district has a crisis response team on standby, and every school has a school-based crisis team in place to support the school's staff and students at a moment's notice. If teachers are comfortable, they are asked to inform their students and share the details of what has taken place. Students are given the details of the death and to whom it has happened. A letter is prepared with the details of the incident and is sent home with students at the end of the day. The school offers counselling support and makes available a grief support room somewhere in the school. This is very much a student-centred approach. Unfortunately, during my career, I was exposed to far too many incidents involving trauma to students and staff. For a number of years, I chaired my school's internal crisis team. It amazes me how, over what I consider to be a very few years, the philosophy of what is best practice after a traumatic event has so greatly evolved. The 'good old days' were not always so good.

The First Kiss

Most boys gradually grow into being interested in girls, while some experience an epiphany. Halfway through grade five, I had my epiphany. At the time, I don't remember thinking anything particular about the girls I knew. I was friends with several of them in my neighbourhood, and we played together the same way I played with the boys. At school, I realized that every girl I knew was smarter than me, but so were all of the boys. For sure, in grade five, I didn't have any of 'those' feelings for girls. That is, until one of them gave me my first kiss.

I think my grade-five teacher, Mrs. Tucker, must have sensed something was going on between Claudia and me. As with my entire life up to this point, most people seemed to know what was going on around me except me. Claudia sat in the seat directly across the aisle from mine. Her mom and my mom were good friends. I talked to Claudia like I talked to all my other classmates, meaning I made jokes and said stupid things. There was nothing particularly special about her, she was just one of the kids in my class. And then one day she got sick, and her mom asked the school to send some work home for her to do while she got well.

I noticed she had been absent for a few days, but I didn't care. Then one day after school, Mrs. Tucker handed me a bag of books and papers and asked me to deliver them to Claudia's house. Because it was a tight-knit community, I knew where she lived, and because it was 1960 and people my age never argued with adults, I said, "Sure."

Of course, the load was not great, as all I had to carry were Claudia's books. It's not like I would ever take any of my own home. I walked to her house with another friend, who continued on his way to his home, and solo, I ventured up the sidewalk to Claudia's front door. I rang the doorbell and the door immediately opened. Clue number one that I missed: Claudia's mom was not surprised to see me. Perhaps I should have recognized the set-up then, but I didn't. Just like I didn't recognize much at that age, or at ages much later than that.

"Hello, Hughie. It's nice to see you. Are you here to see Claudia?"

"No, I'm here to give her this bag." Very smooth, Romeo.

"Wait here and I'll go get her."

My first reaction to this instruction was to say to myself, "Run for your life. She might give you some of her germs," but again, it was 1960, and like every other kid, I did as I was instructed to do by adults.

A few seconds later, Claudia appeared. I was confused. Whenever I didn't feel well, my standard mode of dress was pajamas, dressing gown and slippers. Claudia was in a flower-patterned dress and looked like she was ready to go out somewhere fancy. I was quite certain later that I had been set up, but at the time, I missed that clue as well.

In my suave and charming manner, I stuck the bag out and said, "Here."

"Oh, Hughie, it is so nice of you to bring this to me," Claudia said, and before I could muster a single micro-reflex, she leaned over and kissed my cheek.

I stood in a state of catatonic confusion. This reaction of mine to being startled began at that very moment and would haunt me for the next sixty years of my life.

With great poise, Claudia backed up and slipped away behind her front door. It felt like I stood there for hours, but in reality, I probably left right away to escape my fog of confusion.

I don't remember much about the events of the rest of that day, but one thing is for sure—I never mentioned what happened to my parents. I am pretty sure my mother knew exactly what took place, and it is highly likely my father found out too. Come to think of it, I'd be surprised if Mrs. Tucker wasn't in on it from the beginning. Having my mother work at the school was beginning to get annoying.

The Patrol Boy

During my grade-six year, there was an opportunity for me to apply to become one of the revered 'patrol boys' at Capitol Hill School. In England they are called 'lollipop ladies' (or lollipop men) because the signs they hold out to stop traffic and allow students to safely cross the road remind people of a giant lollipop. Today in the Lower Mainland, many of these car stoppers are either paid adults or student volunteers, and their position is referred to as a 'crossing guard'. The adults are posted on a busy road that leads to the school, and the students are stationed closer to the school on a much quieter road.

Capitol Hill Elementary School is located at the corner of Hastings Street and Holdom Avenue in North Burnaby. During my grade-six year, Hastings Street was two lanes wide and not very busy, and Holdom Avenue was used for local traffic only. The corner had no traffic lights and was controlled by a stop sign for the Holdom traffic.

The Capitol Hill Elementary patrol boys held a lofty status of widespread esteem. In 1961, this was a gendered position due to sexist beliefs. They were charged with stopping the traffic on Hastings and ensuring that students crossed safely to the other side. Patrol boys were subjected to a rigorous selection process, and only the most mature, trustworthy and focused were selected, unless one's mom was the secretary at the school.

We were on duty before and after school and so were allowed to arrive to class late in the mornings and leave class early in the afternoons. It was hard not to let the status go to my head.

My patrol boy uniform was the third uniform I had ever worn. I looked sharp in my Cub Scouts uniform and was proud to wear my soccer uniform, but the only uniform my classmates ever saw me wear was my patrol boy uniform, and that was status. I loved being a patrol boy. However, looking back it scares the hell out of me to think about the risk involved, and I'm glad to know that sixth graders are no longer placed in such danger within the school districts.

I may have been the most unfocused and scatterbrained boy attending Capitol Hill Elementary. I never paid attention to anything. My mind wandered continuously, and yet I was the guy put in charge of stopping cars, trucks and buses that rolled down Hastings Street to make sure my classmates crossed the road safely. What were the teachers thinking? In grade six, I wasn't safe crossing the street by myself, never mind being in charge of the safety of others as they crossed. I actually don't remember a single event from my year as a patrol boy, except the afternoon we got off school early to go see a movie at the theatre.

The reward for our year of hard work being patrol boys and, most importantly, not getting anyone killed or maimed, was the privilege of attending the year-end movie. The bus rolled up at lunchtime, and in front of the entire school, we patrol boys were loaded on for an afternoon of fun. I must have stuck out like the proverbial sore thumb. A bus full of mature, responsible grade sixes and sevens, and then me. I am sure my classmates watched in confusion and wondered how this oversight could have happened.

Seaforth Elementary School

– 1 year –

Both sadly and happily, the last year of my elementary education and the last year of my class-clown career in elementary school was destined not to be at Capitol Hill—sadly, because I would never see most of my close friends again or have the opportunity to get a second kiss from Claudia (my epiphany had become permanent); happily, because my mother was not the secretary at my new school. My parents had bought a piece of property in the faraway outskirts of North Burnaby on Government Road. I was to complete my elementary education at Seaforth Elementary School.

It puzzles me when I encounter parents' concern about the psychological damage their children may experience when the family moves and their children change schools. The truth is that parents think it is a much bigger deal than do their children. After six cozy years of attending the same school with the same group of friends, I didn't skip a beat settling into my new school. And this despite the two schools being as different as two schools could be. Capitol Hill was one of the largest elementary schools in the province. By contrast, my new school, Seaforth Elementary, was one of the smallest elementary schools in the province. It contained seven grade levels and a total of only six classrooms.

The original Seaforth School opened in 1922 as a one-room school and in its first year registered twenty students. Today, the original building can be visited at the Burnaby Village Museum. When I began my grade-seven year, the old school was still located on the Government Road site and was home to a district special education program. The school's most notable alumnus is Canadian crooner Michael Bublé, who recently built a home directly across the street from the school.

The Freedom

The absolute best thing about my new school was that my mother didn't work there. For the first time in six years, I was free. No mom peering through the window of my classroom door, no teachers reporting to my mom on a daily basis about my little indiscretions. This was my first taste of freedom. I was finally on an equal footing with my classmates.

There was no follow-up discussion at home when I forgot to bring my recorder to school for the umpteenth time and was paddled on the backside with a yardstick for it by my music teacher. When I failed my arithmetic test, there was no yelling and sitting at the kitchen table staring blankly at the textbook I obviously didn't understand. When I didn't complete my homework, I didn't get grounded. It was bliss. I was on easy street, that is, until November when I received my first-term report card.

My mom and dad were not impressed with the C- in reading and the C- in science. They were less impressed with the Ds in social studies and arithmetic. I clearly remember them not being happy with the X in work habits. I momentarily considered explaining to them that the X was short for 'excellent', but on my report card, directly above the work habits mark, was a written explanation: G – Superior; N – Satisfactory; X – Improvement needed. I really didn't understand the fuss; I got a G in PE. Who needs socials and arithmetic when their career plan is to become a PE teacher or a professional athlete?

Perhaps this new 'freedom' thing was not as liberating as I had thought it would be. Perhaps I was not ready to be unsupervised quite yet.

The Man-Child

One afternoon, soon after I began my year at Seaforth and just after lunch, there was a knock on our classroom door. There was a muffled conversation between our teacher and another adult. Our teacher closed the door and stood before us. "I need three boys to help out down at the old school." Terrific, I thought, here is my first opportunity to show school leadership. Up went my hand. "Hugh, James and Warren, go down and help out." Most elementary students wait for their grade-seven year for the opportunity to be the 'big ones on campus'. The honour was overwhelming.

A few seconds later, we reached the mysterious, never-spoken-of building that occupied the southeast corner of our school property. My classmates and I had never discussed the old building, and I had never given any thought to what it was. We were met by an adult, whom we assumed to be a teacher, and he thanked us for helping out. All three of us were ready to prove ourselves as competent leaders and prove to our teacher he had chosen well.

"One of our students is refusing to come back to class after lunch. I need you to grab him and bring him back in."

It was 1962 and none of us was going to question him about this being a good or not-good idea. We were all polite and wanting to please. I glanced at James and Warren and could tell they were thinking the same thing I was: You need three of us to bring him back?

The teacher pointed to a large maple tree across the street from the school and identified our prey. "His name is Will, and he is very nice." He might have been nice, but he was also enormous and looked to be about twenty-five years old. We then realized why it was going to take three of us to capture and return him. Obediently but nervously, off we went. We were accustomed to playing tackle

23

football, except after our tackles we always let go of our victim, huddled up and started over again. We knew this was not going to be one of our usual sportsmanlike tackles. Our mission was clearly explained to us. We were instructed to cross the street, grab hold of him, pick him up and carry him back to his classroom.

As we approached, Will did not move a muscle. He did not look at us and he made no attempt to flee. As per our instructions, we pounced on him, lifted and carried him back to his classroom. It was a struggle, but we persevered and the largest and oldest student in all of the Burnaby elementary school system, possibly even including the high school system as well, was safely returned. The three of us must have looked a sight when we returned to our own classroom, as I remember our classmates staring at us with wonderment until the end of the school day when we all had the opportunity to relay, and obviously exaggerate, the story of 'the return of the man-child'. It occurs to me now how lucky we were that as we lugged this giant hulk of a student across Government Road, an RCMP cruiser did not drive by. The optics would not have been good. Most assuredly, this is not something that students would be asked to do today.

It is not that unusual for a special needs student to arbitrarily decide they don't want to return to class after a break. I have observed this behaviour on a number of occasions. I was involved in one such event during my tenure at Sir Winston Churchill Secondary when one of our special education students climbed to the top of a large evergreen tree and decided he preferred his perch to his classroom desk. When he finally decided to return to terra firma, I was there to welcome him back to Earth. When I asked him why he had decided it was better to spend period three atop a giant fir tree rather than in his English class, I was convinced he really didn't have any idea. Sometimes, 'don't ask, don't tell' is a viable strategy.

The Carousel

The relationships students develop at school frequently extend outside the walls of the school building. In my ceaseless effort to make friends, I would do my best to entertain my classmates while in the classroom, but on a few occasions the opportunity arose to extend the entertainment to new and different environments. Seaforth School was, and still is, located two blocks south of the CHAN-TV studio, which first broadcast on Halloween afternoon in 1960 and is now home to Global TV. In 1963, this facility was home to *The Six O'Clock News* with Cameron Bell. It was also home to the hit television shows *All-Star Wrestling*, *The Trading Post* and the beloved *Children's Carousel*.

The *Carousel* was a thirty-minute kids' entertainment show that was broadcast live Monday to Friday from three-thirty to four o'clock. There were games, cartoons, contests and, best of all, free Orange Crush pop and Old Dutch potato chips for the children in attendance. A group of my grade-seven friends discovered that the Friday show was taped and rebroadcast on Sunday afternoons. To be honest, the target audience for this show was a little younger than we were at the time. Most of the kids were driven to the studio by their moms, who sat with them. However, my grade-seven classmates and I discovered that anybody could open the unlocked front door, walk across the foyer and proceed into the studio. At the time, there was very little traffic along this stretch of Lougheed Highway, so our safety-conscious parents were happy to give us permission to jaywalk across the Lougheed to watch the live broadcast of the Friday show and the filming of the Sunday rebroadcast.

Our visit to the *Children's Carousel* became a Friday ritual. Depending on our availability, anywhere from eight to twelve of our Seaforth grade-seven group would head out from school, dash across the Lougheed, clamber up the grassy hill and enjoy the hilarity of the *Carousel*. Oh yes, and stuff ourselves silly with Orange Crush pop and Old Dutch chips. In 1963, there were no selfies or electronic devices that would enable us to view our friends or ourselves on some screen, and no one we knew had ever been on TV, so watching ourselves on the rebroadcast the following Sunday was a big deal. We were practically famous.

The 'guess the cartoon character' segment of the show was the most popular time during the half hour. Hidden behind a four-by-eight-foot piece of plywood was an easily recognized cartoon figure. The sheet of plywood had been cut into twenty-five jigsaw puzzle pieces, each with a number printed on from one to twenty-five. For each game, a monitor was chosen whose job it was to remove the numbered piece after a member of the audience chose it. The audience member could then guess who was under the puzzle. If a contestant guessed correctly, they won a fabulous, no-expense-spared prize, like a glue-it-yourself rocket ship or race car. On one particular Friday afternoon, my classmate and next-door neighbour Diane was chosen as the 'guess the cartoon character' monitor. During the set-up of the puzzle, the show went to commercial break. Without any malice or intent whatsoever, Diane happened to wander behind the puzzle board and noticed that stuck to the frame of the puzzle was a piece of masking tape that had the words *Porky Pig* printed on it in block capital letters. Diane ran over to our group and whispered, "It's Porky Pig, it's Porky Pig," and returned to her position as puzzle monitor.

At the conclusion of the commercial break, the host, Mr. Ron, began the game. Mr. Ron did not particularly like our group. We were polite enough and were never rude or disrespectful, but during our numerous Friday visits to the show, he had made it clear to us that he thought we were a little too old to be attending his kiddies' show and often ignored us and occasionally directed sarcastic remarks at us. I believe he much preferred announcing *All-Star Wrestling*, which was one of the other shows he hosted. He had much more fun hanging out with Canada's greatest athlete, Gene Kiniski, and the 601-pound Haystacks Calhoun than he did hanging out with our smart-aleck grade-seven group. We did not care much for him either, but we tolerated him because of the pop and chips.

As a bit of a dig, Mr. Ron would often begin the puzzle game by asking one of the members of our group to be first to select a number, knowing full well that after only one puzzle piece was removed, you didn't have a snowball's chance of correctly guessing the hidden character. On this particular day, he asked my classmate Paul to select the first number. Uncle Ron picked the wrong guy. Of all of our group, Paul was the one with the most attitude, and he saw this as a chance to get even with Mr. Ron. The happy host looked at Paul and said, "Would you like to pick the first number?" Paul stared at Mr. Ron, hesitated, shrugged his shoulders and said, "Number one."

Mr. Ron was stunned. No one in their right mind ever picked number one. It was a useless number. It was the number of the piece in the upper left corner of the puzzle and always had nothing but blue sky under it. Everyone knew this.

Mr. Ron could not resist a tiny snicker before replying, "Are you sure? Number one usually doesn't give you much information."

"I'm sure," Paul smugly replied.

"Okay, if that's what you want, that's what we'll give you. Diane, please remove puzzle piece number one." And, sure enough, under puzzle piece number one was nothing but blue sky.

Mr. Ron could not resist a chuckle. "Not much to go on there, but you're allowed to make a guess. Who do you think our mystery cartoon character might be?"

Paul made the most of his on-screen opportunity. Like a trained comedic actor, he bided his time. I believe this is called a pregnant pause. He then leaned in for the kill. Enunciating slowly and confidently, he answered, "Porky Pig."

I didn't like him much, but at that moment I truly felt sorry for Mr. Ron. He was lost, bewildered and totally speechless. The segment was supposed to last several minutes, but this one had lasted a mere second. You could see the confusion on his face. "How is this possible?" radiated from his entire being. I believe he wanted to say something like, "How the hell did you do that?" or "You must have cheated." But it was live TV, and frank honesty is a difficult policy

The safe set of stairs from Seaforth to Global TV; in 1962, a slippery
and treacherous path to CHAN-TV

to maintain in that medium, so he sputtered something about Paul being lucky. I remember the word 'congratulations', and then Paul was holding his prize, a model jet plane. A man who was standing on the studio floor wearing a set of headphones and holding a clipboard then loudly said something about another commercial, and Mr. Ron, grinning from ear to ear, looked directly into the camera as if he had never had so much fun and said, "Well, boys and girls, it's time for another commercial!" The little red light on top of the camera turned off, and so did Mr. Ron, presumably to recover and compose himself for what was left of his joyful kids' show.

We continued to visit the CHAN-TV studio on Fridays until we completed grade seven and graduated from elementary school. We stuffed ourselves with pop and chips and won many prizes for the way we skilfully and, most of the time, honestly played the games and contests. On one fortuitous Friday, I was selected to play the watering can game. I was fitted with boots, a raincoat and an oversized sou'wester fishing hat and placed under a can filled with water. If I answered the questions correctly, I would be rewarded with a wonderful prize. If I answered incorrectly, I would get dowsed with water. Just as the game was about to begin, one of my classmates yelled out to Mr. Ron, "He can wiggle his ears. Ask him to wiggle his ears."

Mr. Ron leaned in and asked, "Can you really wiggle your ears?"

Proudly I replied, "Yes."

"Show me."

Sure enough, despite failing social studies and arithmetic, I was a master at wiggling my ears.

At the beginning of the next segment of the *Carousel*, and just before I answered the question incorrectly and was soaked with water, Mr. Ron made an enormous deal about the fact that I could wiggle my ears. The gigantic camera moved right into my face, and there I was on live television about to show the world my greatest, and perhaps only, talent.

I did not disappoint. I performed one of my best wiggles. It was glorious. But my glory came to a crashing halt that Sunday. Up to this point my parents didn't care as much as I thought they should about my career possibilities in entertainment, but that Sunday, for some inexplicable reason, they decided it might be fun to join me and watch the *Carousel*. To their horror they witnessed, along with who knows how many of their friends and family, their son dressed like a Newfoundland fisherman (now fisher) wiggling his ears—and on television, no less. I'm sure this was one of many times I made my parents not so proud. Sorry, Mom and Dad.

The Soccer Superstar

After attending Capitol Hill, where I had been an average athlete in a huge school, I came to the conclusion that I was destined to be the greatest athlete in my new six-room school. In my mind, this had to be the case even though my analysis of this situation was formed after only one week at the school and before tryouts for any school team. I had managed to make a couple of teams at one of the largest elementary schools in the province, and I had actually been subbed in a couple of times with a minute or two left in the game. It was obvious: I was destined to become Seaforth's finest male athlete, better than the other nine grade-seven boys attending the school. More importantly, I was going to be the school's finest player in my sport of passion. I was sure to be the Pelé and the Bobby Charlton of Seaforth Elementary School.

Adding to my confidence, I made the Seaforth Senior Boys soccer team. Making the team was not a challenge. Thirteen grade-six and -seven boys tried out. Thirteen made the team. During our one tryout, I was too busy concentrating on my own amazing skills to notice the skills of any of the other players. I was, for the first time, a first-team player on my school's soccer team. The ecstasy was overwhelming. My world was perfect.

My perfect world did not, however, last long. During our second practice I noticed that one of the other players, one of my new friends, was pretty good at the 'beautiful game'. As a matter of fact, he was very good. I had mixed feelings about this. On the one hand, in the short period of time I had known him, I really quite liked him. He was a really good guy. On the other hand, how dare he steal my glory? Could it be that I was not going to be the best player on the team? Was it possible that he was actually a better soccer player than me? The thought was devastating.

As it turned out, he was quite a bit better than me. During the soccer season, we won every game. He scored every goal. I believe he scored a hat trick, or more, in every game we played. I also recall he scored nine goals, which would be three hat tricks, in one single game.

This future member of the Canadian Soccer Hall of Fame would go on to graduate with me from Seaforth, and we would attend junior high school together. I would get to know him very well and would marvel at the journey that would lead him to soccer stardom.

Cariboo Hill Junior High School

– 3 years –

Our Seaforth group graduated from grade seven and entered the 'big time' of junior high school. In 1963, the Burnaby School District had three senior high schools that registered students in grades eleven and twelve, and five junior high schools that registered students in grades eight, nine and ten. Cariboo Hill Junior High School was only in its second year of operation when I began my grade-eight year. My freedom from parental scrutiny only lasted one year, as my father was the head janitor at my new school. Unfortunately for me, he had the same friendly relationship with the teachers at my new school that my mother had at my elementary school. It was going to take more than one year of freedom for me to be happy with this massive regression of my school independence. The 'getting ratted out' experience I had suffered for six years in elementary school was about to rear its ugly head once again.

On the first day of my junior high education, Cariboo had an enrollment of about 360 students. In the minds of our Seaforth graduating class of 1963, Cariboo was a massive school. Today Cariboo Hill enrolls about 645 students, and, as with all secondary schools in the district, enrolls grades eight to twelve. Notable Cariboo

Hill alumni are world-renowned singer, songwriter and record producer Michael Bublé (recipient of the Order of Canada [OC] and Order of British Columbia [OBC]) and Reid Anderson, former artistic director of the National Ballet of Canada and former artistic director of the Stuttgart Ballet. Glen Anderson, who played sixteen seasons in the NHL and is a member of the Canadian Hockey Hall of Fame, is also a Cariboo grad.

Students from six different elementary feeder schools attended Cariboo. For some students this was an opportunity to develop new friendships. For others, it was a threat to their professional athletic ambitions. I am embarrassed to say I was in the second category.

The Awakening

During my thirteen years of public-school education, I got to know hundreds of my classmates. Only a few have left a lasting impression on me. One such former classmate is 'hat-trick boy'.

During the second week of school, there was an announcement in the daily bulletin advertising tryouts for the school's three boys' soccer teams. (At this time, schools did not register girls' soccer teams. Girls played grass hockey, which is now called field hockey because the 'grass' in grass hockey could be misconstrued and the game called 'pot hockey' or 'dope hockey' or one of several other drug-related names.) The grade-eight boys were invited to try out for the bantam team, the grade nines for the junior team and the grade tens for the senior team. Six of us from the Seaforth team decided to give it a crack and try out.

Unlike the Seaforth tryouts from the previous year, these tryouts were for real. It was possible that not all the boys trying out would make the team. There would be cuts. There would be three tryout practices, of which fifteen boys would be selected to play on the team. The morning after the third practice, a list of team members would be posted in the boys' changing room. I assumed I had joined the 'big time' and I felt certain I was partaking in the identical process that players who tried out for my much beloved Manchester United squad had participated in.

The three tryouts came and went, and I felt like I had as good a chance as any to make the team. The morning after the third tryout, as our bus arrived at the school and came to an almost but not quite complete stop, a number of us stormed off the bus and sprinted into the boys' changing room. As promised, the list was posted. Blind to any other name on the list but my own, I searched frantically for 'H. Greer'. The list was in alphabetical order, and fourth from the top was the only name I cared about. I had made the Cariboo Hill bantam boys' soccer team. A rush of pride overwhelmed me, and then, after taking a few deep breaths and calming my ego, I became modestly interested in who else would be joining me in this illustrious group.

of the six of us from Seaforth were on the list! The only name missing was hat-trick boy. Ha, I thought to myself, I knew he wasn't all that good.

Hat-trick boy was my friend, and I sort of felt sorry for him. He had so much success the year before, and now he was going to have to spend the entire season standing on the sidelines. Oh well, thought I, such is the agony of defeat.

I didn't see him that day until lunch. When I approached him, I assumed he had already learned of his sad fate. I was careful with my words. "Did you see the bantam soccer list?" I began.

"Yes, I did. Great to see all our Seaforth guys made it."

I was confused. "Um, well, almost all of them."

"What do you mean. Who didn't make it?"

"Um, well, you didn't."

"Oh, right. After the third practice, coach asked me to play on the senior team."

And there it was. Like a kick in the groin from a rock-hard soccer boot, the realization that he was indeed that much better than me. We were in grade eight, but he was going to play on the grade-ten team. For the next several decades, I would be continually reminded of my inferiority as hat-trick boy achieved greater and greater soccer fame.

He played all three years on the school's senior team and was top goal-scorer each year. He went on to play in England for Huddersfield Town and Ipswich Town, and then for the Vancouver Whitecaps, where he was a member of the squad from what the ABC sports announcer referred to as the 'village of Vancouver' that in 1979 won an NASL championship. He also played for the LA Aztecs. He played on the Canadian National Men's team for eight years, appearing twenty-four times, and in 2003, was inducted into the Canadian Soccer Hall of Fame. Not too shabby, hat-trick boy. Congratulations on your amazing career, Buzz Parsons.

Grade-eight class photo with Buzz Parsons (second row, next to Mr. Showers) and the author (back row, left end)

The Report Card from Hell

Although I somehow managed to pass all my courses in grade eight, my second year in junior high got off to a very rocky start. I had been assigned the same teacher for English and social studies. She was in her first year of teaching and was the most serious teacher I had ever encountered. She had no sense of humour whatsoever, which was a huge disadvantage to me. For some reason, she didn't think I was funny and early in the year made it clear she did not enjoy my sense of humour, or for that matter, having me in her classes.

One day in social studies, we were being taught the concept of how it is a shorter distance to travel by air via the polar route than to travel in a straight line across the globe. To make her point, Miss P. placed a large globe on her desk and cut a long piece of string. She taped one end of the string to Vancouver and the other end to London, taking the string up and over Greenland and Iceland. She then cut a second piece of string and again stuck it on Vancouver, but his time placed the string in a straight line across Canada and the Atlantic Ocean, all the way to London. She then disconnected the two pieces of string, held them up before our eager eyes and announced, "You see, the string that I used for the polar route is three inches shorter than the string I used to go straight across Canada and the Atlantic Ocean." She appeared very pleased with herself. I then thought I had a valid observation.

"It's almost five thousand miles from Vancouver to London, right?"

"Yes," said Miss P.

"Then what's the big deal about one way being three inches shorter than the other way?" Thirty students burst out laughing.

Over the volume of the raucous laughter, and much to my surprise, I heard, "Get out," and before I could say a word, there I was standing in the empty hall, wondering what had just happened. My stupor was short-lived and replaced with terror when, out of all the members of the Cariboo staff who could have walked down the hall, I saw my father heading toward me. He did not miss a step nor did he give me a glance. He just walked by. For a fleeting split second I wondered if perhaps he had not seen me, but that, I soon realized, was nothing more than pathologically wishful thinking. When I arrived home after school that day it did not take long for me to realize that he had, indeed, seen me.

Looking back, I now understand how a double dose of me in grade nine would have been a bit too much to bear, especially for my first-year, highly anxious teacher. My scolding after my father discovered I had been kicked out of class was nothing compared to the hell that broke loose at home when he read the comments on my first-term report card for English and social studies.

"In English and social studies Hugh is too talkative in class and lacks self-discipline. He is unruly."

It wasn't pretty. The first thing my father said was, "Go to your room and bring me your dictionary." Dutifully and filled with terror, I obeyed. "Look up 'unruly' and read it to me."

In the most quivering voice imaginable, I read, "Unruly means lacking in restraint or not submitting to authority. An unruly person refuses to obey authority and is incapable of controlling oneself or being controlled by others." My ex-navy father was not impressed.

Without going into the gory details of the next several days, weeks and months of my miserable life, things were uncomfortably tense at home until I received my second-term report card. "Hugh's behavior and attitude in English and social studies have shown great improvement." I am in no way suggesting that scaring the crap out of your child is an appropriate way to produce the change a parent seeks. However, there is evidence this method of parental discipline can sometimes be effective.

If the parent wishes to consult with any member of the staff please telephone the school for an appointment.

SCHOOL PHONE 522-7901

Remarks

FIRST REPORT *In English and social studies Hugh is too talkative in class and lacks self-discipline. He is unruly. He must work hard to improve his French.*

My grade-nine first-term 'report card from hell'. Not my proudest moment; not my father's calmest moment.

The Rare Good Decision

During my grade-ten year, I learned many valuable lessons. A few of them in the classroom, most of them in the gym. The gym was a safe and happy place for me, unlike the classroom, which was embarrassment-prone and nerve-racking. I felt lost in my classrooms. Everyone seemed to know what was going on except me. I did poorly on tests and when called upon to answer questions, seldom knew the correct answer. I hated my time in class. The gym, on the other hand, was where I knew what to do. I was happy and confident. In the winter of my final year of junior high school and after the completion of soccer season where Buzz and I had been reunited, Buzz playing on the team for his third year and me for the first time, it was basketball season. The Cariboo Hill senior boys' basketball team was average at best, but we loved practising and playing, and we had a kind and fair-minded man as our coach, who also happened to be our PE teacher. Mr. Showers was only in his fourth year of teaching and believed in fair play and equal playing time. He had been a great high school athlete at Oak Bay High School and in 2020, was inducted into the Oak Bay High School Sports Hall of Fame. During the years he taught us, he played professional lacrosse in the Western Lacrosse Association for the Victoria Shamrocks, and many of us from Cariboo made it a point to attend games he played at Queen's Park Arena when the Shamrocks visited and played the New Westminster Salmonbellies. He was a great role model. I had decided by this time that I wanted to be just like him and become a PE teacher. I am pleased to say that since I left junior high school fifty-six years ago, Mr. Showers has remained a very good friend to my parents and to me, and I still see him several times a year. I am also pleased to say, because of his inspiration, I did indeed begin my career in teaching as a PE teacher.

He taught all the boys' PE classes and shared the gym with the girls' PE teacher, Miss McCauley. Miss McCauley was a large, imposing Australian woman who scared the crap out of the boys.

The girls seemed fine with her, but we grade-ten males kept our distance. When I look back at it, I think Mr. Showers found her a bit scary as well.

In September of our grade-ten year, Miss McCauley started a ballroom dance club. She began by advertising it in the traditional way, via the morning bulletin. The new club registered twelve girls. This arrangement was, of course, not at all satisfactory for Miss McCauley or for her twelve girls, who lacked dancing partners. As a result, the grade-ten boys came under increasing pressure from the very scary Miss McCauley to join the ballroom dance club. We were regularly cornered in the hall and cafeteria by her and told, in no uncertain terms, that it was our duty to join the club. If we did not, she said, she would be very unhappy and so would the girls, some of whom, she was aware, we had become quite interested in as a result of our social and sexual development. The consensus from our peer group was that although some of the girls were looking quite good, it would not be worth the agony and humiliation of dancing with them. The club therefore continued for several more months with just the twelve girls.

One day after basketball practice, about halfway through our season, Mr. Showers sat us down and presented us with a 'wonderful opportunity'.

"I think you boys should join the ballroom dance club."

We were, without exception, a group of respectful fifteen-year-olds, so we politely listened to our coach's sales pitch, not being clever enough to connect the dots about where this was coming from or where this might be headed. We decided as a group that even though Mr. Showers was a great guy, there was no way we were going to defame the gym floor, which was meant to be used for basketball, floor hockey and volleyball, and not for such a frivolous activity as ballroom dancing.

Another week went by and we were again subjected to another after-practice talk. This time, Mr. Showers was more serious and intense.

"Look, you guys, I need you to go to the next ballroom dancing practice."

We all sat and stared at him and waited for some kind of explanation. I think he must have read our minds.

"Miss McCauley is going to kill me if I don't convince you guys to go, and I sort of promised her that if you didn't go, I would fold the team and cancel the rest of the basketball season."

We were horrified. Cancel the rest of the season? Unimaginable.

So, it being 1965 and we being obedient fifteen-year-olds who had just unwittingly been blackmailed, at the next ballroom dancing club practice, there were twelve new members.

The first meeting of the new and improved Cariboo Hill ballroom dance club began exactly the way all our school dances began—boys up against the wall on one side of the gym and the girls against the wall on the opposite side. However, unlike the school dances where nothing happened until the girls crossed the floor *en masse* and picked a boy to dance with, one brave member of the boys' basketball team made the first move. Against all odds and to the astonishment of everyone present, including Mr. Showers and Miss McCauley, I confidently and purposefully strutted across the floor. The entire room froze until I got to the other side and politely asked, "Barb, will you be my partner?"

You see, as out of character as this move was for me, and as insecure as I was in interacting with the opposite sex, I knew from discussions with her and a few of her friends that Barb was a very accomplished dancer. I also knew that I was not. So what better strategy than to partner up with the best female dancer in grade ten? The outcome was brilliant. For the next five months, Barb led and I followed. She was magnificent. She not only pushed and pulled me around the floor, she also whispered a running commentary into my ear as we gracefully floated across the gym like Fred and Ginger. "Now turn left, now go backward, now bring your right foot forward." I had picked the right partner and, for one of the few times in my life, had made a good decision.

The culmination of our dance season was an evening performance for parents. The girls dressed up in their finest gowns, and we boys all looked very smart in our Beatles blazers. I might not have been the best soccer player or best basketball player on our school teams, but I was, on this night, the best male ballroom dancer in the building.

In 1965, my father was forty-three years old, and right up until he died at age ninety-five, I don't believe he ever got over what he witnessed that night. After watching me play soccer and basketball for so many years—and on a good day be mediocre—he could not believe what he saw. I know this because on the way home in the car after the performance, he didn't say a word about what he witnessed that evening, nor did he mention it again for the remaining fifty-two years of his life.

Cariboo Hill senior boys' basketball team, a.k.a. the Cariboo Hill ballroom dance club. Author is last 'dancer' on the right.

The Girl Fight

Looking back at my time at Cariboo, I realize it must have been frustrating for the teachers to be restricted to teaching only junior-level courses, especially when their colleagues at three other schools in the district were assigned to teach all senior-level courses. However, on the plus side, in the 1960s, classroom management challenges did not exist at Cariboo. Students were polite, cooperative and followed the rules. Good behaviour was the norm, with a few notable exceptions.

Today, school teams travel for tournaments and exhibition games all over the world. Rugby teams travel to Wales, basketball teams to Hawaii, and I have even heard of a high school cricket team travelling to India. In 1965, our grade-ten boys' basketball team members were delighted to be told we were playing in a tournament in beautiful Powell River, BC. Even better, the cheerleaders were coming with us.

I don't remember much about the trip. I have no idea if we won any of our games or lost them all, but what is firmly etched in my memory is what happened when our bus returned to the school on Sunday afternoon.

We arrived early, and as a result, none of the parents had yet arrived to pick us up. Most of us were busy grabbing our luggage from under the bus when all of a sudden, all hell broke loose. For the previous couple of days something had been brewing between two of the cheerleaders, and it came to a head shortly after our arrival.

I had seen a few boy-versus-boy fights, and I had even been in a couple myself. My most memorable fight took place on the last day of grade ten on the bus ride home. My friend Dennis was sitting directly behind me and was, as usual, 'horsing around'. Just as I turned to see what was going on, Dennis flailed out his arm and smacked me right in the mouth. It was obvious to all my classmates on the bus, and also to me, that this had not been an intentional assault. However, the blow was severe enough to split my lip. I took the palm of my hand, wiped my chin and, to my amazement, discovered a considerable amount of blood. I had no choice but to retaliate. This is my story and I am sticking to it.

So I punched him in the face. A split second later, we were rolling around in the aisle of the bus while my classmates and neighbours looked on in horror. From what I remember, neither of us landed another blow, as the aisle was pretty narrow and we were jammed in tight.

The bus came to a sudden halt, the bus driver walked down the aisle and tossed us out the open back door. There we both were, sitting on the boulevard as the bus drove away. Talk about feeling stupid. We stared at each other and realized that there was no use continuing this nonsense, as we had lost our audience. I cannot recall any conversation between us as we walked home together, but I do remember arriving home, putting ice on my lip, not saying a word to my mom and going for a bike ride with Dennis that afternoon.

It was a time when there was instant forgetting after boys had a fight. It was also a time when we knew that if one participant stopped fighting, the fight was over. There was never any thought of weapons or of spectators getting involved. Is it wrong to call this 'safe fighting'?

Although I had participated in a few of these types of minor skirmishes and had been a spectator at a couple, I had never witnessed two girls engaged in a punch-up. It was not pretty. This was a serious battle. There was hair-pulling, screaming, kicking, wild punches and then the most remarkable thing—when the teachers arrived and began to yell at the combatants to stop, nothing. The girls just kept going as if they were deaf. Eventually the girls fell to the ground and began rolling around over each other. Finally, exhaustion set in and both of them were left motionless, lying on their backs. None of the rest of us, the boys or the girls, had ever seen anything like it. The lesson was that girls don't fight the same way boys fight. They fight worse.

Many years later, I would attempt to break up a similar fight but would forget this lesson and suffer the consequences.

The Shattering

My three years at Cariboo went better than most people who knew me would have anticipated. The school was safe, people seemed to like me and I managed, on most occasions, to slip through the cracks and stay out of trouble. None of my group of friends ever got into trouble. The one exception to this was the day I witnessed my friend Gary shatter one of the school's largest windows. Oh, how I ended up wishing I had been anywhere else but there.

Gary, like the rest of my group of friends, was polite, respectful and well-behaved. He also, like most of my friends, got much better marks than me. Unfortunately, on this particular day, what could have happened to any one of us happened to him.

It was lunchtime and we were hanging out in the second-floor hall in front of the library. Along the other side of the hall, across from the library, was a row of plate glass windows that looked down onto the courtyard. A small group of us stood in front of the windows, just talking as we usually did. That was, until one of our female classmates, for some inexplicable reason, lunged playfully at Gary. Reflex kicked in and Gary thrust himself backwards to avoid contact. He was successful in avoiding the human contact but not successful in avoiding backing up into the window, causing it to explode into thousands of little pieces and fall to the courtyard below. Fortunately, the courtyard was closed on this day, and there was no one below who might have been seriously injured.

Unsurprisingly, a stunned, silent disbelief overcame our group. Then lo and behold, who should appear on the scene but my father. It was like the man had radar. He was not pleased. In his equally unsurprising and custodial manner, he gruffly inquired, "What the hell just happened here?"

Although I had witnessed the event, my father, as usual, was not interested in my observations or opinion. He accepted the 'it was a mistake' explanation from other witnesses but turned to Gary. "We're going to have to go down to the office and talk to the principal about this." So off they went, one of my closest friends and my dad, to discuss this act of delinquency with our principal. I felt sick.

What was described to me later by my friend, who I felt certain would shortly become my former friend, was that as they were waiting to see the principal, my father decided to give Gary some advice.

"What are you going to say when you get in there?"

"I guess that I'm sorry."

"Then what?"

"I don't know."

"You're going to say that you will pay for the damage."

"Oh. How much will it cost?"

"A large piece of glass like that is not cheap. It will be about twenty bucks." A whole lot of money in 1965. We had a school counsellor, but I guess Dad thought he was up to the task of counselling my friend.

So, dutifully, after my father's sage advice, Gary entered the principal's office, apologized and offered to pay the twenty dollars. My dad was waiting in the general office as Gary exited the principal's office and asked him how it had gone.

"He was really nice about it and said it would all be okay if I paid the twenty dollars."

To which my father replied, "Twenty dollars? What's wrong with you? You should have offered him ten."

This was my father in a nutshell. I loved him and was proud of him, but I was not always enamoured with his twisted sense of humour, and this time his humour was at the expense of one of my best friends. I could hardly wait for grade ten to be over and for me to once again live a parent-free school life.

The Long Walk Home

One would assume that I would get a ride to school and back home each day with my dad. After all, he worked at the school and we lived in the same home. However, he began his workday at a ridiculously early time. I believe he usually arrived at the school around 6:15

and usually left around 3:15. Neither of these times worked for my schedule, so every morning and every afternoon, before and after school, I took the public bus.

The stop for the bus that went to the school was directly in front of our house, but to catch the after-school bus required a four-block walk to the nearest stop. In 1965, Cariboo Hill was out in the boonies and did not have the frequent bus service it has today. After a basketball practice or game, we would often catch the 6:00 bus, which was the last bus of the day. On one particular, dark, wet afternoon, my friend Paul and I arrived at the bus stop at 6:05. We had missed the last bus.

The sensible thing would have been to call one of our parents and ask them to come and pick us up. In my case, it would have been worth the evening's grumble about how I should be more aware of the time and once again hear the story of how my dad walked from Capitol Hill in North Burnaby to Kitsilano to visit my mom when they were courting. Apparently, it was eighteen miles uphill . . . both ways.

For some inexplicable reason, neither Paul nor I thought it would be a good idea to phone and ask to be picked up. I have no recollection whose idea it was, but we decided to walk. The first thirty minutes of our journey home went great. It was all downhill and well lit along Cariboo Road until we reached the Cariboo Road overpass, which crossed over Highway 401 (now called Highway 1). I then had a brilliant idea. If we walked along the highway and turned to the right, we would end up almost in my backyard. I knew I was going to be in some amount of trouble because I had missed the last bus and it was already twenty minutes past the time I would have been home. This shortcut would save us a great deal of time. So off we went, marching along the highway. To be fair, this was not as foolish an idea as it would be today, as there was virtually no traffic on the highway at the time, and all we had to do was walk along the shoulder and make an educated guess where to turn.

After about twenty minutes of highway walking, we decided it was time to make our turn. As we walked deeper and deeper into the

46

forest that bordered the highway, the walk turned into a trudge. The ground became softer and wetter, and soon we were over our shoes in water and making very little progress. Eventually, and much later than we should have, we decided the prudent thing would be to turn back before we got completely swallowed up by the dense forest and underfoot muck.

We struggled back to the highway, turned left and began our return to the Cariboo overpass. By this time, it was pitch dark along the highway, but we could see the lights on the overpass and walked with pace toward them. As we got closer to the overpass, we also noticed the red flashing lights of an emergency vehicle.

A short time later we arrived at the overpass, scrambled up the hill to the road and began the remainder of our walk home. We noticed the flashing red lights were coming from an RCMP cruiser that was parked on the shoulder of the road at the opposite end of the overpass. We also noticed that as soon as we appeared on the road, the cruiser did a quick one-eighty and began to drive in our direction. The officer stopped beside us, rolled down his window and asked, "Would your names happen to be Paul and Hugh?"

My expected arrival time home had been 6:20, and it was now 8:10. After my dad had driven all over Cariboo Hill and surrounding areas without locating us, he phoned the police and they were out looking for us. Sitting in the police car as the nice officer drove us home, I was so relieved and so cold and wet that I completely ignored what I knew was about to happen when I finally did arrive home. If I had been sharper, I would have begged the officer not to leave me but instead come into the house and protect me.

The next couple of hours were ugly, to say the least. My dad did his usual yelling thing and my mom did her usual crying thing. They were a great team at making me feel both frightened and guilty at the same time.

After things had calmed down a little, and I had finished my cold, dry dinner that had sat for two hours, and I had taken a hot bath, we all sat down at the kitchen table for a rational conversation. It began with my dad asking me what the hell was wrong with me, followed by my mom asking me what on earth I had been thinking. I reiterated the plan and both my dad and mom sat in stunned disbelief.

"In the pitch dark, you thought it was a good idea to take a walk along the Trans-Canada Highway?" Dad began.

"Yes, that's what we thought," I replied.

My dad then turned to my mom and asked, "Do we have a map of Burnaby in this house?"

"Yes, in the car, I believe," was her reply.

"Would you go and get it, please."

A very short time later, my mom reappeared with map in hand. She opened it up and spread it out on the table. Of course, to do this she had to remove all the food-related items as the 'old school' paper map covered the entire surface of our kitchen table. We all stared at it for several seconds before my dad continued.

"That's what I thought," and he traced my route with his finger. "You came down Cariboo Road, turned along the highway and you were going to cut across into our backyard."

And then I saw it. I thought I was going to be sick, but with how they were feeling about me, puking on their map was not going to improve my situation. I had made a slight miscalculation. Directly between the highway and our home, right where we began our cut-through, was a small obstacle in the form of 3.11 kilometres of water called Burnaby Lake. As it turned out, unlike asking Barb to be my dance partner, this was not one of my better ideas.

The next day at school, I saw my friend Paul and gave him a blow-by-blow summary of my evening. When I finished, I asked him how much trouble he had gotten in, to which he casually replied, "When I got home my mom and dad were out, so they don't know what time I got home." Sometimes there is just no justice in a boy's life.

The Inauspicious Ending

The remainder of my grade-ten year was relatively uneventful. I failed two out of my eight courses but was delighted to discover that I could repeat French 10 the following year, in grade eleven, and would not have to attend summer school. Thankfully, failing Power Mechanics 10 would not jeopardize my academic future or my chances of becoming a PE teacher. The only consequence of failing power mechanics was that once again I had embarrassed my dad, as my PM10 teacher was one of his best friends. Awkward for them both, I am sure.

When I look at the final marks on my grade-ten report card and see the two FAILs printed in block capital letters, as well as the *P* in English 10, which meant I had just barely scraped through, I am mystified at why I chose the friends I did during my time at Cariboo Hill, or perhaps why they chose me as a friend. All my friends were really smart and achieved excellent grades, which no doubt added to my feelings of academic inadequacy. Bill has a degree in pharmacy and ended up being the head of pharmacy at a large Vancouver hospital. Dave has a degree in electrical engineering and moved to Sydney, Australia, where he ran a sound studio that recorded Olivia Newton John. And there was my closest friend, Gary, who managed to recover from the trauma of breaking the largest window at Cariboo Hill and went on to do his PhD at Simon Fraser University and become the director of the Centre for Teaching and Academic Growth and later the Institute for Scholarship of Teaching and Learning at the University of British Columbia. I don't know what that entails, but it certainly sounds impressive.

Sometime in the spring of my grade-ten year, about a dozen of us who lived in the Government Road neighbourhood were offered a surprising choice. Because Burnaby North was crowded and Burnaby Central had space to spare, we could choose which of the two schools we wanted to attend. Despite popular opinion, school choice is not such a new concept after all. As most of my close friends were not given the choice and were mandated to attend Central, I chose to go with them, a curious choice given how academically mismatched I was with most of them.

I was convinced that my move to senior high school was going to be academically challenging and that I would be lucky to last a month before being tossed out. I was certain that in no way was I ready to attend senior high, much less pass any courses. There were no other options, however, so I spent the summer in constant fear of what was to come and hoped the summer would never end. Just my luck, the summer did end, and in September, off I went to the much bigger and more daunting world of senior high school.

Burnaby Central Senior High School

– 2 years –

In 1966, Central had a student population of about 1,100 students and registered students in grades eleven and twelve. There was also a class of grade thirteen, an anomaly in the Burnaby District that contributed enormously to making Central an athletic powerhouse. Students in grade thirteen required an extra year to graduate and were, naturally, a year older than the grade twelves. As Central was the only school in Burnaby to have a grade-thirteen class, the athletic program was enriched by students who were eligible to play three years of senior high competition.

This advantage produced some very successful Central teams, and over the years, Burnaby Central has graduated numerous outstanding athletes, many of them in the sport of soccer. Seven professional soccer players are listed on their website as graduates.

One of my classmates, whom I don't recall being a great athlete but do remember being a very nice person, was my friend Sandra. She invited me to my first-ever formal event. It was an installation ceremony for the local chapter of Job's Daughters. This organization is advertised as "a youth organization for girls and young women aged ten to twenty." It purports to "teach the values of leadership, public speaking, charity and respect." I had never heard of it, but when I informed my parents that I was to attend this function, I discovered that my father had heard of it. "It's a bloody cult, you know. What are you doing going to a cult meeting?"

Sandra was being installed as the Bethel Queen, or maybe Princess, I don't remember. What I do remember is that I was mandated to dress in a suit and tie, which I wore for the first time in my life. I was, after all, seventeen years old and only in grade eleven. My extensive wardrobe consisted primarily of blue jeans and T-shirts. The 'suit and tie' concept was totally foreign to me and presented a major obstacle to accepting an invitation to such a gala event. Along with the fact that I didn't have the slightest idea how to behave in such a formal setting. I was terrified of the 'how to eat' etiquette piece. I wasn't a slob when I ate but had watched several shows on television from England that showed formal eating behaviour and knew I was not anywhere near that standard.

The formal part of the evening reminded me a great deal of a wedding. The important people up at the front reciting vows and making promises while being observed with awe by the invited guests. The girls looked magnificent in their formal ball gowns, and I got to eat crustless sandwiches during the event—another first for me. I had no idea there was such a thing.

To this day, I am overwhelmed with the amount of memorizing Sandra was required to do and how perfectly she recited it. By being elected to the position of Honoured Queen, she was promising to uphold the values of the organization and to lead the individual chapter, referred to as the Bethel. She had memorized the required thirty pages of promises from the Supreme Book of Ceremonies and recited them flawlessly.

Although I don't remember Sandra as a terrific athlete, she did produce one, and gifted both Canada and the world with her daughter: Christine Sinclair (OC), fourteen-time Canadian Soccer Player of the Year, seven-time FIFA Player of the Year, captain of Canada's 2020 women's Olympic gold medal team and arguably the greatest women's soccer player of all time.

Alphonso Davies, Bayern Munich soccer sensation, also attended Central. This great school has not only educated many extraordinary athletes, but also students who have excelled in other fields, such as Iron Chef winner Rob Feenie and actor, comedian, author, producer and activist Michael J. Fox (OC).

The Math 11 Inspiration

My two years at Burnaby Central Senior High School were relatively uneventful and spectacularly unrewarding. During my entire time attending school, math was a nightmare for me. In every grade, I just barely passed and spent the entire time in math class feeling lost. I did, however, occasionally have fun in math class. In term two of my grade-nine year, my class did a geometry unit. For what seemed like weeks on end, we drew figures and cut them out to form geometric shapes. Near the end of the unit, we advanced to creating three-dimensional shapes from cardboard. In an attempt to teach us the profoundly important principles of geometry, we were tasked to build spheres, cylinders, cubes, tetrahedrons and even something called an octahedron. Apparently, learning to do this would enhance my brain and enable me to understand spatial relationships and the properties of two- and three-dimensional shapes. The precision and concentration to do this was far too difficult for my lack of coordination (noted on my grade-two report card), so I decided it would be much more fun to create a shape that had never been created before. I made a house.

I was very proud of my house. It looked great. It had windows, a front door with a path leading up to it and even had a chimney. I cut carefully, glued with great precision and after its completion, in accordance with our instructions, I attached a string to the top of it so it could hang from the lights of our classroom. Unfortunately, Mr. Sylvester, my math teacher, was not impressed with my efforts.

By this point in Math 9, Mr. Sylvester and I had experienced a few minor hiccups around the issue of my behaviour and my wayward mouth. He was not a huge fan of anything I did or said. As mentioned, at the end of the last class of the geometry unit, we were asked to hang our geometric figures from the ceiling. Today health and safety guidelines would not allow such a blatantly dangerous practice like standing on the top of our desks, but as always, we did what we were told. I hung my house, the bell rang ending the period, and I departed for my next class. When I returned two days later for my next math class, my house was gone, but all my classmates' figures were still hanging. I looked around the room and located my pride and joy on Mr. Sylvester's desk. I knew it was not there as an exceptional model of what he wanted, but I was not going to inquire about its location. It sat on his desk for a long time, and when all the other geometric figures were returned to my classmates, I got mine back as well. My math teacher was not amused. He was not amused to the extent that he gave me zero out of twenty-five for my creation. I assume he missed the potential of my architectural ability.

In grade eleven, two years after my geometry fiasco, I did experience my single most enjoyable math class. I learned a lot that day, as well. Mr. McAteer was a wonderful math teacher. When he taught math, it actually made sense to me. I suppose the Burnaby School District agreed with my assessment, as Mr. McAteer was eventually promoted to the position of secondary school principal. He also served as the president of the BC Principals' and Vice-Principals' Association.

He happened to be an acquaintance of the author of our Math 11 textbook and invited her to our class to teach a lesson. It was an amazing experience for me. Mary Dolciani presented a masterful lesson. She was engaging, funny and personable. It may be the best single lesson I ever received in school. Most impressively, she conducted the entire lesson without using a copy of the textbook. She made reference to it multiple times but didn't look at it once. I guess if you write a book, you should know what's in it. Still, remembering every equation and every question on every page is very impressive. It was an inspiration for me to see how a teacher could teach with such skill and engagement.

I had, for some time, toyed with the idea of becoming a teacher. In grade eight, I thought Mr. Showers's job of teaching PE looked very attractive, but because I knew becoming a teacher required a university degree, and I was barely passing my junior high school courses, I had always considered the prospect of becoming a teacher beyond my academic reach. But this one-time math lesson with Dr. Dolciani reignited my interest. I decided I wanted to be that person who could turn uninspired, struggling students on to learning. Perhaps it was time to leave the class clown behind and become more serious and focused in pursuit of higher education.

I would continue for some time to 'goof off' and entertain my classmates, but I came to decide that I wanted to be a teacher and that I would do whatever it took to be one. If I could accomplish this lofty goal with *my* track record, I would become an inspiration to others who had not experienced a great deal of early success in their school endeavours. Perhaps I could even inspire the teachers of challenging students to not give up on them and to maintain hope for their success. Not only did I learn a little math that day, but that one lesson cemented the strength of my ambitions to become the best teacher I could be.

For the first time in my life, it occurred to me that I had the potential to channel my skills as a class clown into becoming an effective teacher. I began to realize that many of the skills required to be an excellent teacher were, ironically, the skills required to be an excellent class clown. Both roles required a sense of timing and the ability to entertain and engage and to communicate effectively. Just because I was not a great student did not mean I could not be a great teacher.

The Great Deal

At this point in my life, I was neither an athlete nor a scholar and felt like the invisible man. My only goal was to graduate with a grade point average that would grant me admission into UBC so I could get on with becoming a teacher. In British Columbia, then as now, one of the requirements to graduate was to pass a grade eleven-level science course. I chose Biology 11 because someone had told me it was the easiest of the three science electives. My three term marks were D, E, D, and my final mark was an F. Imagine the marks I would have received if I had taken chemistry or physics, supposedly the two harder courses.

Looking at my report card some fifty-four years later, I find it quite curious that there is not one comment on my report card from my science teacher. Another 'not best practice' example. I was sentenced to four weeks of summer school. I hated it like nothing I had hated in my life. School in the winter was bad enough, but sitting in a classroom during the hot, sunny days of summer was, to me, cruel and unusual punishment. My mother hated it too because she lost the use of her car from nine o'clock to noon, Monday to Friday.

My Bio 11 teacher was a very nice lady. It certainly was not Mrs. Mason's fault that I did not hand in any labs, nor was it her fault that I failed the majority of my exams. Come to think of it, I may have failed every one of them. Learning biology was like learning a new language. It made no sense to me whatsoever, memorizing all new names for the parts of the body that already had perfectly good ones. Why did something I had known for sixteen years as my bum suddenly have three different names in biology class? To me it was my bum, occasionally my ass, never my gluteus maximus or my gluteus medius or my gluteus minimus. Under what circumstance would I need to know that my butt crack is my 'intergluteal cleft'?

You can imagine what went through my mind when on my first day of summer school, in walked Mrs. Mason. On the plus side, I was pretty sure I would be seeing the same lessons, same labs and most importantly the same tests that I had seen during the previous school year. On the minus side, I knew Mrs. Mason was not my biggest fan. Besides failing all the tests and not handing in any labs, I may have been, on occasion, a bit of a smart aleck in class, and I may have mentioned, on more than one occasion, the stupidity of renaming all the parts of my body. On a few occasions, I may have even mentioned by name the inappropriate version of 'intergluteal cleft', which resulted in me spending some time in the hall.

Like a convict requesting parole for good behaviour, I dutifully attended each and every class of Bio 11 at summer school. I even handed in most of my labs. I believe I also passed a test or two. But at the end of the course, the 50 percent I was longing for was just not there. I knew my parents would be upset. Especially my mom, who had spent five mornings a week, for an entire month, isolated from the outside world without her car.

On the last day of summer school, after receiving the bad news that 44 percent was not a passing grade and just as I was about to exit the classroom, I heard Mrs. Mason say, "Hugh, before you leave, can I have a word with you, please?" I really was not in the mood for a lecture, as I knew I was going to get a couple of them that night at home, but as the polite, if not very bright, young man that I was, over I went for my telling off.

Grade-eleven report card; destined not to become a biology teacher.

"Next year I am going to be teaching all three classes of Biology 12. I would like to make you a deal. If you promise me you will *not* take Biology 12 next year, I will give you credit for Biology 11."

Can you imagine my utter ecstasy? I couldn't believe my luck. Before she had time to finish pronouncing the *n* in 'eleven', I spat out, "Okay, deal!"

My graduation transcript has the words "Biology 11, 50%, credit granted" forever inscribed on it. Sometimes, it's better to be lucky than smart.

The Wildcat Athletes

At the time, Burnaby Central Senior High School happened to have an inordinate number of outstanding athletes—athletes who, after graduating from Central, achieved fame and athletic success. This made it difficult and almost impossible for the likes of me to continue the even modest athletic success I'd experienced at Cariboo. The competition was so challenging that I didn't even bother trying out for the soccer team. To this day, I count it as another one of my classic blunders. I did, however, try out for the basketball team and got unceremoniously cut after the first practice and asked if I wanted to referee the games instead of playing in them. Ouch!

Looking back, it was a very high bar to make the senior boys' basketball team. The 1968 Burnaby Central Wildcats senior boys' basketball team was a force. In those days, games were played in eight-minute quarters. The Central senior boys' basketball team still holds the record for most points in a thirty-two–minute game, by defeating archrival Burnaby South 115 to 48. The team also finished third in the 1969 AAA boys' provincial tournament. Alex Devlin was on this team. He became an NAIA all-star at Simon Fraser University (SFU), played on the Canadian National Team at the 1976 Summer Olympics, was invited to the Portland Trailblazers rookie camp and is in the BC and Canadian basketball halls of fame. Rod Matheson was on this team too. He went on to play at UBC and was the starting guard on the 1972 undefeated Canadian university championship team. And I thought I had a shot at making this team. What was I thinking?

Not only did this basketball-crazed school have these outstanding players during my two years there, but it also included my classmate, Bill Disbrow, who went on to become one of British Columbia's most successful high school boys' basketball coaches. During Bill's tenure as coach of the Richmond Colts senior boys' AAA team, he led them to ten provincial championship appearances and won the tournament five times. In 2009, he was inducted into the BC Basketball Hall of Fame.

Another of my classmates and one of my close friends in high school was Reid. Today he would be referred to as 'visually impaired' or 'sight challenged', but in 1967, he was blind. Normally Reid would have attended one of the schools for the blind, but he was exceptionally independent and able to function without a great deal of support. Today, he would be offered many types of support. Perhaps from someone called a certified orientation and mobility specialist, or some other itinerant support worker to help him out, but in 1967–68, he managed all on his own. Not only did he manage, but as a member of our school's wrestling team, he excelled.

Reid had amazing upper body strength. He was the only member of the wrestling team who could climb a rope to the girders of the gym ceiling using only his hands, without the aid of his legs. He made it look effortless. The wrestling coach was Mr. McCritchey. He was also the school's football coach and revelled in his reputation of being mean and aggressive. After having him as my PE teacher for a year and being the athletic trainer for his football team, I came to know him as quite the opposite, but for some reason he enjoyed yelling at students and equally enjoyed being feared by them. He played no favourites and, as a result, Reid was given no special treatment on the wrestling team. This was not a time when 'adapted instruction' was a thing. Nonetheless, Mr. McCritchey was not without skills in creating ingenious opportunities for Reid. Reid worked out with the rest of the team and participated in weightlifting, rope climbing and most of the other fitness training the team was required to do. However, running wind sprints wall to wall across the gym posed a problem for him. In 1967, holding hands with your teammate was never going to be a thing, so Mr. McCritchey devised a plan for Reid. While the rest of the team sprinted across the gym, Reid would go upstairs to the bleachers and run back and forth up there. He would rub his hand across the top of the railing and as he got close to the wall, his hand would cross the piece of string that Mr. McCritchey had tied to it.

Something else that had not been invented yet was the concept of political correctness. We once told Reid that we were going to cut off the string and watch him collide into the wall. "How funny would that be?" we asked him. Like most sighted students would, he replied by smiling and giving us the finger. He was just Reid, one of the guys. He was never 'blind Reid'.

Reid not only had an amazing positive attitude toward his disability but also an amazing sense of humour. He cracked us up with his stories and jokes about being blind. He never made us laugh harder than the time he competed in a wrestling match against Centennial High School from Coquitlam.

Reid had a cane that folded up nicely and could fit into his back pocket. When he needed to use it, he would whip it out, snap it somehow and it would assemble into a regular white cane. On this occasion, when it came time for Reid to wrestle, he asked one of his teammates to hold on to the contraption. He then asked another one of his teammates to point him in the direction of his opponent. Reid knew exactly how far it was from the edge of the wrestling mat to the centre, where his opponent would be waiting. He walked confidently to the centre, shook the boy's hand and began the bout.

A very short time later, Reid pinned his opponent and the match was over. After shaking hands with his rival, Reid then turned and walked off the mat to where he knew his teammate was waiting with his cane. He then held out his hand, accepted the cane, turned and faced his opponent and flipped it open. The look on the other wrestler's face was remarkable, but the real joy for us came when we looked over at his Centennial teammates. Their faces of confusion and disbelief were almost more than we could handle. Reid had just provided us with one of our greatest high school memories.

REID POYNTER: "I don't know." This year's Boys' Sports Rep., Reid plans to become a fantastic lawyer. He hates getting lost in the halls.

My friend Reid displays his humour about being blind in his write-up in our grade-twelve yearbook.

The Most Popular Fool

One cold, rainy February day during lunch, our annual staff-vs.-student basketball game took place in the gym. The place was jam-packed with students and members of staff. The game was a very competitive event, and to my great joy, I had been asked to referee it.

I would have much rather been playing in the game than refereeing it, but earlier in the year, after a series of tryouts and being closely evaluated by the school's coaching staff, I had been unceremoniously cut from the squad. An ego-bruising lowlight of my high school athletic career but in retrospect, given the quality of the players on the team, understandable and appropriate.

With the score tied and about two minutes left in the game, the dreaded Mr. McCritchey, who was on the court and playing at the time, accosted me, told me he was going to commit a foul the next opportunity he had and ordered me to give him a 'technical foul' for unsportsmanlike conduct. I was, without warning, plummeted into a classic 'between a rock and a hard place' situation. Don't do as he ordered and face his wrath, or do as he ordered and . . . well, face his wrath.

I thought it would be better for me to 'T him up', meaning give him the technical foul, as this would lead to massive approval from my classmates. So, as prearranged, the most feared teacher in the building fouled his check, and I blew my whistle. I then, not for the first or last time in my life, entered my own personal twilight zone. He walked right up to me and got into my face, yelling, "Now give me the technical foul." I blew my whistle again, pointed at him and made the technical foul signal. The gym went insane. Everyone, including the teachers, yelled and screamed their approval. As if this wasn't weird enough, Mr. McCritchey then ordered me to eject him. He wanted me to throw him out of the game. I would normally have needed some time to process such a monumental decision, but on this occasion, overwhelmed with testosterone and adrenalin, I did not hesitate. I blew my whistle again and made the enormous NBA gesture of tossing him out. He stared right into my eyes, and for a moment I felt like I was about to meet my maker, but instead he whispered, "Nice one, Greer. Thanks."

I may not have been a scholar or an athlete, but at that moment I became the most popular student attending Burnaby Central High School. Hundreds of my classmates became my adoring fans. They were ecstatic. I was their hero. I was the bravest student at the school. Only two of us knew the truth, and I was certain neither one of us was about to spill the beans. My day only got better when I arrived in class, right after lunch, and was greeted with a standing ovation by my History 12 classmates. My teacher, however, was not so enamoured of my lunchtime performance.

"Hugh, what on earth is wrong with you? That man is going to spend the rest of the year torturing you."

Turns out this was a universal belief around the school, and not only did all my teachers share it, but so did my adoring fans, who, as it turns out, were not as adoring as I'd thought but rather amazed at my stupidity.

For weeks after the game, I was asked over and over again if I was scared that Mr. McCritchey was going to take his anger and hatred out on me, and every time I answered with bravado, "I can deal with him." The truth is, Mr. McCritchey never again mentioned the incident, and to be honest, I believe he treated me better after the big game than he did before it. I had helped him to solidify his reputation as being nasty and hot-tempered, and I believe he appreciated my help.

The Travesty

My two years at Central were not without some amusing moments. Near the end of June of my graduation year, the grads were directed to the gym for the annual awards ceremony. During the ceremony, most of my friends received an award in some category for their contribution to the school during the previous two years. I, on the other hand, sat and watched as they walked up to the stage to receive their awards. Awards were given for a myriad of reasons. Academic, service, athletic and even an award for the safest driver.

My friend Andy received this last award. The award was given to the grade-twelve student who demonstrated safe, courteous and skilful driving while driving to and from school, and it was awarded by the British Columbia Automobile Association (BCAA). During the ceremony, we all wondered how anyone in our graduating class could have been identified as driving in a safe, courteous and skilful manner. During the preamble to the actual presentation, the BCAA representative disclosed that the association had placed an observer (later labelled 'spy' by our group of friends) in the student parking lot, and on several occasions observed student drivers entering and leaving the lot. Apparently, Andy was good at this.

If you ask 100 drivers if they are above average, average or below average drivers, 100 of them will answer, "above average." This is true now and was true in 1968. After the criteria was read, all of us who had a driver's licence and had ever driven to school were sure we were going to win the award. And then we heard Andy's name.

Andy was a popular and likeable member of our grad class, but when it was announced that he had won the award for being some superstar driver, virtually every grade twelve in the gym started booing and heckled him as he walked to the stage to receive his award. Our grad class was composed of polite and respectful young men and women who had caused very few problems in the school during the previous two years, but we were outraged. This was a joke and everyone in the gym knew it, even the teachers, especially my French teacher. You see, my French teacher was Andy's mom, and every morning when Andy drove into the parking lot and every afternoon when he drove out of the parking lot, his mother was sitting right next to him. How else but with extreme care does a sixteen-year-old drive when their mother is sitting next to them? Just one more moment of injustice in my sad high school career.

The Fluke

Inexplicably, I passed all my courses at the end of grade twelve. I received my transcript at the beginning of August and was puzzled to see that I had passed History 12 "by adjudication." I had no idea what that meant. After asking some of my parents' friends who were high school teachers, I learned that when the provincial History 12 final exam had been marked, too many students had failed, so the Ministry of Education markers marked them all again and lowered the standard to pass. I was in the 'lower standard' group. I really didn't give a damn how I had passed, only that I had, so I completed and sent in my application to attend UBC and train as the PE teacher I had wanted to be since meeting Mr. Showers in grade eight. The chances of me completing five years of academic university rigour was a long shot, but so was graduating from high school, and somehow that had worked out for me.

About two weeks later, I got my reply. "We are pleased to inform you that your application to attend the University of British Columbia, Faculty of Education, has been accepted. Congratulations."

There is no doubt that one significant factor that enabled me to be accepted was how much lower academic requirements were at this time. Today, an academic average of between 75 and 80 percent is required. My grade-twelve report card shows an academic average closer to 50 percent. I apologize to my fellow grads, but a second significant factor must have been that 1968 was a very lean year in BC for high school graduates.

Academy Award–winning actress Audrey Hepburn is quoted as saying, "Nothing is impossible, the word itself says, 'I'm possible'!"

I wish I had seen this quote before I went off to what I was sure was my inevitable doom.

University of British Columbia

– 5 years –

The Family First

I was the first person in my family to attend university. As a result, I had no frame of reference and no family mentor to prepare me for this experience. Without knowing a thing about being a university student, I had convinced myself that my chances of success were slim and there was no way I could go the distance and actually complete my degree. For me, just getting into the place was an enormous accomplishment.

My mother lamented to me that if times had been different, she would have loved to attend university and study creative writing. She certainly had the aptitude for it and made it clear that she was proud and envious of me and hoped I would achieve the outcome that would lead to my dream job. My father, in his usual style, said very little. He was a difficult man to read. He never said a word to me about university, but during the five years I attended, several of his friends informed me that he had told them he was proud of me and, although not optimistic, hoped I would do well. He did, however, congratulate me for working part-time at the sawmill and earning enough money on my own to be able to pay for my tuition and books. "If you're going to be successful in this life, you have to make it on your own." My interpretation of his words led me to believe that he was greatly relieved that he did not have to pay for any of this nonsense.

After studying the university calendar and making no sense of it whatsoever, I decided to make an appointment with a university counsellor. She was very helpful and clearly understood me. She told me exactly what courses I needed to take. I considered my university experience as a means to an end. This was job training. Don't give me any highfalutin, idealistic mumbo-jumbo about intellectual growth. I want to be a PE teacher. Tell me how I do this, and she did.

In late August, I ventured out to campus. After spending the entire day lining up to get the computer punch cards I required to enrol in the courses I needed in first year, I built myself a nice little timetable. I hand-printed a copy for my parents to place on our fridge door, just like when I attended junior and senior high school. They always wanted to know what courses I was taking and on what days I was attending them so they could ask me if I had any homework. I was hoping these enquiries would not continue once I began university, but tradition is tradition. Proudly I displayed my university timetable on the fridge door where my parents could adoringly worship it, or maybe look at it and shake their heads in disbelief.

English 100	M W F	8:30 a.m.	Buchanan 100
Math 110	Tu W F	1:30 p.m.	Math 110
French 110	M Tu Th	10:30 a.m.	Angus 100
Economics 100	Tu Th F	9:30 a.m.	Economics 105
Dancing 100 (Sep–Dec)	M W Th	2:30 p.m.	Armories Building
Swimming 100 (Sep–Dec)	M Tu Th	11:30 a.m.	War Memorial Pool
Golf 100 (Jan–Apr)	M W F	12:30 p.m.	Armories Building

My mother's reaction to seeing her son's university timetable posted on the fridge for all to see was predictable. The first thing she did was remove it and recopy it in much larger print. She raised its location so it was directly at eye level and removed everything else from the fridge door. I knew this was for the benefit of her friends who might be visiting for a cup of coffee or any other reason they would have to enter our home and kitchen. But I also knew the more prominent location was specifically for any of the members of our family who might visit, so they could easily view the sacred document. For my mother, nothing was better than communicating to our family, "Here is my son's *university* timetable. He is the first member of our family to attend *university*."

On the other hand, my father's reaction had a different tone. "What the hell? Dancing, swimming and golf. Are you going to university or have you joined a country club?" I knew what he meant was "I'm proud of you, son. Well done." This is my story, anyway, and I'm sticking to it.

The Supply and Demand

The first year came and went, and I was not, as anticipated by most who knew me (myself included), kicked out at the end of the year. I only failed one course, Economics 100. Failing the course never upset me. What, to this day, I fail to understand is why I ever chose it. It was an elective. Given my lack of success during my entire life with anything to do with numbers, what was I thinking? Graphs, numbers, the principle of supply and demand, stuff I had no interest in and certainly had no aptitude for. It brought back terrifying memories of my two attempts to pass Biology 11. Everything I had known by one name suddenly had another. Why after calling it 'money' my whole life was I now forced to call it 'currency'? What's wrong with calling it 'stuff I own'? Now it's 'my assets'. And in what upside-down world is 'bull' the opposite of 'bear'?

As a result of my failure to grasp even the simplest of economic concepts—and also my failure to attend class for the last three months of the course—I earned a miserable 44 percent in the course and was placed on something called 'academic probation'. All I needed to do the following year was not fail a course. I was optimistic. I had achieved success! After an entire year of attending university, I had not been kicked out.

The 'Real Deal' Teacher

It was early in my second year that I became truly excited about my choice of career and knew I was on the right track. I was only fifteen months out of high school and only nineteen years old, but I was going to be a teacher. Well, I was going to be a student teacher. Beginning in September and for the entire year, all second-year education students were to be placed in a school and bussed to that school to be given the opportunity to 'teach'.

My placement was at White Rock Junior High School. I had never heard of it but was delighted to be given the opportunity to prove to everyone that I was ready and able to be a teacher. I was quite certain that the next four years of sitting in a classroom at UBC would be a total waste of my time. I was ready now, just show me the gym and let me do my magic.

I carefully dressed the part of a PE teacher. I was convinced that if I dressed like Mr. Showers, I would teach like Mr. Showers. I would be brilliant. New white Adidas gym shoes, track pants with an orange stripe down the side and a white collared golf shirt. It would be impossible for me to be any more confident. I was a legend in my own mind. That is, until my first visit to WRJH and my introduction to my teaching assignment.

As a requirement to enter the Faculty of Education at UBC, I was required to choose two subjects to train in and be qualified to teach. Obviously PE was my first choice, but a second choice was a major problem for me. I wasn't good at anything else. I certainly was not going to take courses in biology again, and anything to do with numbers was out of the question. I cannot remember the process my mind went through, but my second teaching major somehow became Guidance.

My sponsor teacher for both my PE and Guidance practicums was a very happy, positive, mid-thirties jock-type fellow who had been assigned to teach PE and Guidance in what is referred to now as the 'special needs' class or the class with 'designated students' but was then referred to as (please forgive me) the 'occ block'. This unfortunate name was short for 'occupational block'. This particular group of students was made up of those who struggled academically and had been timetabled into modified academic classes and given industrial education (now tech studies) electives. The students in this class were also given time in a work experience placement and spent several weeks each term in a real working environment. Many of them were terrific at work. Most of them were horrible at school. It had somehow been determined that I was going to teach these young fellows PE and Guidance.

The classes were called PE 10X and Gu 10X on their timetables. Most of them hated PE, and all of them hated Guidance. I was confident that I could make the PE classes somewhat enjoyable and was sure I could win them over, but I had no idea how to control them for sixty minutes in a Guidance class. That was, until my sponsor teacher was kind enough to enlighten me.

In the vastness of pedagogical jargon, the term 'best practice' is often used. Well-respected educators Andy Hargreaves and Michael Fullan define best practice in education as "existing practices that already possess a high level of widely-agreed effectiveness." To me this means 'stuff you do in the classroom that works'. It turns out that at White Rock Junior High School in 1969, best practice for teaching my assigned Guidance class of special needs fifteen-year-old boys was to show them a film. In every class. A film of any kind. The subject matter of the film did not matter. Just a film on a reel. This best practice also dictated that when the film was finished, the teacher would not rewind the film but thread it back into the projector and play it backwards. The 'carrot' for the students was, if they behaved well during the showing of the film through its first run, they could see it backwards. If they misbehaved, the film would be rewound in the normal way and shown again in the traditional manner. All the students in the Guidance 10X class wanted to see the film in reverse.

As good educational role modelling, my sponsor teacher allowed me to witness a 'best practice' model lesson before I attempted one myself. It was magic. Twenty-five 'difficult' students all engaged in the lesson. They quietly watched the film that had no possible interest or relevance to them. I think I remember it having something to do with water safety. They had behaved well. Then gales of laughter as they watched it in reverse. I seem to remember a part of the film that involved someone jumping off a diving board. The first time through, no reaction. In reverse, when the individual flew out of the water and up onto the board and then walked backward along the board, then down the ladder onto the pool deck, there were screams of hilarity. Gut-grabbing, tear-causing, side-splitting laughter. As all teachers know, timing a lesson is crucial. This lesson was timed to perfection. The last swimmer climbed backwards out of the pool, dried himself off with a large beach towel and entered the waiting bus, backwards of course, after which we saw the bus drive away, naturally in reverse, and the bell rang to end the class. The students left looking happier than after any class I had ever walked out of as a student. The model of a successful lesson. My sponsor teacher could not have looked more satisfied. He had presented the quintessential lesson for his new and impressionable student teacher.

On the bus ride back to UBC, I sat in silent contemplation. Was this really teaching? Was this what I was expected to do? Confusion gripped my total being. There was only one thing to do to help alleviate my dilemma. So off to the Student Union Building (SUB) I went and drank vast quantities of beer.

If I thought teaching the Guidance class was going to be a challenge, I was in for an awakening when I was allowed the opportunity to teach the same students in the 'occ block' (sorry again) PE class.

I was certain the PE class was going to be much more aligned with my sensibilities. Unlike the Guidance class, the PE class was sure to make sense to me. Fifteen-year-old boys need physical exercise. They need to run off their testosterone until they are on the verge of puking. I had learned this at Burnaby Central in my own PE classes.

Again, I was offered the opportunity to observe my sponsor teacher as he taught the class, before I was afforded the opportunity to take charge myself. Unlike my own PE classes in high school, where students were severely chastised if they arrived to class in other than the required clothing, no proper gym strip was required. Proper running shoes, blue shorts and a white T-shirt were always the required and appropriate order of the day at Cariboo and Central. Apparently, for this 'special' class, anything would do. Bare feet, socks, jeans and any description of shirt was okay. I knew that the adage 'when in Rome, do as the Romans do' was a prerequisite when a student teacher taught their sponsor teacher's class. So I asked no questions and I made no comments. I didn't like it, but I accepted the PE dress code. I entered a world I did not know existed.

I had spent hundreds, probably thousands of hours in high school gyms, and the number one priority for my instructors had always been safety. My teachers had always emphasized safety. "We do it this way because it's safer." "You must wear this because it's safer." "The spotter is here for your safety." 'My' class at WRJH seemed not to require the same standards of safety as my PE classes had and, as I observed later in my practicum, not the same standards as the other PE classes at White Rock Junior High. The safety instructions usually issued before any activity were omitted. On the day I observed the class, my sponsor teacher got out the equipment and more or less said, "Go for it." No lesson plan, no instructions, nothing. Just "go play."

My observation class was a floor hockey lesson. The equipment was safe enough. The plastic sticks and plastic balls looked to be in good repair. What could possibly happen? During my observation class, nothing. During my first teaching class, calamity.

The Tuesday following my observation, I was ready to begin my career as a PE teacher. I set up the class exactly as my sponsor had done. The same equipment, the same rules of play, the same location. The same everything except result. I knew the stocking feet thing was not a good idea, but in spite of my outward confidence, I was too unsure of myself to make any changes to the procedures used by my sponsor. About halfway through the lesson, one of the sock boys was running full speed after the ball with one of his classmates in hot pursuit. Just as sock boy arrived at the ball, his pursuer gave him a hefty shove in the back. Because sock boy had no traction, the push in the back sent him hurtling headfirst into the corner of the stage. Poor sock boy flopped to the floor like a blob of Jell-O. He didn't move or make a sound. Every student in the class froze, as did their student teacher. Sock boy rolled over and I saw, to my horror, that he was covered in blood. I had never seen so much blood. I remember feeling a small sense of relief that at least he had rolled over on his own and was not dead, but there was still so much blood. I am not exactly sure what took place during the next several minutes. I recall my sponsor teacher magically arriving and telling me not to move sock boy because he could have a head or neck injury.

What seemed a lifetime later the paramedics arrived and sock boy, who had now become 'the student I broke', was about to be taken away in an ambulance. Things did not improve for me when, after my broken student had been lifted on to the stretcher, I watched him exit the gym and move directly past the school principal, who was holding the door open. I was quite sure, in all my course materials, I had not read, "When you are student teaching, a good opportunity to meet your school principal for the first time is just after a student in your class has suffered a serious injury and the principal is holding the door open for the paramedics as they carry the stretcher containing the student you have broken." I think Hargreaves and Fullan would agree, this is not best practice.

I continued to show films forward and backward to my Guidance class, and sock boy returned to school without any permanent damage.

I avoided breaking any more of my students for the duration of my student teaching at WRJH. Remarkably, I received a first-class evaluation for my student teaching practicum, and three years later was given another opportunity to 'teach'.

Unfortunately, breaking sock boy would not be the only time that I would break a student during my student teaching experience. Like the proverbial bad penny, the injury jinx would rear its ugly head on more than one occasion, and on one memorable day, not once but twice.

The 'Oh No, Not Again' Day

During my fourth year, I was assigned to Eric Hamber Secondary in Vancouver for my next teaching practicum.

At the time, Bob Pennyway was a full-time boys' PE teacher at the school and the best sponsor teacher a student teacher could have. He kept the most accurate records of attendance and achievement in the entire Vancouver School District. Not only the most accurate, but the neatest. As a hobby, he created stained glass artwork. The detail and precision needed to construct stained glass carried over to his record keeping at school. He was also very patient with and supportive of his students and student teachers. I was most fortunate to be assigned as Bob's student teacher for my second practicum.

I observed him teach and was terrifically impressed. His lessons were always thoughtfully organized, and unlike my first sponsor teacher, he emphasized safety. After I had observed a few of his classes, he assigned me to teach a three-week wrestling unit for his two grade-nine classes. He spent time with me organizing the lessons and kept emphasizing the safety procedures I should have in place. In the written lesson plans that I prepared and shared with Bob, I even added a section for safety. He was impressed. Impressed until I actually taught the third class in my unit.

The first two classes went well. I began with some gentle stretching, asked my class to bring out the mats and unroll them. Then a few more stretches on the mats and the introduction and demonstration of two wrestling moves per class. After the instruction, the boys were asked to practise the moves with a partner, but only at half intensity. Each class ended with a one-on-one match between two equally sized opponents. It was masterful teaching, until it wasn't. With about twenty minutes remaining in the third lesson of the unit, it all went wrong.

The first I heard of trouble was when one of the boys came over to me as I was observing a match on one of the other mats. "Sir, I think Peter has hurt himself."

No problem, I thought. A minor sprain or maybe the wind knocked out of him. I sauntered over to the mat where Peter had been wrestling and now was lying flat on his back, and asked him what the problem was. He told me his knee hurt so I gently rolled up the leg of his sweatpants. The first problem was that I could not find his kneecap. It took me longer than it should have to locate it, and when I did, I was pretty sure it was not supposed to be on the outside of his leg. I was quite sure it was supposed to be in the front. But there it was, in all its agony, ninety degrees from where it was supposed to be, and where I had never seen any other kneecap in my entire life. Another confusing observation I made, and another thing I had never seen before, was that poor Peter was as white as a ghost, despite appearing to be in relatively little pain. Very confusing, not only because this gruesome injury seemed to be causing Peter limited amounts of pain, but because Peter's skin colour had turned ashen white. I knew this was not okay. He was of Chinese descent. Not having a clue what to do except not move him, I asked one of the students to run to the staff room and get Mr. Pennyway. I was sure Bob would know what to do. Thankfully, he did. He was so calm. He looked at Peter's wayward kneecap, and then he looked at his pale, anemic-looking face and said, "I'm going to call for an ambulance. He's gone into shock." Oh my God, I thought, sock boy all over again. My first thought was to plead with Bob to keep the principal out of the gym until the ambulance left. Grossly selfish, I know, but it was what came racing into my mind at the moment.

The ambulance came, Peter went and the bell rang to end the class and begin the lunch break. I was shaken but confident all would be well, because Bob told me it would, and Bob was good at what he did.

The staff room at Hamber was segregated by gender in 1972 and was not a place that welcomed female members of staff, nor was it for the weak in character. It was a place of brutal teasing, and once in a while, cruel insults. To use today's language, it was a place of bullying. Word had spread fast about my wrestling disaster, and I knew I was destined to be the brunt of the male staff's sadistic teasing. No more "Hi, Hugh" or "How's it going, Mr. Greer?" I was subjected to "Any 911 calls lately, Killer?" and "Great way to decrease your class size. I should have thought of that myself." Looking back, all good-natured, but for me, way too soon.

I was shaken but not broken. I viewed this as an opportunity to show them all that I was made of strong stuff. I was to teach the same lesson to another grade-nine class after lunch, and this would prove that Peter's injury was a fluke. I was going to redeem myself and prove to all the doubters and hecklers in the staff room that I was not a wimp. I could come back from this minor hiccup and come away from the experience a better and stronger teacher. It turned out that I was quite mistaken.

Just as the morning lesson had begun well, so did the afternoon lesson. Same smooth introduction and instruction. Mats out and some 'controlled' one-on-one practice. Then the opportunity to wrestle against an opponent.

My teaching future then entered a downward spiral when I heard "Sir, I think René has hurt himself." My head swivelled to where I knew René was wrestling, and I was relieved to see him standing on his feet. Good, I thought, he can't be that badly hurt. I calmly walked over to him and asked him if he was okay. He stared at me, unable to speak. He then glanced down at his elbow. Just as Peter's kneecap had not been located where it was supposed to be, the end of René's elbow was not where it should have been either. And just as Peter had dislocated one of his parts, René had done the same thing to his elbow, which had popped itself out of its socket and was now located behind his upper arm. It actually looked more gross than Peter's kneecap relocation.

I didn't panic. I just made the same decision that I had made in the morning. "Go to the staff room and get Mr. Pennyway."

Bob assured me that René was not suffering from shock and that we did not need to call an ambulance. Thank goodness for small mercies. We led René to the nurse's office where the nurse applied ice to his deformed extremity. The secretary called his mom and she arrived moments later and drove him to the hospital emergency department where they sedated René and relocated his elbow.

Later that day, I discovered I had seriously misjudged myself. I was not made of strong stuff at all. When Bob suggested I go home and take the rest of the day off and that he would finish the class, I jumped at the opportunity. I really couldn't face the staff room again. I knew my tormentors would be at full throttle and that I could not survive a round two of their beating.

Somehow, even after this disastrous day, I managed to do quite well on my practicum and was informed by Bob at the end of it that I was the best student teacher he had ever had. Poor Bob, he must have had some very poor student teachers up to this point in his career.

The Foot in the Mouth

The remainder of my student teaching time at Hamber went without serious injury, but not without embarrassment. My sponsor teacher for the Guidance section of my practicum was one of the school's counsellors. Bill was a former PE teacher and now was a full-time counsellor. He had been a great athlete, excelling at softball and playing varsity basketball at UBC, and was to become men's champion at the Beach Grove Golf Club. He was very supportive of me in spite of my early faux pas.

The first day I met Bill, we sat down in his office and had a 'get to know you' chat. During this talk, he asked me several questions about my background, interests and hopes for my future. It was a good, solid introductory counselling meeting. During the meeting, he enquired where I had gone to high school, to which I proudly answered, "Burnaby Central."

"Were you ever taught there by Mr. Olenick?"

"Yes, he was one my PE teachers," and off I went on an ill-advised tirade about how much I did not like the man or enjoy his class. I then asked, "Do you know him?"

"Yes, I do, he was the best man at my wedding."

I now realize that during my time at Central I must have missed a crucial piece of evidence regarding his teaching ability. 'Mr. O' went on to teach at Langara College and in 2013, was awarded the Queen Elizabeth Silver Jubilee Medal. In 2014, he was awarded the Faculty Emeritus, Kinesiology Award in recognition of his outstanding work. Sorry, Mr. O.

The Contrast

I loved teaching and couldn't wait to get on with it as a career. I endured a few more courses back at UBC. The requirement for my final practicum was to be placed for one month somewhere out of the Lower Mainland. I was assigned to Merritt Secondary School (MSS).

The town of Merritt is 270 kilometres northeast of Vancouver. Its economy is driven by ranching, farming, forestry and tourism, and it is very much a working-class town.

In 1973, MSS had a student population of about 600 students who were from diverse cultural and socio-economic backgrounds. I immediately discovered the students were cooperative, respectful and a dream to teach. The staff was generally happy. Surprisingly, I learned far less about teaching during my four weeks there than I did about the nuances of living in a small town. This was my first experience living in a small community, and it left a lasting impression. I did learn some things that would enable me to be a better teacher, but I learned a great deal more about racism and drinking beer.

No matter which one of the eighteen secondary schools in Vancouver a student teacher is placed in, they are going to be introduced to students from many different ethnic backgrounds. Hamber had a significant Jewish population in the seventies, as well as a significant Asian presence. I quickly learned that no matter what a student's background, I could not make any assumptions about how they would behave or how well they would learn. Every ethnic group had its superstars, and every group had its pains in the ass.

Unlike Hamber, MSS did not have a noticeable population of either Asian or Jewish students. A significant number of students came from what was referred to then as East Indian and Native Indian backgrounds, today referred to as South Asian and Indigenous backgrounds. I had been sheltered while growing up in predominantly WASP Burnaby, and the part of my orientation to Merritt Secondary that included the 'them' and 'us' thing was very new and upsetting to me. Several members of the staff at the school made it very clear to me that 'we' were to drink in the Grasslands Pub because 'they' drank at the Merritt Hotel. I am ashamed to admit that, true to my student teaching philosophy of 'when in Rome . . .', I went along with what my teaching colleagues advised and drank with 'us', not 'them', during my time in Merritt.

And, oh my goodness, did we drink. Every day after school there was a teacher activity. We played volleyball in the gym or played a round of golf at the local course. We kicked around a soccer ball and went for long bike rides. The activities always ended with all of us consuming vast amounts of beer, needless to say, at the Grasslands, not the hotel. I believe I drank more beer in four weeks during this practicum than I drank in my previous four years of university.

It is my sincere hope and optimistic belief that today in Merritt things are much different. It has been a long time since I taught there, and I am confident that a great deal of awareness and education has taken place since my time student teaching there. I sure hope so.

Despite my overindulgence in alcohol and my severe discomfort with the prevalence of racism, I managed to pass my final practicum and complete my bachelor of education degree and subsequently was granted my British Columbia teaching certificate.

My mother could not hide her pride and peppered me with questions. "When is your graduation? Are parents invited? Where is it going to be? Do you get to wear one of those long robes and that funny-looking flat hat?"

I never heard him say it, but I think with some certainty that my father's reaction was much the same as mine: Will wonders never cease?

The Cart Before the Horse

To add another 'twilight zone' event to this time in my life, I had been offered a full-time teaching position with the Vancouver School District even before I had begun my final practicum.

During my fifth and final year at UBC, I had been required to take a methods course in teaching Guidance. It was one of the most useful courses I took during my program, and it was taught by one of the most exceptional educators I have ever known.

Bob Carkner had been a high school counsellor in Vancouver and in 1973 was the Coordinator of Guidance and Counselling Services for the Vancouver School Board. He was also the instructor of my Guidance methods class at UBC. He had noticed my efforts and decided he wanted me to work in Vancouver in an experimental program that was to begin in September, following my graduation. Ironically, the program was to be at my practicum school, Eric Hamber. Two of the counsellors at Hamber were retiring, and the idea was to replace them with two full-time Guidance teachers. This would allow the remaining counsellors to focus their entire time on counselling and not lesson preparation and classroom teaching. Somehow, he had convinced the people in the human resources department at the school board to hire me for this new full-time Guidance position.

It seemed strange to me that I had been offered a job before passing my final practicum, but it got a lot stranger when I met with the woman at the school board who did the hiring. Mrs. Fosbrooke was a legend at the school board. Everyone liked and respected her, and it seemed that everyone who had been hired to the district during the past several decades had been interviewed by her. She was quite candid with me that my interview with her was the first she had carried out with an applicant who had already been offered a job. Usually, she casually stated, the interview took place before a job was offered, not after.

We had a really nice chat, and she wished me well in my career. While I was driving home after the interview, I wondered if this was to be my destiny. A one-of-a-kind teacher. Breaking new ground, setting new precedents. As it turned out, it was not me who was to accomplish this, but the man who had offered me the job.

Bob Carkner went on to be a superstar educator. After his time in Vancouver, he moved to the Richmond School District, where he was principal at several Richmond secondary schools. He also established projects in Guatemala and Vietnam that provided opportunities for Richmond students to improve the world by building and maintaining orphanages. He created the Richmond mini-basketball program, which, for years, provided great opportunities to young players and provided Richmond's secondary schools with a plethora of outstanding ball players. To acknowledge his contributions to education, Bob was awarded an honorary doctor of laws degree and the Order of Canada. It was an honour to have known him. Thank you, Bob, for making me a better teacher.

As the years went by, however, I often wondered how such an exceptional educator could make such an enormous mistake and think it was a good idea to hire me for this experimental position. No one is perfect, I guess.

Part 2

The Teaching Years

Eric Hamber Secondary

– 3 years –

The year I began 'real' teaching, meaning the year I began getting paid to be a teacher, was 1973. I was back at Eric Hamber Secondary, where I had been a student teacher. Built in 1962, it was one of the newest secondary schools in Vancouver. At the time, Hamber's most notable graduate was Patty Loverock, who was one of Canada's elite 100- and 200-metre sprinters and went on to compete in the 1976 Olympic Games.

Eric Hamber Secondary School was named after Eric Werge Hamber, fifteenth Lieutenant-Governor of British Columbia and sole private Canadian guest, along with his wife, to attend the wedding of Queen Elizabeth II and Prince Philip. Hamber was an avid horse-racing enthusiast and always dressed his horses in blue and maroon silks. Today, Eric Hamber Secondary's sports uniforms are blue and maroon.

Hamber registered approximately 1,800 students when I arrived. There was a significant Filipino and Asian population at this time, as well as a large number of Jewish students.

The Ominous Prediction

It was great to have the opportunity to return to Hamber to begin my teaching career. I knew several of the teachers and recognized many of my former students. There was a sense of comfort on the first day of school, September 4, 1973, as I entered the building and took my seat in the lecture hall for the traditional morning staff meeting.

My first teaching assignment was twenty-one hours of Guidance per week. I was assigned my own counselling office, but was told in no uncertain terms that I was to do no counselling. This made sense to me, as I was in my first year of teaching, had no coursework in counselling and was only twenty-three years old. I thought I had died and gone to heaven. At the time, jobs in Vancouver were scarce, and I was going to start my career at a school I understood, with staff members I knew and, most impressively, in my own office, which had a door with my name on it. I also had my own telephone extension.

It didn't take long for me to question the desirability of my new job. During the morning staff meeting, one of my colleagues asked to take a look at the written copy of my timetable. Some thirty minutes later it reappeared with twenty-five names and dates written on it. Apparently, twenty-five of my new colleagues had put a dollar each in a pool and had written the date they thought I would have my nervous breakdown and quit. Closest to the date of my anticipated demise was going to win the money. My colleagues had come to the conclusion that mine was an impossible timetable, and I had been severely set up.

As it turned out, the teaching load itself was not all that bad. I had only four lesson preparations per week. The difficulty for me was that each lesson was repeated five or six times. The boredom factor was terrible. By the time I had watched the film about boys becoming men six times, I wanted to scratch my eyes out. I was the only teacher in the school who taught a 'boys only' load. This was a challenge. Twenty-one hours per week teaching boys thirteen to seventeen years of age the subject they considered the most useless on their timetable and, to make things worse, in the same block that they were scheduled into PE. So, in their minds, they were stuck taking a Guidance class instead of their much beloved PE class. It is no wonder twenty-five of my colleagues thought it was only a matter of time before I cracked.

Against overwhelming consensus, I hung in there for the entire year, and none of my naysayers ever saw a penny in winnings. It was of no surprise to anyone that after only one year, the full-time Guidance teaching model was abandoned, and the school returned to the traditional model of the counsellor who was responsible for a specific grade teaching Guidance to the students in that grade.

Although my teaching load had been eliminated after only one year, I was offered an opportunity to stay at Hamber. I had majored in PE and Guidance, but the next year I was offered four blocks of English and one block of PE. I had not taken an English course since my third year at university and had never taken a methods course in English. Regardless, I began my career as an English teacher. This was the way it was in 1974.

NAME Mr. H. Greer			CLASS Oct 5, 1973		ROOM 367
SUBJECTS Gu 8, 9, 10, 11					
Sept/73		SEMESTER I			23

	A	Gu 9	B	Gu 11	C	Gu 8	D	Gu 9	E
DAY 1									
DAY 2	B Gu 9		C Gu 10		D Gu 11		E Gu 10		A Gu 10
DAY 3	C Gu 8		D Gu 9		E Gu 9		A Gu 11		B Gu 10
DAY 4	D Gu 8		E Gu 8		A Gu 11		B Gu 11		C
DAY 5	E	Gu 9	A	Sup.	B	Gu 8	C	Gu 8	D

My first teaching timetable: the 'one and done' experiment

The Philosopher

My next two years at Hamber were enjoyable but difficult. Every lesson I taught was a new prep, and I discovered I was the world's slowest marker. I don't know if my marking speed would have been faster if I had been a trained teacher of English, but it felt like every spare second of time I had was consumed by marking the always-present set of papers. Marking consumed my life. During the third week of September, soon after my introduction into the world of teaching English, a colleague invited me to go with him to Exhibition Race Track to watch the horse races. During the nine-race program, which lasted about six hours, I spent eighteen minutes selecting horses to bet on, forty minutes lining up to place the bets and twenty-seven minutes watching the horses run around the track. That left me 275 minutes to do my marking. My colleague Bruce, who was a full-time PE teacher at Hamber and who was one of Hamber's great characters, was so disgusted by this that he said he would not go to the track with me ever again unless I was 'essay-free'. He told me I was an embarrassment to him and all betters at the race track.

All schools have their characters who develop a sense of entitlement as the years pass. Bruce was a special kind of man. 'Special', of course, can mean any number of things. He was wonderful with the students. He was a supportive PE teacher who encouraged all the students in his classes, regardless of their ability. He was a fair and kind coach to the students who played on his school teams. However, he was quite a different person to the adults in his life. When I arrived at Hamber, Bruce had several colleagues whom he refused to speak to, or who refused to speak to him. Typical of many but not all PE teachers, things in 'Bruce's world' were right or wrong, black or white, in bounds or out of bounds. No in-between. If you pissed off Bruce, you were given a life sentence.

Bruce was always willing to share his philosophical points of view with anyone who would listen. He had his own designated seat in the staff room that no one dared sit in, and he had his handpicked group of followers who had been given permission to sit with him. Several staff members referred to Bruce and his group as Spanky and Our Gang. One of Bruce's more well-known philosophical beliefs was 'Clerking beats working'. Quite simply, Bruce believed that it was easier to do the required paperwork that went along with the job than it was to actually teach the students. Unlike so many of his colleagues, Bruce enjoyed collating marks, filling out report cards and taking inventory of each and every piece of athletic equipment in the building. A very unique point of view from a very unique individual.

Another of his famous sayings was 'Bullshit baffles brains'. When I first heard Bruce utter this phrase, it sounded rather cynical to me. I wasn't sure I knew what he meant. However, as the years passed, and I saw how some decisions were made and how some things were done in my career, I discovered exactly what he meant. On many occasions, I observed that he was quite correct.

The Creative Learning Resource

Over the course of my career, I encountered and interacted with thousands, perhaps tens of thousands, of students. Now that I am retired, I only remember a small percentage of them and for all sorts of different reasons. One such student was in my English 9 class at Hamber during my second year of teaching.

Five years of training as a teacher had not really prepared me for the multitude of different learning styles and learning disabilities I was going to encounter. I had no training in teaching students with learning disabilities. I had never heard of attention deficit disorder, hyperactivity or a medication called Ritalin and had never been given any information on how to effectively teach students who may have had these conditions or been on this medication. Looking back, I am quite sure Anthony had them all.

Anthony was a delightful fourteen-year-old grade-nine student who was in one of my English 9 classes. He was polite, smart and had a wonderful sense of humour. His sister was in grade eleven and in another one of my classes. She, like her brother, was a great kid. She was Anthony's greatest ally. She mentored him, protected him and loved him to bits. Unfortunately, during the time Anthony was in my class, he was on his own, and to describe him as a student with a short attention span would not come close to describing his behaviour. In the staff room, behind the closed door, I had heard him described as a "complete loon" and "off the wall." I made it my mission to support him and his learning in any way I could.

Although I liked him, he constantly drove me crazy. It was impossible to keep him focused. Any tiny movement anywhere in the room, out in the hall or outside the window drew his attention, and he was gone from the activities in the class. I moved him to the front of the room, hoping he could focus a bit better. I moved him away from the door and windows hoping for the same thing. I had no success. He always managed to find some movement to draw his attention away from me and what I was saying. I would invite him to rejoin me and he would, but my requests often produced mocking giggles from other students, which I knew embarrassed him. For several weeks I tried without success to keep him focused, and then, an epiphany. A moment of sudden and great opportunity presented itself. It happened as the students were working, and I was mindlessly gazing out my classroom window down onto the staff parking lot.

A delivery truck had pulled in to the parking lot, and I saw two burly young men removing several large cardboard boxes from the back of the truck. Each box had a picture of a refrigerator on two of its sides. After class, I made haste downstairs to the foods classroom, where I assumed the fridges were to be unloaded. Standing there in front of me was the solution to Anthony's learning struggles. A row of several empty cardboard boxes.

I asked the delivery guys if I could have one of the boxes and if they would be good enough to remove one of the four sides. They looked a bit puzzled but indicated they were happy to accommodate my request, and I was even happier when, at the beginning of Anthony's next English class, he and his desk fit perfectly inside the box.

Before you judge me and accuse me of cruel and inhumane behaviour toward my student and report me to the Ministry of Education, please understand, Anthony fully supported this idea. As a matter of fact, when I suggested to him that this might help his learning and that he could, at any time, come out, he willingly inserted himself in the box.

I would like to believe that this was a positive experience for Anthony. He was much more focused from inside the box and easily passed the course. I believe he ended up with a *B*. I assume he did not suffer any permanent emotional damage or I would have heard about it by now. Would I use this technique now? Probably not, but 1974 was a much different time in education, and I sleep well at night believing this was a positive experience for Anthony and that he holds no ill will toward me. This 'inside the box' experiment was the first of my very few 'thinking outside the box' moments.

The Clueless One

I knew from the beginning of my career that there was much more to the job than the classroom teaching part. I coached teams, sponsored clubs and supervised student activities. At one of the first school dances I supervised, I observed one of my students behaving in a rather unusual manner. After five years of university and a combined total of nine weeks of student teaching, plus just over a year of full-time experience, I felt I was able to recognize student behaviour that was under the influence of alcohol. On this occasion, I was sure that my student Abby was pissed. I reported this to Mr. O'Brien, one of the vice-principals (I found him more than a little intimidating and never could refer to him as anything but "Mr. O'Brien"). He promptly escorted her to the side of the gym, spoke to her and escorted her to his office. Unlike my own feelings toward him, Abby didn't seem intimidated by him in the least. She actually told him how great he was and gave him a hug. No Breathalyzer test required after that.

I completed my shift of supervision and drove home. The next morning, during first period, Mr. O'Brien telephoned my room and asked me to pay him a visit at the beginning of the lunch hour. He began our meeting by complimenting me on my observational acuity and requested that I write a statement explaining exactly what I had seen and deliver it to him before I left at the end of the day. Apparently Abby's mom was not happy and was under the impression that there had been many students at the dance under the influence and her daughter had been singled out.

I diligently completed my assignment and, after the day's classes, submitted it, as requested, on my way to my team's basketball practice. After practice, I checked my letter box and found a note from Mr. O'Brien summoning me to his office to meet with him and Abby's mom at 8:00 a.m. the next morning. The thought of even entering his office made me feel very anxious. Little did I know that thirty-three years later, the name above his office door would be mine, and I would be the one asking teachers to join me for a meeting. I hope I never made a teacher feel as anxious about entering my office as Mr. O'Brien made me feel about entering his.

Abby's mom was not happy. She had demanded the meeting. This was to be my first parent discipline meeting, and I was terrified.

First of all, I was terrified of Mr. O'Brien and his office. Second, I was terrified of the notion of a student discipline meeting with a parent. But I had been ordered, so it was to be.

Mr. O'Brien's words of wisdom and mentorship to me before the meeting were "Don't speak. Let me do the talking."

"Fine by me," I agreed.

Abby's mom was a large, daunting woman who wore layers of makeup and had jet-black dyed hair. I wondered if she had prepared for the meeting the way warriors prepare to do battle. If her purpose was to intimidate me, it definitely worked. She wanted to know why I had taken it upon myself to report only her daughter to the administration and not all the other students who had been drinking.

I looked at Mr. O'Brien for permission to speak. After receiving a subtle nod, I responded, "She was the only one I noticed."

"Is it possible that you singled her out because you are anti-Semitic, Mr. Greer?"

I began to wonder what Abby had told her mom about all this.

At twenty-four, I was far from a man of the world. I had led a sheltered life and was unaware of many of the ways of life. It is fair to say that I was extremely naive. I had never heard the word 'anti-Semitic' and had no idea what it meant. Call me ignorant, call me stupid, but this is the truth. I then made a horrible mistake. I spoke without getting the nod from Mr. O'Brien.

"I'm sorry, but I don't know what that word means."

Abby's mom went beet red. She clenched her teeth and her fists. I froze in disbelief, not having a single clue what I had said wrong. "How dare you mock me," she hissed.

'Mock' I did know the meaning of, but I certainly did not feel I had done that. At least, not intentionally.

Mr. O'Brien then did what vice-principals are supposed to do. He took charge and protected me from further damage. He stood up and asked me to leave his office. There was only one thing for me to do, so I stood up and headed directly back to my classroom and looked up 'anti-Semitic' in my dictionary. Oh, I thought to myself, I guess Abby is Jewish. Brilliant deduction, Sherlock.

I was not privy to what happened after that. In the morning I found a note in my letter box from Mr. O'Brien thanking me for my time. My first student discipline meeting had not gone all that well. I would like to think the other dozens, maybe even hundreds, of student discipline meetings I was involved in after that went a little better. Honestly, looking back, some did, but many didn't.

The Field Trip

During my second year of teaching at Hamber, I was asked by the track-and-field and swim team coaches if I was interested in helping

92

chaperone the teams to Hawaii. Three teachers, two parents, seventy-five high school students and me, staying in a Honolulu hotel over spring break. What could possibly go wrong?

What went wrong came to me right out of the blue and was not what I ever could have anticipated in a million years. The students, with few exceptions, behaved well, and the track-and-field and swim competitions went as expected. We got our rear ends severely kicked by the host school. In spite of the humiliation, a good time was had by all. That is, until twenty minutes into our flight home, when we heard this thunderous bang followed shortly after by an announcement from the captain instructing us to pay close attention to the flight attendants as they gave us instructions as to how to assume the crash position.

Our students were great. They remained calm and listened intently to the instructions. We were informed that instead of landing in Seattle, as scheduled, our plane was making an emergency landing in Hilo, on the Big Island. A short time later, as we all assumed 'the position', we experienced the most terrifying landing imaginable. To this day I cannot understand how that 747 did not shake apart. The vibration and noise from the aircraft were like a volcanic eruption, which was appropriate given our location. Finally, after taxiing down the runway for what seemed like hours, but in reality was probably less than a minute, we came to a stop. I heard some quiet praying and some whimpering. Not being of a religious persuasion, I admit I place myself firmly into the latter category.

We were then informed that during our take off from Honolulu, the airplane lost its hydraulic system, and the captain was forced to land the plane manually, with only the use of the plane's foot brakes. Quite a feat, apparently. At the conclusion of the announcement, the passengers erupted into applause. We were instructed to exit the plane and told we would be taken by taxi to the Hilo Lagoon Hotel, where we would be hosted, at no charge, until the plane was repaired, at which point we would be able to complete our journey home. Another burst of applause, led by the Hamber students, who immediately recognized this as another day in paradise and, with any luck, an extra day of spring break holiday. As it turned out, it was actually three more days in paradise and two extra days of spring break.

Finally, at about 11:00 in the evening we got our students settled into their rooms. This procedure did not take as long as usual, as departing the airport was expedited because without the use of the plane's hydraulics, it was impossible to access our luggage. We were stuck with only what we had carried on. My first thought was about needing a bathing suit. A minor irritation. It never occurred to me that not having their luggage would cause such extreme trauma for several of our students.

At 9:00 the following morning, we met with our students and informed them that we would be grounded and staying at the hotel until a part for the hydraulic system of the aircraft was flown in from New York. All would be well. The airline was paying for the rooms and food for our group. We soon discovered that neither the airline, nor the hotel, had any idea about how much food seventy-five ravenous teenagers could eat. The students had been buying their own food while in Honolulu, and most of them had chosen souvenirs over food and had run out of money several days before our departure. They were starving. The breakfast buffet became a Hamber eating frenzy. Just as a tray of scrambled eggs was refilled, it was quickly emptied, then the bacon tray was refilled and emptied. Then there were no more sausages and then no toast and so on and so on. It must have appeared to the staff and hotel guests that these kids had not eaten in a month. To me this was all very amusing and not entirely unexpected, but I would receive a deeper lesson yet on adolescent behaviour later that day.

I was relaxing in my room after buying a bathing suit at the hotel gift shop and spending some time lounging by the pool thinking how well things had been going, when my life suddenly became anything but relaxing. Earlier in the day, our students had been complimented by the hotel staff on their excellent behaviour, and I had slipped into a false sense of security that our trip would be a resounding success and this minor glitch was nothing to worry about. And then there was a knock on my door.

"Can we come in and talk with you, sir?" whispered the designated spokesperson for three of our grade-eleven girls. All three of my visitors had facial expressions that indicated impending doom.

"Of course. Come in," I replied with some trepidation.

"We have to get our luggage. It's really important," she continued.

"I don't think that's possible. As we told you, until the hydraulics are repaired, we can't access any of our luggage."

"You don't understand. We really need our luggage."

Despite being scared stiff of their response, I continued with my best empathic voice. "Okay, then, help me understand."

The three girls took turns looking at one another after which, ironically, there was a pregnant pause. One of the two girls who had not spoken looked at the spokesperson and said, "Go ahead. Tell him."

"It's like this. Our birth control pills are in our suitcases, and we really need them."

Just like that, my mind jettisoned back to Mr. O'Brien's office and the interview with Abby's mom. How could I be so naive? How could I not know the meaning of the word, 'anti-Semitic' and how could I not know that grade-eleven girls would be having sex in Hawaii? More importantly, what the hell was I going to say now?

I suppose I sputtered out something that made sense to my visitors, although I don't remember what. I do remember thinking that they seemed to be happy enough when they left. I, on the other hand, was not happy. How could I be surprised with this? It was 1974, and young people in high school were having sex. I had been their Guidance teacher. I was the teacher who had taught them about birth control and sexually transmitted diseases. I should be happy and proud that they were comfortable enough with their relationship with me to choose to speak to me in their hour of need. I was anything but. I was pissed. Why were these grade-eleven girls having sex, and at twenty-four years of age, I wasn't? Not only was I not having sex, I had never even had sex. What the hell was wrong with me?

Two days later, we flew home without access to our luggage. There would be no long-term repercussions from the unavailable birth control trauma. For several weeks after, every time I saw one of the three girls at school, I would do my best not to stare at their midsection but often couldn't stop myself. Only after a few weeks with no evidence of the dreaded bump did my paranoia subside. My annoyance at the 'why them and not me?' situation, however, was another matter. Talk about being a late bloomer.

The Stag

At the beginning of my second year at Hamber, my old friend Gary, of shattered window-fame at Cariboo Hill, joined our staff. He was soon to be married, and he had asked me to be his best man. Both Gary and I liked the students at Hamber, and most of them liked us. Gary and I were young, friendly and easy to get along with. We both had conversations with our students that I would not recommend teachers have today. The conversations were not inappropriate, just a little too casual and informal.

Somehow, after one of these not-recommended conversations, several of the students discovered that Gary was soon to be married, and I was going to be his best man. During this one particular conversation I had with several of the grade-ten boys, I was asked if I was going to organize a stag party for Gary. I had assumed I would but had not gotten around to planning any of the details, so in my most cautious and noncommittal voice responded, "Yes, I guess so."

"Where will you have it, sir?" Ted inquired. Ted was a great kid. He was one of my favourite students. He was funny, friendly, and always appropriate, which made him very likeable. He was in one of my English 10 classes.

"Well, I haven't got that far along in the planning yet, Ted." I really hadn't, but more to the point, I really didn't want to discuss the details of my stag party planning with one of my students.

"You know, sir, my family owns the Penthouse Night Club. You would have a really great time there."

Ted was fifteen years old and was in grade ten, but he wanted to help me organize my friend's stag party. This was not at all comfortable for me. My comfort level dropped even more when, the next day, Ted remained after class, reached into his pocket and handed me a wad of tickets.

"Here, take these tickets for the club. Just tell me the date, and I will make sure everyone has a terrific time."

I did my usual thing. I sat there speechless with my mouth hanging open. My grade-ten student had just handed me tickets to Vancouver's most well-known strip club. Despite the fact that it was 1975, and things were a little more casual than they are today, this was not a good thing.

However, in the absence of a better plan, I let Ted know the date, and when we arrived, we were shown to a reserved table directly in front of the stage. I am sure the servers and entertainers had been prepped, and they treated us like royalty. It was the best stag ever. I was the best best man ever. I really knew how to organize a stag. All I had to do was make a casual comment to one of my grade-ten students. Who'd have thought?

The One of Many Hamber Stories

All schools have their own unique stories that reflect the history and culture of the school. Through the years, these stories morph into legends that are passed down from generation to generation. Hamber had more than its share.

One of Hamber's most famous and amusing stories is about a new immigrant family who one day came to the school to register their son into grade nine. The vice-principal at the time was Mr. Winteringham. Mr. Winteringham was a wonderful, compassionate man and always put students first in all of his duties as vice-principal. The story goes like this.

The Kumar family had moved into the Hamber catchment and were in Mr. Winteringham's office filling in registration paperwork.

"Good morning, Mr. and Mrs. Kumar."

"Good morning, Mr. Winteringham."

"This is your son?"

"Yes, it is."

"What's his name?"

"Ashit."

Without a second's hesitation, "Welcome to Hamber, Ashit."

Mr. Winteringham completed the necessary paperwork before addressing the elephant in the room.

"So, Mr. and Mrs. Kumar, I would like to discuss your son's name. Here at the school, we must register the student with the name on his or her birth certificate, but we can call them any name we agree to if that name is a more appropriate choice for the student." To be expected, there were blank looks from the Kumars. "Your son's name in the English language is going to draw some negative attention and may get him teased and even bullied by some of the other students. I would like to suggest you go home tonight and come up with another name that we can call him."

Mr. and Mrs. Kumar were very appreciative of the vice-principal's concern for their son and agreed to send a new name, in writing, with Ashit the next morning. Problem solved.

True to the agreement, Ashit appeared at Mr. Winteringham's office first thing the next morning with written confirmation of his new name. The family had spent a considerable amount of time discussing the matter and had agreed on a new name. Unfortunately, when Mr. Winteringham had met with the family, he omitted one small detail about the impending name change.

> *Dear Mr. Winteringham,*
>
> *We, Ashit Kumar's mother and father, agree that from this date our son may be called "Ashit Brown."*
>
> *Sincerely,*
>
> *Mr. and Mrs. Kumar*

I loved my time at Hamber, and after three years of teaching, I knew I had chosen the right career. Confident in my life's path, I was anxious to improve my skills and become the best teacher I could become. However, at the age of twenty-six, I came to the realization that it was time for me to grow up a little. What better way to accomplish this than to buy a backpack and a pup tent and travel around the world? I applied for and received a one-year leave of absence and spent the next twelve months visiting twenty-three countries.

Prince of Wales Secondary

- 4 Years -

The year I spent travelling was a year without a winter, as I followed summer from the northern hemisphere to the southern hemisphere and then back again to the north. I saw amazing sights, experienced incredible adventures and met many marvellous people. I also decided teaching was the life career for me. I missed teaching during this time, but I especially missed the young men and women who entertained me and kept me energized. At the end of my year of travelling, I was looking forward to returning to work and being more mature in myself and skilful at my craft.

In August of 1977, after travelling for twelve months, I arrived home to find a letter from the Vancouver School Board informing me that I had been assigned to teach at Point Grey Secondary School. To my utter bewilderment, my teaching assignment was seven blocks of English. As I still considered myself to be a PE teacher, I had anticipated a load that was appropriate for my training. Unexpectedly, one of Point Grey's English teachers had been diagnosed with an eye problem and had requested a full-time PE load. He was given 'my' load and I his because I had taught a couple of English classes at

Hamber and was considered, by the Vancouver School Board, to be a qualified and experienced English teacher. Not for the first time, and certainly not for the last, they were wrong.

The Short Stay

I spent the month of September planning my units, getting to know my students and developing relationships with the staff, and then it all went up in smoke. At precisely 3:00 p.m. on the last Friday in September, after settling in to my new school and teaching assignment, my classroom phone rang. It was the school secretary. I was to meet with the principal at 3:30 p.m.

He was as considerate as he could be as he delivered the bad news. Point Grey's projections were wrong. They had predicted that more students would show up than actually had. In Vancouver, all schools are required, in the spring, to project the number of students they think will arrive at school in September. Point Grey had guessed, or as they say at the school board, 'projected', incorrectly. The result of this 'mis-guess' meant Point Grey was going to lose a teacher. As a result of my low seniority, I was that teacher. I was to report to Prince of Wales on Monday morning. Prince of Wales had 'under-guessed' and needed another teacher.

I negotiated with the principal to meet with my Point Grey students first thing the next Monday morning to explain to them why they now had a new English teacher and to give me the opportunity to explain why I was leaving. I was not interested in my former students going home after school on Monday and telling their parents their English teacher was so bad, he got fired. Believable, perhaps, but not accurate. After the meeting, I drove down the Arbutus Street hill to begin the first day of my four years at Prince of Wales. I was hopeful that the disappointment of being transferred to another school after only one month would be offset by getting a more suitable timetable at my new school. I was wrong again.

Prince of Wales Secondary (P.W.) is a west-side school, socio-economically and culturally much like Eric Hamber. It has always been, and remains today, an academically driven school. P.W. parents have high academic expectations of their children and demand top-quality teaching from the staff. P.W. also has an impressive list of alumni.

Andrea Neil is a P.W. grad. She appeared 132 times for Canada's national women's soccer team and is the first woman inducted for soccer into the Canadian Sports Hall of Fame. Broadcaster Rafe Mair was a P.W. grad. Mair was a Social Credit Member of the Legislative Assembly (MLA) from 1975 to 1981 and was a well-known radio personality and political commentator. Spencer Chandra Herbert, MLA for Vancouver–West End, who was elected in 2008 and re-elected in 2009, 2013, 2017 and 2020, is also a P.W. grad. Perhaps the best known of the P.W. alumni is Kim Campbell, PC, CC, OBC, QC and (as of the time of writing) Canada's only woman prime minister. She was also P.W.'s first female students' council president.

Unlike my first day at Hamber, I did not know a single teacher at P.W. The bizarre nature of the assignment of courses I was allocated to teach continued. Even though my degree was in PE and Guidance, my teaching load consisted of all English and social studies classes. I will never understand what qualified me to teach social studies. It had been ten years since I had taken my last social studies class, and that was in grade eleven at Burnaby Central.

I was fortunate to have a department head in English who was prepared to overlook my lack of experience and deficit of method courses in the subject. He appeared supportive of adding me to his department. He was polite and respectful, and I assumed he managed to come to peace with this situation, even knowing I was one of 'those jocks'. I had, after all, taught the subject for two whole years. It turned out this was not the reason he so graciously accepted this situation. As fortune would have it, his daughter had been in my English 11 class during the previous month at Point Grey and had shared with him that I was not a complete idiot. She may have even said something more complimentary.

The social studies assignment, however, was another story, as was my department head's reaction to me joining his department. "Oh, God no! Are you kidding me?" were his exact words. I'm sure what he meant was "Welcome to the department." I hadn't the foggiest idea about the curriculum or the methodology. My entire knowledge of world history was based on my own high school social studies courses and my father's description of the Second World War, and how he single-handedly won the war without any help from anyone. I knew Dad would insist I refer to it as "WWII, the big one." I knew even less geography. Again, I was lucky and was introduced to an experienced full-time member of the social studies department who offered to mentor me. I would once again survive.

The New Best Friend

I bumbled through my first year of teaching social studies and English at P.W. and was blessed when, in September of 1977, my soon-to-be close friend Dave arrived as the new vice-principal. During the next four decades, Dave and I would travel together, play golf together, win and lose vast quantities of money at our once-per-month nickel-and-dime poker games and, for seven years, share a grade as vice-principal and counsellor at another Vancouver secondary school. In 1978, however, I knew nothing about him except he couldn't manage to get any heat into my classroom.

My classroom at the time was the farthest away from the school's boiler room and was ridiculously cold for half of the year. After the Remembrance Day holiday, and during an unusually cold stretch of weather, my room was unbearably cold. I seem to remember the thermostat in my room registering 52 degrees Fahrenheit. I wrote a couple of notes to Dave informing him of this and received replies that I felt were somewhat dismissive. I instituted the 'it's okay if you're five minutes late for class' policy for my students, to allow them to go to their lockers to put on a coat before arriving to my class. During a conversation with the teacher across the hall from me, who suffered the same heat dysfunction, I was informed that if I took the cover off the thermostat and attached a rubber band to the little flipper thing inside, it would permanently open a supply of heat to my room. The next day I brought a mini screwdriver to school and removed the front cover from the thermostat. I then attached a rubber band and voila, instant heat came pouring out of my registers. Problem solved, until three days later when I received a memo from Dave. "Hugh, please see me after school today so we can discuss the heat situation in your room."

My first thought was to send a reply memo stating, "What heat situation? I have lots of heat," but not knowing Dave or his sense of humour, or lack thereof, I decided it would be wiser to just show up to his office as requested.

After school that day, Dave informed me that the custodian who cleaned my room had informed the building engineer that I had rigged up this elastic band thermostat contraption. The building engineer then informed Dave that doing this would put the entire integrity of the building's heating supply in jeopardy and that the offending elastic band had to be removed. "Really?" I questioned. "You know this is an elastic band we are talking about here, not a nuclear meltdown."

"Just get rid of it" was his stern reply.

I dutifully removed the elastic band, anticipating that within a very short period of time, my room would be inspected by the custodian, building engineer and vice-principal. The next day my classroom was back to its former igloo status. I could not understand why I had been targeted and not the teacher across the hall, so I asked him. "Oh, I guess I forgot to tell you that you needed to replace the front cover before you leave for the day." Yup, I guess you did.

After stewing about it all evening, the next day I wrote Dave a note. I was only twenty-eight years old and full of enthusiasm. Translated, this means 'arrogant'. I wrote Dave a note indicating that if this heat problem was not resolved soon, I would bring my classes down to the office where it was nice and warm and teach them there. I placed it in Dave's letter box at the lunch break. During my afternoon classes,

I rethought the wording of my note and came to the conclusion, yet again, that I was an idiot. It was too late, however, to do anything about it. I had cast my fate. I was doomed to be told off. Perhaps even sent to the principal's office for discipline. For two hours I imagined multiple scenarios, and none of them worked out well for me.

Before leaving for the day, I mustered up enough courage to do what I always did on my way out of the building. I walked through the office and checked my letter box. In it I found Dave's reply. With great precision, he had whittled a mini campfire and delicately placed it on the inside flap of a package of matches. Below his 'solution' to my problem was written, "Here, I hope this helps keep your room warm." There and then, I decided this was someone I wanted to get to know. He was definitely my kind of guy. He reminded me a lot of myself. Witty, sarcastic and a bit of a jerk.

The City Champions

My teaching load at P.W. never did reflect my training, nor my desire to teach PE. I continued to be assigned English and social studies classes and most years a block of Psychology 11. As a result of being excluded from the PE department, I turned my attention to coaching. Coaching teams in high school is totally voluntary and gives teachers an opportunity to interact with students in a much different way than in the classroom. P.W. was a rugby school and chose not to register soccer teams in the interschool leagues. As a result, I was not able to coach the sport I enjoyed the most and in which I had the greatest coaching expertise. So I decided I would volunteer to coach basketball. I wasn't much of a basketball player in high school, but I had taken a university course in basketball coaching so I figure I was qualified enough. I coached a couple of the boys' teams and then was asked if I would like to coach the junior girls' team. The junior girls' age group usually puts them in grade ten. One of the school's PE teachers was going to coach the juvenile girls' team, which was made up of mostly grade nines, then the following year she wanted to continue with them and coach them as juniors. The plan was for her to coach the senior team the year after that and thus allow me the opportunity, after my junior season, to coach at the senior level. I thought this was a great deal, and I agreed to it without hesitation.

I had been told by one of my teaching colleagues that this PE teacher/coach who was going to move up with her team was someone who had a great deal of experience and success as a basketball player and coach, but I had never heard of her. Her name was Darlene. This would be yet another one of those naïveté experiences in my young career. Something I should have known, or at least looked into, but didn't. I now lament having ignored the opportunity to learn from her and increase my coaching expertise. If only I had been more 'with it'.

As it turns out, this Darlene person was Darlene Currie. And yes, she does have some experience and success playing and coaching the game of basketball. In fact, Darlene played for Canada in three Pan American Games. In 1970, she was named head coach of the Canadian women's national basketball team. In 1971, she took the Canadian women to Brazil for their first appearance in the modern era at the FIBA World Basketball Championships. She was inducted into the Canadian Basketball Hall of Fame in 1994 and, in 2019, was inducted into the British Columbia Sports Hall of Fame as a builder of the game of basketball.

As a high school coach, Darlene was amazing. She was brilliant with the girls on her teams, and although I did not realize her pedigree, I did manage to gain some valuable experience simply by watching her coach. Her unintentional mentoring was so good, my junior girls' team won the 1978 Vancouver City Championship. However, this did not come about without some major controversy.

The Vancouver Junior Girls' Basketball League is divided into west-side teams and east-side teams. This structure is in place to reduce travel to and from games, especially in the winter when it gets dark early, and the girls end up forced to take the bus across town after their games. There were, and continue to be, some not-so-subtle differences in the style of play from each side of the city. West-side players tend to be more timid and less aggressive on the basketball court. As a coach, one of my challenges was to convince the girls to be more aggressive without playing dirty. During the season, we had great success in league play against the other west-side teams and advanced to the city finals against the winners of the east-side division. Unlike the P.W. girls, the Templeton junior girls' basketball team did not suffer from a lack of aggressive play. Their coach was an elite athlete who played for many years on Canada's national women's softball team. Her team reflected her competitiveness.

The format of the finals was best of three. The first team to win two games would become city champion. The first game was played at P.W., and we lost it in a very uneventful game by three points. I must admit, after that loss, I thought our chances of winning the next two games were remote, especially with the next game being played at Templeton. The Templeton gym was a less than friendly environment to bring west-side girls into. As with the first game played at P.W., we would have one paid professional referee provided by the referees' association and one student referee, provided by the home school.

The first half of the second game finished without incident, with our girls trailing by a point. The Templeton centre, who after grad- uating from high school was awarded a basketball scholarship and played for four years in the United States, was having a great game, so at half-time, I made a couple of minor adjustments. I changed our defence to a formation where we could double-team her. I positioned one of our girls in front of her and one checking her from the back. Early in the second half, the first time their centre was passed the ball, she pivoted around and collided into our player checking from the back. The professional referee called an offensive foul against the Templeton centre. This was her third foul of the game. I could tell that the Templeton coach did not like the call, but she restrained her displeasure for the moment, and I made a big deal of congratulating our defenders on their great defence.

Several minutes later, the exact same thing happened with the exact same result, only this time the offending player said something rather uncomplimentary to the referee, and he gave her a technical foul for unsportsmanlike conduct. This was her fifth and disqualifying foul. She was done for the game. I could not have been happier, and her coach could not have been less happy.

The Templeton coach was incensed, so much so that she threw her water bottle onto the court, perilously close to the professional referee. To no one's surprise, she too was issued a technical foul. Then it got even goofier. She verbally abused the referee until she finally spurted out, "You are biased against me. You have always hated me. I am not going to continue to be treated like this. We are not going to play anymore."

Without a second's delay, the referee blew his whistle and loudly announced that the game was over and the official score would be recorded as P.W. 2 – Temp 0.

I lined my players up for the traditional end of game handshake, and I heard the coach say to her team, "Get into the locker room. We are not shaking hands with those cheaters."

The P.W. parents who were in attendance and who had provided transportation to the game looked stunned but remained silent. I gathered the parents and players around and pleaded, "Get your things, get into your cars and get out of here." The one and only time all season I issued a direct order to the team.

That night, I called my principal at his home and gave him a brief description of the events of the afternoon. Shortly after, I received a call from the head of the referees' association asking me to provide him with a detailed, written summary of what had taken place.

Two days later, I received a copy of a letter written by the Templeton coach detailing how incompetent the professional referee had been and how poorly behaved the P.W. players had been. She also mentioned that the P.W. coach (that would be me) had lost control of his players. There was also a demand from the coach that the referee for the next game under no circumstances be the same person who had refereed the previous game. Somehow, and not from me, a copy of the letter was given to one of our parents who was in attendance at the game. She shared it with the other parents who had also attended the game, which resulted in a steady stream of phone calls to the P.W. principal supporting and congratulating the behaviour of all members of our team and, I assume, describing more accurately the events of two days previous.

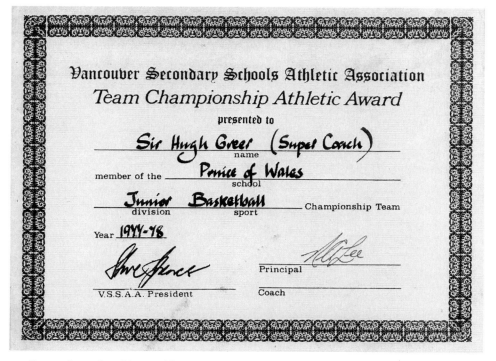

Team championship certificate, including athletic association president's attempt at humour

The next and deciding game was to be played in a neutral gym and refereed by one professional referee and one student from the neutral school. On game day, the Point Grey gym was completely packed with interested onlookers. The word had spread. The principal from P.W. and the principal from Templeton were there, as was the district coordinator of athletics for the Vancouver School Board. Every one of our players had at least one parent there and a host of friends who had come to support them. I had no doubt that this was to be an eventless game, won by the better team, and would involve no controversy. Then in walked the referee from the professional association.

In 1978, and for many of the previous years, the head referee in charge of allocating officials was a man named Gordie McDonald. He ruled with an iron fist, or in this case an iron whistle. Nobody told Gordie what to do. Nobody ordered Gordie to do anything. He was strong, stubborn and could be vindictive. All of us involved in the local basketball scene knew this. I can only assume that in her fit of anger, the Templeton coach had a brief brain freeze when she wrote the letter and forgot this, because in came the same referee who had refereed the previous game. I was not the least surprised to see him. The Templeton coach froze in disbelief. I chuckled with satisfaction. Then, nothing. Not a word. I can only assume she accepted her fate.

It was not the only time she was forced to accept defeat that afternoon, as the P.W. junior girls did themselves proud and played a tremendous game. Final score: P.W. 36 – Temp 33. At the end of the game, another refusal to shake hands. In the words of John Wooden, legendary basketball coach of the UCLA Bruins, "Things turn out best for people who make the best of the way things turn out."

The Abduction

As well as teaching and coaching during my years at P.W., I completed a master of education degree in counselling psychology. A requirement of the degree was to complete a practicum course. The most obvious and straightforward plan for me was to work with one of the counsellors at the school. I approached a member of the counselling department whom I thought I could most relate to and asked him if he was willing to be my practicum supervisor. He was. The parameters from my university supervisor for how the practicum should be organized were very vague. I felt I had a free hand for how I could structure my work. I decided to use the student teaching practicum model of observing and teaching (in this case, counselling) while being observed, and then take over. I completed exactly one observation before a list of twelve students appeared in my letter box. Somehow, I had been assigned to be their counsellor. Somehow the observation stage of my practicum was over after one session, and I was now able to take on unsupervised counselling of these twelve students. I put this down to rapid growth of my counselling skills. What else could it be?

Kevin was one of the students I had been assigned to counsel. He was a grade-eight boy whose father had been a counsellor at another school in the district. His father had recently and suddenly passed away. Kevin's issue, which I was assigned to 'fix', was that he wouldn't come to school.

My vast experience in counselling told me there must be something happening at school that was keeping Kevin from attending. Perhaps he was being bullied. Maybe he was embarrassed because he was failing his courses. There had to be a reason why this kid would not come to school. I interviewed his teachers, his friends and even students in his grade who didn't even know him. Nothing. I read up on school truancy, hoping to formulate a theory and then put a plan in place that would get Kevin back to school. I then decided a home visit and interview with his mom might be helpful.

Wouldn't you know it, according to his mom, Kevin's psychiatrist believed that Kevin's refusal to attend school had nothing to do with school. Maybe I needed more training after all to be good at this. Maybe a couple of theory courses and a course in interviewing was not enough to make me a counsellor. Kevin's psychiatric assessment indicated that he was suffering from 'separation anxiety'. Kevin's dad had died very suddenly. Kevin went off to school one morning, and when he got home he was told his dad had died. As a result, he was afraid to leave the house in case when he returned home someone was going to tell him his mom had also died. So I went back to the textbooks from my counselling program and looked up 'separation anxiety' and sure enough, it made sense. Now having a diagnosis, I turned my attention to the treatment. The treatment recommendation from the psychiatrist and the literature was to get him to school, no matter what. It didn't really matter if he attended any of his classes, the important thing was to get him in the building each day and out of his home. It was also important that he stayed at school the whole day.

P.W. has about eighteen exit doors. If I could even manage to get Kevin in the building, how the hell was I going to keep him there? Ironically, the keeping him there was not as difficult as the getting him there.

Kevin's vice-principal had been a friend and colleague of Kevin's dad. He had also been my sponsor teacher when I student-taught at Windermere Secondary, and I respected and liked him very much. He had been a counsellor for many years, and I felt fortunate that I was going to work with him to support Kevin. The counsellor/vice-principal relationship is unique in high schools. Each member of the team has a different role, but both are working to achieve the same outcome. Before supporting Kevin, Clive and I were always on the same page. While working with Kevin to help him succeed, we were also on the same page. What could we do to help Kevin succeed? The answer was obvious. No matter what it took, get him to school. Good thing Clive owned a Volkswagen van.

After a brief consultation meeting with Clive, Operation Kevin began at 8:15 Monday morning. The house phone in my classroom rang. It was Clive. "Kevin's mom just phoned. Kevin is refusing to come to school."

My first-period class was to begin in thirty minutes, but if we were quick we could drive to Kevin's home and back and I wouldn't be late. The driving there and the driving back was easy; the part we underestimated was the getting Kevin into the van.

When we arrived, Kevin was in the downstairs rec room. He was dressed for school and happily sitting on the couch, reading a book. He was not shocked to see us. His mother had told him we were coming. Both Clive and I did our best 'counselling/empathy/convincing' thing to get him to come with us. It quickly became obvious that he wasn't going to budge. We were running out of time. We had to get him in the van and back to school without delay. Clive was first to speak. "Mr. Greer, do you want the legs or the arms?"

We hadn't discussed the 'pick him up and carry him' strategy, but we were out of options, and Kevin's mom's body language appeared to support the idea. I replied, "Arms." Clive and I pounced. Together, we carried a fiercely resistant and surprisingly strong thirteen-year-old out of the house. It all seemed to be going quite well until we encountered one of the neighbours, who was out walking her dog. The optics of what we were doing were not great. Two grown men carrying a young boy who appeared to be fighting for his life and then throwing him into a van.

Fortunately, dog-walking lady knew Kevin's mom, and when Mom calmly said, "Good morning, everything okay?," dog walker decided it was prudent to mind her own business and continue on her way. Given some of the other possibilities, I think Clive and I were lucky that day.

With Kevin securely in the van, his mom handed me his lunch and we quickly returned to school. To our great surprise, when we arrived at the school, Kevin got out of the van and calmly walked into the office. I was relieved that Clive and I were not going to be forced to perform our 'lift and carry' in front of the many students who were arriving to school at that time. I could just imagine the dinner conversation that evening at one or more of our students' homes.

"How was your day at school today, dear?"

"Not bad. This morning I saw my vice-principal and my English teacher drag a grade-eight boy out of a Volkswagen van and carry him screaming and fighting into the school. Mr. Hughes and Mr. Greer are a lot stronger than I thought they were."

Kevin spent the day sitting in the main office reading his favourite book. For the next several months Kevin came to school every day and gradually began attending more and more of his classes. He arrived each morning in a variety of ways. Some days he walked, some days his mom drove him and some days Clive and I returned to the scene of the crime and performed our 'grab and go'.

There was one morning when Kevin decided he was not walking, getting driven by his mom or having a ride in the van. Fortunately, I was only involved as an observer on this occasion. This particular morning, Kevin was adamant that he was not going to school. His mom decided it was time for drastic measures and called the school and requested 'team grab and go'. When Clive and I arrived, Kevin was not hunkered down in any of his usual places. He had decided to wait for us in a new, quite ingenious location. He was sitting atop the family's backyard cherry tree. This tree was enormous. I remember Clive looking up at Kevin and then turning to me and saying, "I don't climb trees."

Kevin's mom overheard Clive and assured him that there would be no need to climb the monster, as she had called the fire department and they were on the way. Not missing the absurdity of the situation, Clive called the school and asked the secretary to get a teacher to cover my first period class and then said to me, "There is no way either of us is missing this."

A short time later a VFD ladder truck arrived with the usual contingent of young, fit firefighters. Without any hesitation, they deployed the ladder to the top of the tree. Up went one of the firefighters and soon after, down he came, with Kevin in tow. It was amazing how calm and orderly the 'rescue' had been. My amazement only grew during the weeks after the 'great cherry tree rescue of 1980'. After that morning, Kevin never missed a day at school. He got up each morning and walked himself not just into the building but into his classes.

This 'cure' for Kevin's separation anxiety was not the result of my counselling expertise or months of a carefully devised counselling strategy, it was the result of Kevin being helped by one young, kind firefighter risking his own safety, and it only took twenty minutes.

The Ingenious Ones

As with its legends, every school has its own unique reputation of grad pranks. Grad pranks come in all degrees of originality and effort. In the 1980s, Prince of Wales was famous, or infamous, for its creative and carefully planned grad pranks. Each P.W. grad class had enormous pressure placed on it from previous grad classes to continue the tradition of pranking the school. I certainly was not able to express my honest opinion about the P.W. grad pranks while I was there as a staff member, but I am now comfortable to state that I thought many of them were really terrific.

The Volkswagen with the school's flagpole protruding through the middle of it certainly earned my admiration. Obviously, the idea had been plagiarized from the UBC engineers, who have for decades suspended Volkswagen Beetles from many different locations around the Lower Mainland, including the Lions Gate Bridge. My personal favorite P.W. prank is still the brick walls in front of the doors.

Sometime during a Friday in June, one or more of our grads had attached a piece of wire to the opening handle of a teacher's window on the second floor of the building and dangled the wire outside the window. The teacher they chose was popular with the senior students, and they knew he would appreciate their choice. During the weekend, a group of grads climbed up a ladder and pulled the attached wire, which opened the window. The grads managed to get the window open without breaking it or causing any damage. Several members of this industrious group climbed in the window and entered the classroom. Other equally, or maybe even more, industrious members of the party laboriously carried dozens of concrete blocks up the ladder while their co-conspirators on the ground mixed a batch of concrete.

Inside the classroom, after carefully placing tarps on the floor so as not to cause any damage, a group of 'masonry' grads constructed two separate block walls, one inside the classroom door leading from the hall and one in front of the door connecting the adjoining classroom. The grads departed via the window and even closed it behind them.

Monday morning, the targeted but honoured teacher unlocked and opened his door, only to stare at a solid block wall. Thinking he could outsmart his pranksters, the teacher entered the adjoining classroom and opened the shared door, only to find an identical wall.

Word spread throughout the building, and room 205 became not only the most popular room in the school, but also the location of a grad-prank legend. At about 10:00 a.m., six Vancouver School Board workers arrived with a sledgehammer and wheelbarrow and spent the next three hours dismantling the structures and removing the blocks from the building. This prank was so impressive on so many levels. It involved ingenuity, creativity and originality. The most impressive part, however, was that this prank caused no damage to the school whatsoever. Congratulations, P.W. grads of 1980. Well done!

The Tragedy of Ted

Ted was a student in my first period English 10 class. He sat in the first-row, second desk from the front. The last time I saw him was during his Friday class. The next night, as his parents were hosting a dinner party upstairs, Ted died by suicide in the family basement.

Monday morning was unbearable. The entire school had learned of this tragedy from the weekend news or from friends, classmates and colleagues. Every student who walked into the classroom stared at Ted's empty desk in disbelief. How could this happen? Ted was great. He was happy, he played on the school's basketball team, he had a girlfriend, he was normal.

I chose not to ignore the obvious and attempted to provide some comfort to my students and some understanding of what had happened. I fear my efforts were sadly lacking, as I was in total shock and had no understanding myself as to why it had happened. It was impossible to explain the tragedy to my students when I couldn't explain it to myself.

Somehow, we got through the class, and as the days passed, we gained some understanding. We learned that Ted had displayed several clues of what he was considering. He had broken up with his girlfriend, been cut from the basketball team, returned his textbooks, emptied his locker and officially signed out of the school. A number of years later, I would show a video to my guidance classes on the topic of suicide prevention and identifying the signs. One of the case studies featured Ted's story. It was comforting to think that maybe some good might come from Ted's tragic death.

I had no idea what to do about Ted's desk. There was no way I was going to assign it to another student, but during every class, its emptiness stared at all of us. So it sat empty for the rest of the semester. When the next semester began, and for the next three years that I taught in the room, I was the only one who knew that the second desk from the front, in the first row, had belonged to Ted. In my mind it always would.

Prince of Wales Mini School

– 1 year –

The Prince of Wales Mini School is located on the grounds of P.W. Secondary School and is home to approximately 120 students in grades eight through twelve. As part of the application process, students are tested and interviewed and accepted only if it is thought they could be successful in an academically enriched environment. 'Mini' students take a combination of enriched academic courses, which are taught in the annex by 'Mini' teachers, and regular elective courses, which students attend at the main school. After four years teaching at the main school, I decided it was time for a change and applied to move across the field and teach at the Mini. At the time I filled out my application, I was applying for a teaching load only and had no idea I was about to be asked if I also wanted the position of head teacher.

The Promotion Reversal

It had never entered my mind that I would be qualified to be appointed head teacher at the Mini. I had never taught enriched courses, nor had I received any training in enrichment methodology. Unsolicited, I was invited into my principal's office to discuss this possibility with him and the two vice-principals, Dave and Clive. I was told that the school was in need of some 'working-together improvement', and it was felt my skills and counselling training would be an asset. The six teachers at the Mini were an eclectic mix of competent individuals, with the key word being 'individuals'. There was a great deal of good teaching going on at the school but not a lot of cooperating and collegiality.

I was interviewed by the departing head teacher, Norm; the P.W. principal; and another teacher on staff at the Mini. The next day, I was offered both the teaching and head teacher positions. The day after my interview, I met with a school board painter to discuss the colour of paint I wanted in my new office. At the end of June, I left for summer holidays, excited about my new adventure. Excited until Norm phoned me three weeks later and informed me that my job was gone. The school board had decided to make cuts at the board level, and there was a district consultant for science and math who needed a job. He had been appointed to the head teacher position, and it was hoped I would be happy teaching the humanities classes and not be upset with losing my new head-teacher job. What could I say? I needed a job and it was a done deal. Thanks, VSB.

I did decide to make the change and transfer to the Mini in spite of what I thought was a royal screwing. I had lost my position at the main school, so the only other option was to accept a teaching load of whatever was left over after the normal procedure of placements that had taken place in the spring. The thought of that did not put me in a happy place. With as much goodwill and enthusiasm as I could muster, I got ready to teach the gifted learners at the Prince of Wales Mini School.

My first challenge was not with the students but with the ghost of my predecessor. The teacher who had taught the humanities classes for the previous six years was not at all similar to me and my methods or my personality. He was much more of what I will generously refer to as a free spirit. At no time during my teaching career was I called a free spirit.

The students discovered that I was somewhat more formal than their previous year's teacher and did not hold back making comparisons between us. After all, these were gifted, freethinking, outspoken young scholars.

There was one specific story the students described in great detail that encapsulates the difference between the two of us. Apparently, said teacher had read that it was possible to absorb nutrients directly through one's scalp and into one's brain. He explained in great detail what he had read and then proceeded to demonstrate. Perhaps a great lesson on the surface, but my perception of the greatness disappeared when I was informed that the demonstration involved massaging yogurt into his scalp one morning and leaving it there for the entire day.

In spite of the fact that the process would have worked much better on my scalp because I had no hair to obstruct the absorption, I was not about to perform any circus tricks for these students, and I am pretty sure they knew it.

The Not-So-Gifted Gifted

It was a steep learning curve for me, getting to understand the gifted learner. In theory, all the students at the Mini were really smart and able to learn quickly and thoroughly, but as I soon learned, not all gifted students are created equal.

At the end of June, of my one and only year teaching at the Mini, I was designated to chaperone a group of thirty students as they hiked through the West Coast Trail on Vancouver Island. The three teachers who were to accompany the group met with the students several times to discuss appropriate preparations for such a physically demanding venture. We talked about footwear, food, backpacks, tents, first-aid essentials and covered all the topics we thought were necessary. As it turned out, these 'gifted' adolescents had gaps in their giftedness.

In the morning of the first day of our adventure, one of the grade-eight boys attempted to step over a log, slipped and fell onto his back. He did not appear to be hurt but was having an impossible time righting himself and getting back onto his feet. A couple of the senior students helped him up, and I noticed how large his backpack appeared. I took the backpack from him and could barely lift it. As part of their preparation, we had shared with the students a formula that compared body weight to the maximum weight their backpack should be. In his 'gifted' wisdom, this young brainiac had loaded his backpack with at least three times more weight than he should have and somehow thought he was going to complete a seven-day, 100-kilometre hike.

The silver lining in this came about as we watched the senior students come to his rescue. Without being asked, they each took a few items and carried them for the duration of the hike. Without this generosity and compassion, our grade-eight gifted lad would not have had a chance of completing the hike. I dare say, he might still be lying on his back in the first few metres of the West Coast Trail.

Another 'lack of giftedness' scenario unfolded gradually during the hike. We had discussed nutrition several times with our group and decided not to check what food they had actually brought with them but to trust their good judgment. Sometime during day four, some of the grade-ten boys, who were in the same food prep group, discovered there was no way they had enough food to get them through to day seven. In a panic, they approached me with their dilemma.

"Well, boys, here is what I think you should do. Have a chat with some of the girls. I am pretty sure they have packed enough food for themselves and probably have more than they will need. They may choose to share with you."

Sure enough, the girls did have extra food, and they were generous enough to share with the boys during the remainder of the hike. On the last day of the hike, I overheard a couple of the boys discussing how lucky they had been to have the girls look after them. "We would have been totally screwed if the girls hadn't taken care of us."

To which I replied, "You just learned a lifelong lesson. Get used to it, boys."

The best 'giftedness gap' experience came on the fifth day of our hike. We stopped hiking at around four o'clock and pitched our tents. I watched the students set up their tents about three metres back from the water's edge. I was amazed, and to be honest quite amused, but said nothing. I had set up my tent about twenty metres back from theirs. I was surprised that they did not ask me why I had pitched my tent so far away from theirs and so much farther from the water's edge.

A couple of hours later, I was sitting on a log in front of my tent, enjoying a cup of tea, and heard all kinds of yelling and shouting. The penny had dropped. Not one of these gifted learners had noticed that they had placed their tents well below the high-water mark. Every one of them had missed the obvious clue of the seaweed and driftwood at the high-tide line. Feverishly, they dismantled their tents, gathered all their belongings and relocated farther up the beach. I watched, yet again, in amazement. They had indeed moved up the beach from the incoming tide but were still well below the level of the high-tide debris. An hour later it was like watching an episode of *The Three Stooges*. More yelling, more shouting and yet another relocation, this time beside their 'ungifted' teacher. Sometimes a person has to experience to learn.

The Principal Prank

Even though I had completed my master's degree in counselling, I was still happy to continue the joy of classroom teaching. Several people found this a bit unusual and felt I should use the knowledge I had gained and apply for a counselling job. After one year of teaching at the Mini, I discovered I was not suited to teach the gifted, so after nine years of classroom teaching, I decided I would like the opportunity to work as a counsellor, and I let my wishes be known to my principal and anyone else who cared. My principal at P.W. felt it was time for me to make the change and so did his friend, the principal at John Oliver Secondary (J.O.). My P.W. principal also knew that once a year a group of teachers from Eric Hamber left work at noon to travel to Portland to watch an NBA game, play golf and act like children. I had become part of this group during my time at Hamber and was not about to give it up simply because I now was teaching at P.W. The plan was to get dropped off at school in the morning with our golf clubs, get someone to cover our afternoon classes and then discreetly leave the building at 12:00 sharp. Gordy from Hamber had a big van, and he was happy to drive us. Super secret spy stuff if we kept it to ourselves. Not so secret if our principal found out about it.

Norm was a great principal and wonderful man. He was my principal at P.W. for all six years I was there and became a friend and member of the poker group I played in. He did not often display a sense of humour, but he certainly had one.

The day of the Portland trip, I scurried down to the boys' PE office just after the lunch bell rang to retrieve my golf clubs, which I had cleverly located there. Clubs over my shoulder and overnight bag in hand, I exited the office and turned to leave the gym and meet up with Gordy and the boys. I was about halfway to my weekend adventure when I heard Norm's voice from the other end of the gym.

As innocently as can be, he asked, "Oh, hi, Hugh, do you have a minute?"

I hesitated for a moment and contemplated answering, "No, I'm in a hurry, Norm" but thought better of it. "Oh, sure, Norm. What can I do for you?"

I thought it was strange when he didn't question the golf bag and overnight case but rather began questioning me about my future in counselling. "You've finished your master's in counselling, haven't you?"

"Yeah, a couple of years ago."

"And you're interested in a counselling job for next year?"

"Yes, I am going to apply if there are any."

"Well, I just got off the phone with the principal at J.O., and he is looking for a counsellor for next year. I told him you were interested, and I have arranged for you to be interviewed by him at 3:30 today."

Uh-oh. At 3:30 this afternoon I was going to be driving down the I-5, halfway between Seattle and Portland, not sitting in front of the J.O. principal. What to do, what to do?

I stood and stared at Norm for what seemed like an eternity. Then, before I had the opportunity to dig a massive hole by lying or saying something stupid, Norm, in his usual classy manner, started to laugh and sputtered out, "Oh, did I say this afternoon? I meant Monday afternoon." He then turned and started to walk out of the gym while I continued to stand in petrified terror. Just before he opened the door to leave the gym, he turned and said, "Say 'hi' to the boys for me, and enjoy the game."

I did say hi for him, and I did enjoy the game. Over the following thirty-seven years, I never forgot this interaction with this lovely man.

The following Monday, I did interview for the job at J.O. and, after six years at P.W., accepted a full-time counselling position at my first non-west-side school.

Part 3

The Counselling Years and the Exchange Year

John Oliver Secondary

– 4 years –

John Oliver Secondary School is one of Vancouver's oldest high schools, opening its doors for the first time in 1921. It is neither a stereotypical west-side school nor a stereotypical east-side school. It is more a 'south-side' school, that is to say, somewhere between the stereotype associated with west- and east-side schools. Socio-economically, its student population is somewhat middle-of-the-road. For many years J.O. had a significant Mennonite population made up of blond-haired, blue-eyed, well-behaved young people who won every choir competition they entered because many of them had sung in their church choir from a young age. In 1982, when I joined the J.O. staff, the most noticeable and significant population was made up of South Asian Sikh students or—as they proudly referred to themselves—'the browns'.

Notable alumni of J.O. include Walter Gage, who had a fifty-year career at the University of British Columbia, during which time he rose from undergraduate student to university president. Jimmy Pattison, OC, OBC and multi-millionaire philanthropist, graduated from J.O., and more recently, Evander Kane, NHL hockey star, attended the school.

The interview on Monday afternoon after my trip to Portland was for the grade-nine boys counselling position, because, of course, in 1982 men could only counsel boys. The principal informed me that there were two other candidates for the position, and I was the third to be interviewed. I think it would be fair to describe my meeting with him as an 'old-time interview'. At the time there was no contract to follow, no department head included in the process and no staff committee rep involved in the selection, just the principal. He would arbitrarily make the decision as to who got the job. During the interview, I was asked three questions. I remember them vividly.

1. "P.W. has a very good rugby program. Do you coach rugby at P.W.?"
2. "If you get this job, would you be willing to coach rugby here?"
3. "What other teams have you coached besides rugby?"

Obediently, because I wanted the job, I answered all the questions. I had no idea that years later, when I would be interviewing candidates for positions, I would have been severely reprimanded for asking a question that had anything to do with coaching.

Apparently I gave the correct answers, because after my third answer I was told, "The job is counselling grade-nine boys if you want it." I was confused.

"What about the other two applicants?" I asked innocently.

The reply was strong and swift. "Neither of them will coach rugby. I need a rugby coach because all we have here is football, and I hate football." So, the following September, I began my four years of counselling at John Oliver Secondary.

I also began a most unsuccessful tenure as a high school rugby coach. I had played rugby at Cariboo Hill for three years and was an average player at best. I fear I was less than average as a rugby coach, but it did not matter a bit for my new principal, who was just happy that I showed up for practices and games and shared his dislike of football.

The First Student

Even though it did not have a window, I did have my very own counselling office. I also had my very own group of students whom I could guide to success. I was ready to be a counsellor. I was ready for anything. Anything, that is, until I met my very first J.O. student.

At J.O. there were a group of teachers who had been teaching there for some considerable length of time and possessed a sense of entitlement. They were referred to by the staff as the 'senior senators'. In the staff room, this illustrious group had their own designated chairs at their own designated table. One afternoon, during the first week of school in September, one of the 'senators' telephoned my office. She was sending me a grade-nine boy who needed a 'talking to'. "No problem. I can do that," I confidently replied.

Mitchell looked like one of the Greasers from the novel *The Outsiders*. His hair was jet-black and slicked back. He was wearing a tattered T-shirt, and exposed across the front of the shirt for all to read was the issue that required I give Mitchell a 'talking to'.

In large, bold letters across the front I saw

F C K
All that's missing is U

Nothing new here. As a classroom teacher, I had dealt with inappropriate T-shirts before. Easy solution. Win-win. Turn the shirt inside out, return to class and promise never to wear it to school again. Done and dusted. My first counselling success. Until I took a detour and decided to take a minute to get to know my student a little better. I started by asking the usual ice-breaker type questions. "How's your timetable? What are your electives? What are your interests?" Then subtly moving to a few more personal questions. "Do you have brothers or sisters here at the school? Where were you born? What do your mom and dad do?" And down the rabbit hole I went. I discovered there was more to this counselling thing than just asking a few questions.

Very casually, Mitchell informed me, "I don't live with my parents, I live with my grandparents."

"That's interesting. Why not your mom and dad?"

"My mom is dead."

"Oh, I'm sorry to hear that. How long has she been gone?"

"She's not gone, she's dead."

"Sorry, how long has your mom been dead?"

"Seven years."

"And what about your dad?"

"My dad's in jail."

"Wow, that's a lot for you to deal with. Sounds like you have had to grow up fast."

"I guess."

"If you don't mind me asking, why is your father in jail?"

"He killed my mom."

How could I have done this again? How could I be so unprepared for this moment? I was back in Hawaii reliving the "We really need our suitcases" conversation with the grade-eleven girls. I was back in Mr. O'Brien's office with Abby's mom, having the "I have never heard the word anti-Semitic" nightmare. The feeling of inadequacy was unbearable. I mumbled something and sent Mitchell back to class. In spite of my clumsy start with him, Mitchell and I became close during the next four years. We had many personal conversations, and I am proud that he was a member of the J.O. graduating class of 1986. Thanks for giving me a second chance, Mitch.

I learned several valuable lessons from my relationship with Mitch, and, fortunately, they occurred early in my counselling career. One such lesson was that I could never expect to be prepared for where a conversation with my students might lead. It was going to be necessary for me to be an on-the-spot thinker and sometimes be quick with a counselling strategy to support the needs of my students.

Another lesson was not to be too hard on myself if I got off to a rocky start with a student. Moving from grade to grade with a group of students as they advanced through their five years of secondary schooling was going to be a long process, and I didn't need to connect with all of them the first time I met them. I had time and needed to be patient with developing a relationship that could be helpful and meaningful to them. Thanks again, Mitch.

The Barn

The students at J.O. were great and their parents very supportive. As with all schools, the teaching staff had its mix of superstars and strugglers, but unlike most schools, J.O. had a separate building with teachers who saw the world from their very own unique prism. One of the biggest challenges the school faced the year I started there was dealing with a group of teachers who taught in 'the barn'. The John Oliver barn is, in reality, a three-storey, eight-classroom annex that is located on the J.O. site but is its own separate building. For many years, teachers who chose to teach in 'the barn' viewed themselves as outcasts from the rest of the school staff. They requested to teach in 'the barn' to be away from supervising eyes. Ironically, although they had little time for their colleagues who taught in the main building, most of them were excellent teachers who happened to be very opinionated and did not like prying administrators or counsellors. They believed the barn teachers were 'real' teachers. No BS, no politics. They either liked you or disliked you, no in-between. They taught in the barn, they ate lunch in the barn and, whenever possible, avoided coming into the main building. At staff meetings, they sat in the back of the room like a bunch of misbehaving students. In fact, that is exactly what they were: 'misbehavers'. Most of them disliked school administrators, and several of the administrators over the years disliked them.

An infamous J.O. story that I am sure has morphed into a less than accurate legend is the story of one of the principals offering a staff member $100 to burn the barn to the ground. The story goes that one night during a school dance, after a particularly rough day of conflict with one of the barn teachers, the principal and three of the school's teachers passed by the barn during their supervision rounds.

The principal reached into his pocket, counted out five twenty-dollar bills and announced, "I will pay $100 to whoever burns that thing to the ground."

The barn still proudly stands today at J.O., and as the years pass, it earns a greater and more elaborate reputation.

The barn reputation and the teachers who taught in it during my four years at J.O. remind me of the idiom about peeling back the layers of an onion. Underneath the negativity displayed by this particular group of teachers was a sincere and skilful desire to provide the best education possible for students.

The infamous J.O. barn still proudly standing today

The President of Teaching

The following year at J.O. we were granted a new principal. Jim Killeen was a brilliant man. He was the first two-term president of the British Columbia Teachers' Federation, had been president of the Canadian Teachers' Federation and president of the World

Confederation of the Organization of the Teaching Profession. In 1986, he received the G.A. Ferguson Award for outstanding achievement in the field of education. More impressive to me, he was a man of great wisdom, who always seemed to be able to isolate and verbally capture any situation.

One morning as I was heading toward the building from the parking lot, I came upon two of our teachers standing nose to nose, screaming at each other. One was the band teacher and the other the choirmaster. They were in the process of loading the bus with the school's sound equipment before departing for Whistler to participate in a music festival. The issue at hand was who exactly owned the speakers that they both needed to use at the festival. It was well known amongst the teaching staff that the two combatants did not get along, but I had no idea how antagonistic their relationship had become. There they were, at 7:30 in the morning, in the school parking lot, in front of several dozen students, yelling and screaming at each other about a couple of speakers. Rather than intervene and attempt to play peacemaker, I decided to continue into the building and share this situation with the wise and all-knowing Mr. Killeen. Jim's mind worked at warp speed. The second I finished describing what I had seen, he looked at me and, slowly and without emotion, said, "You know, Hugh, I always expect children to act like children, and I always expect adults to act like adults. The children very seldom let me down." A line I never forgot and used many times during my career.

The Mad Bomber

A secondary school is an unpredictable environment. When bad things happen at a school, the people who work there are usually very skilled at discovering who is responsible. This includes such incidents as vandalism, theft and student misbehaviour. With support from staff, students and sometimes the community, the school generally finds out what happened and who was responsible. However, solving these incidents is not a perfect science, and every once in a while the identity of the person or persons responsible is never discovered. At J.O., the identity of 'the mad bomber' was never discovered.

The mad bomber terrorized John Oliver for about six months. The first bomb exploded in the dumpster at the back of the school. It didn't cause any damage, but the rear half of the school felt the vibration, and most of the school heard the blast. A few days later, another bomb exploded, this time in the elevator. The location of the second one created more concern, as more people in the building could feel it and hear it, and it filled the second floor with smoke. An added concern was that the bomb triggered the smoke alarm, and we all ended up out on the street while the fire department investigated the smoke. We were forced to wait outside until the Vancouver Fire Department was sure it was safe for the administrators to give the 'all clear' signal to allow the students and staff to reenter the building.

The second detonation also initiated a police investigation. At our next staff meeting we were told the Vancouver Police Department's bomb squad had determined that the bomb was a homemade pipe bomb. The good news, we were told, was that the bomb did not contain projectiles, which would create a much more serious, even deadly, scenario. This good news did not reassure us. We still had a bomber on the loose, and there was no reason to believe they would not strike again.

Several weeks passed and we were all grateful that we had not heard again from the mad bomber. Just when we thought all was well, they struck again. This time, I was personally involved.

I had just walked out of the counselling centre and was on my way down the second-floor hall when bomb number three exploded in the boys' washroom. The washroom was about five metres in front of me. I heard the blast and then a split second later saw the washroom door fly open. Very shortly after, a gust of smoke and then the fire alarm. In my usual quick-thinking manner, I stood frozen in my tracks. During neither my teaching nor my counselling training had I been taught what to do when a bomb exploded directly in front of me.

After regaining some semblance of composure, I cautiously made my way to the washroom door and pushed it open. I meekly called, "Anyone in here?" Hearing nothing, I walked across the hall and entered the band room. I instructed the students to exit by the rear door of the classroom. After working with the band teacher to make sure all the students were out of the room, I made my way down to the office to report what I had witnessed. Later in the afternoon, I was interviewed by the Vancouver Police Department but was of absolutely no help. I did, however, get an opportunity during the interview to be escorted by the police to the scene of the crime and view the damage. Apparently, this bomb had been placed in one of the stalls directly under one of the toilets. The explosion completely destroyed the toilet and had launched dozens of pieces of shredded porcelain at great velocity throughout the room. I could see pieces of the shrapnel embedded in the walls.

Fortunately this was the last attack from the mad bomber, who apparently felt their work at J.O. was done and decided to retire. Although I was shaken by my bomb experience, I remember using the expression 'scared the crap out of me' during my interview with the police. When I shared the incident with one of my friends and recounted the incident and my interview with the police, he pointed out that I was not nearly as impacted as any student would have been if they had been sitting on the toilet at the time of the explosion. Unlike my idiomatic description, this would have quite literally scared the crap out of them, or worse, seriously injured them.

The takeaway was that the profession of teaching is much more challenging than classroom instruction alone. Working in a school setting is about relationships, emotions management, constantly updating best practices and even staying vigilant. Teachers today should be aware and prepared for the unexpected from time to time. In other words, always expect the unexpected.

The Worst Possible Ending

My four years at John Oliver were enjoyable and passed by quickly. The grade nines I began my counselling career with were the grads of '86. In June of 1986, as the school year came to a close, I believed the memories of my time at J.O. would be wonderful and positive. Unfortunately, I was wrong.

It was the last Thursday in June and the second-last day of my tenure at J.O. Our entire staff was at a hotel in Richmond enjoying the annual year-end party. Earlier in the day, we had distributed the school yearbook. While we were partying in Richmond, many of the students were sitting on the school playing field signing each other's books. One of my grads decided it would be fun to drive his car onto the playing field and do a few 'doughnuts'. He momentarily lost control of his car and ran into a small group of grade-nine girls who were sitting in the field signing each other's yearbooks. To everyone's horror, the car came to rest directly on top of one of the girls. After several students attempted to lift the car off the trapped girl, a couple of them ran into the school to get help, but no one was in the office and none of the teachers were in their building. Eventually, one of the students located a custodian who ran out to the field and was horrified to discover what had taken place. He immediately ran back into the school, called 9-1-1 and summoned several of his coworkers to come and help. The custodians and several of the students tried in vain to lift the car off the girl, but to no avail. By the time the first responders arrived, the young girl had suffocated and was pronounced dead at the scene.

Needless to say, the next day, the last day of school, a traditionally happy day, the school was filled with grief and disbelief. I learned the name of the student who had been driving the car and felt sick. I had been his counsellor for four years and had known him as a really great kid. Responsible, sensible and mature, and all it took for him to permanently scar the rest of his life was a split-second lack of judgment on the last day of his high school career.

Eventually, because of the fallout from his actions that day, he was forced to flee the country and return to his country of birth. So many people were impacted by this event. So many people destined to suffer for the rest of their lives. This was one of the most horrible days of my eleven thousand. Sadly, this day would not be the last time in my career when unbearable grief would rock the school where I worked.

I would not return to John Oliver again until many years had passed. Earlier in the year I had applied for and been granted another one-year leave of absence, this time through the League for the Exchange of Commonwealth Teachers. My wife and I were about to pack up our lives, including our two daughters, recently turned four and not yet one, for a year of teaching and living in Cornwall, England.

Helston Comprehensive School

– 1 year –

The Commonwealth Teacher Exchange Programme (CTEP) was founded in 1918. It provides teachers with an opportunity to exchange jobs with teachers who work in other countries. Exchanges typically last for one year but have been known to extend to a second. Frequently, these exchanges involve switching houses and cars as well as jobs. Most exchanges take place between Canada, Australia and the United Kingdom. For Canadians, the Australian exchange is a little awkward because the Australian school year terminates at the end of the calendar year, whereas the end of the UK school year coincides with the Canadian school year.

I was originally matched with a teacher who taught in Romford, England, a large town east of London. My teaching exchange partner subsequently withdrew his application, and, after several weeks of being in limbo, I was offered a second exchange. I was told over and over again by dozens of people how lucky I was to be heading to Cornwall, England. It turned out that I was far more than lucky. I was blessed. Blessed with the opportunity to teach and live in this amazing county and experience what was to be one of the best years of my life.

THE LEAGUE FOR THE EXCHANGE
OF COMMONWEALTH TEACHERS

Patron: H. M. QUEEN ELIZABETH THE QUEEN MOTHER

This is to certify that <u>Mr Hugh W Greer</u>

has served as an exchange teacher in

<u>Cornwall, United Kingdom</u> *during 19* 86/7

through the auspices of the

League for the Exchange of Commonwealth Teachers

and the Departments of Education of the United Kingdom

Chairman   **Executive Secretary**

Commonwealth Exchange League certificate. Thanks, Your Majesty.

Cornwall is England's most isolated county and is tucked away in the most southerly and westerly part of England. Land's End is a famous Cornish landmark and is located at the last piece of land in the country. The Cornish are proudly independent. They have their own language, parliament and flag. They even have their own anthem, "Trelawny." Many 'real' Cornish have a passionate sense of independence and believe Cornwall should be its own country, not just its own county. On more than one occasion, I was asked if I was disappointed to be sent to Cornwall when I had applied for an exchange in England. Although I recognized this as a joke, as time passed and I discovered more about the culture of the county, it became apparent that there was more than a grain of seriousness in the question.

I was assigned to teach at Helston Comprehensive School. The original school built on the property was opened in 1905 and was called the Helston County Grammar School. In 2019, most of the comprehensive school was torn down and according to its website was replaced with a "£17 million purpose-built school." What is a 'purpose-built school'? It sounds a lot like a 'loft church', something else I don't understand.

The 'English' Assignment

As most Canadians are aware, our judicial and educational systems are both modelled after the English systems. That's why I was surprised to discover how vastly different teaching in Cornwall was from teaching in Vancouver. One startling difference was how the students at my Cornish school were assigned to their classes. The classes in Vancouver schools are randomly put together by a computer program. At Helston Comprehensive School, grade-wide final exams were administered at the end of each year. The results of these exams were used to compose the classes for the following year. The top thirty students were timetabled into the 'top set' class, the next thirty into the 'second set' class and so on. The bottom groups were made up of fewer students in recognition of their special learning needs. After eleven years of counselling, I returned to the classroom as a full-time teacher of English. My track record of being assigned teaching loads that had little or nothing to do with my training continued even eight thousand kilometres from home. My Helston School teaching assignment consisted of six 'bottom set' groups for English class, and the room assigned to me was the school cafeteria. I also was assigned a class of 'computer learning', whatever that was. I soon discovered it was a class for the bottom set students and was supposed to give them some extra support. It was in line with what was called SDC at J.O., or Skills Development Centre.

I'm not sure about the pedagogical wisdom of assigning me this load, but it occurs to me that the administration of the school didn't think a teacher from Canada could measure up to the job of teaching average or above average students, and only someone educated in England could teach English to the English.

It would have been welcome information if someone had let me know in advance that the majority of the students in my classes had special needs. I'm not sure if it would have made any difference to their education or my teaching, but it would have saved me from embarrassing myself the day I asked my colleagues about the composition of my classes. Soon after beginning my tenure at Helston School, but having had time to discover the school was filled with delightful, smart, respectful young students, I naively remarked, "I am confused about how many disabled students I have in my classes. I am not used to this."

"What do you mean?"

"In one class, I have a student with a club foot, in another a student with a cleft palate and I think the rest of them are learning disabled. All my classes have multiple special needs students in them." I was certainly not expecting the answer I received: "Inbreeding, Hugh boy, inbreeding."

"Inbreeding?"

"Of course. This is a small county. Not much of a gene pool. Cousins have been marrying cousins around here for generations. On top of that, you have all the thick ones."

"The thick ones?"

"You know, 'thick as two short planks'. All the bottom groupers."

The penny had dropped. I had been given the fifteen students who had scored the lowest marks on the previous year's final exams. I was terrified. How was I going to help these poor kids? Teaching special needs students, in any country, is a skill that requires specialized training and a unique aptitude. I had neither. I also had no materials or resources. The teaching part of my exchange turned out to be the greatest challenge of my career. I had been given a dozen or so students who knew they were the bottom set in the grade. Having been banished to the cafeteria for their classes, they felt they were not even worthy of a real classroom.

I had Nigel, whose nickname was Jetlag because he appeared to be permanently suffering from this usually temporary condition. I had Daniel, whose nickname was Stinky because he had once or twice, years before my time at the school, pooped himself. And I had Martha, nicknamed Bubbles, who continually produced snot bubbles no matter how many times she blew her nose.

I also had Mark. He was in my fourth-form English class, the Canadian equivalent to grade nine. Soon into my time at Helston School, he looked at me during class one morning with apparent confusion and asked, "Sir, why have you come here?"

"What do you mean, Mark?"

"Well, why have you left your country and your school and your home to come and teach us?"

The educator in me took over. This was to be a wonderful 'teach-able moment'. "When you travel you get to witness how other people live and it enriches your own life. I want to become as knowledge-able as I can about the world and enrich my own life. What do you want from your life, Mark?"

It took him very little time to formulate his answer. Apparently he had already contemplated his life's plan. "I want to be like my dad and my granddad. At the end of each day, I want to have enough pocket money to go to my local and buy a pint and a bag of crisps." And once again I was speechless.

Several weeks later, Mark was suspended from school and never returned. Unfortunately the incident that got him suspended happened during my class. My students were sitting at one of the cafeteria tables quietly reading when I heard some mumbling and a word I had never heard before, 'gypo'. Like a Scud missile, Mark launched himself across the cafeteria table and grabbed one of the other students by his throat and started throwing punches like he was a prizefighter. It was all over in the blink of an eye, but the damage had been done. Apparently, the absolute worst thing you could call members of Mark's family, or any Cornishman, was 'gypo', short for 'gypsy'.

By 1986, there had been an influx of Eastern European families into the county. The modus operandi for many of them was to buy a small caravan, or camping trailer, tow it into a farmer's field in the middle of the night and remove the wheels and axels. With great haste, the wheels and axels were sold to anyone who would be willing to pay a few pounds for them. The idea was not necessarily to make money from these parts but to no longer have them anywhere near the family's new home. Of course, the farmers were livid when they discovered a trailer full of people living in their field. They ordered the trespassers, or 'gypsies' as they were commonly called, to leave. The answer was, "We can't. We have no way of moving our home." There were hundreds of these homes scattered over the fields in the county. The locals hated the 'gypos', and the word became the worst insult imaginable to any local like Mark. I felt bad about losing Mark and often wonder if he achieved his life's goal and sits every night in his local, enjoying a pint and a bag of crisps.

The Heads

The position of principal in British schools has the title 'headmaster' or 'headmistress'. Helston School's headmaster, Mr. Worrall, was a benevolent English gentleman who had graciously welcomed me to the school and given me a very informative tour of the building. Shortly after I began teaching at Helston School, I noticed he would appear at staff meetings but was seldom seen at the school any other time. After a couple of months of repeatedly walking by his vacant office, I enquired about his frequent absence, hoping he was not seriously ill. To my great relief and even greater surprise, it turned out that Mr. Worrall was also Justice Worrall, local town magistrate. He was often not available to attend to his responsibilities as headmaster because he was sitting on the bench passing judgment on Helston town citizens who had not behaved well. This was an interesting combination of jobs, secondary school principal and local town judge. I wondered then, and I continue to wonder now, if any of the school's teachers had ever appeared in court and how that may have affected their chances of promotion at the school.

Three mornings per week at Helston School, the day would begin with a single-grade assembly. Once per week the entire school, which was made up of the third, fourth and fifth forms, was summoned to the auditorium, which I reverently referred to as 'the great hall'. In the Canadian system these three grades are equivalent to grades eight, nine and ten. All assemblies began the same way. The students assembled in the auditorium and stood in neat rows according to their homeroom class, known as their 'tutor group'. The head-of-school position was somewhere between headmaster and deputy head of school and was 'second-in-command'. To begin each assembly, the head of school, Mr. Truscott, appeared from his office and stood on the landing above the 'great hall', where the students stood in wondrous anticipation. He conducted the assemblies with an iron fist. The first order of business was to sing a hymn. It did not matter one's religion, all were to sing the Christian hymn. The school's music teacher sat dutifully at the piano awaiting his orders. Like magic, the words for the hymn of the day were lowered from the ceiling. As the students sang, the head of school paraded up and down the rows of children and ordered them to sing louder. "You, boy, louder! I can't hear you, girl!" At the conclusion of the hymn, a designated student read a passage from the Bible. I wonder what was going through the minds of the Jewish, Muslim and other non-Christian students who were forced to sing the hymns and listen to the Bible passage, or worse, read one. Then, the 'Alan Show' began.

I liked Alan. He treated me respectfully and was always friendly to me. To the students he was officious and was 'he who must be obeyed'. He was the head of school. This was a big deal. Each assembly contained a 'telling-off' of some kind. From his position on high, he would lament about how poorly the students were behaving or how they all needed to study harder, or he would describe in great detail some unacceptable incident that had recently taken place at the school. The students stood obediently and never flinched. I waited day after day, but not once did I hear a snicker or see a yawn. I often wondered if this was fear I was seeing or respect. I now believe it was the former. Alan was not a large man, but he was a man not to be disrespected.

One morning, during full school assembly, after the hymn and the Bible reading, Alan disappeared into his office. A deathly silence fell over the student body. They stared at his office door with great concern. They knew something was up, and it was not something good. When he reappeared, he had his arms wrapped around a disfigured locker door. He was incensed that some student had vandalized school property. As he stood in front of the entire student population, he shouted, "What kind of a horrible boy or horrible girl would do such a thing? What would the parents think of their child's behaviour? It's disgusting, is what it is. A student who behaves in such a terrible manner does not deserve to attend this school," and on he went for some time. He began to sweat and turn red in the face. I became concerned he was about to have a heart attack, but still, not a snicker from anyone. As time went on and I saw the show multiple times, I became convinced that, indeed, it was a show. Alan was a master actor. After I got to know him and became comfortable with our relationship, I questioned him one day about using so much time in assembly rather than using the time for teaching, which could possibly lead to learning. There was no hesitation. "Chaos, my young Canadian friend, chaos." I still don't know what he meant.

I enjoyed many philosophical conversations with Alan about education. Permanently-embedded in my memory is the discussion we had about his predecessor. Johnny was Alan's role model, and, during his career as head of Helston School, he had the advantage of being able to administer corporal punishment to the students. Mercifully and coincidentally, corporal punishment in British schools was banned in 1986, the year of my teaching exchange at Helston School.

In British Columbia, the strap, which was the implement used to administer corporal punishment in schools, was banned in 1973, the year I began teaching.

During Johnny's day, corporal punishment at the school had been administered using 'the switch'. Johnny had masterful ways of getting the truth out of students when they behaved badly. One Johnny story Alan shared with me involved two boys and some stolen property. Neither boy would admit to the theft, but Johnny was sure one or both of them was responsible. Johnny was after a confession.

As the two lads waited in terror, sitting on chairs in front of Johnny's office, Johnny appeared. "You, boy, into my office." The other boy was ordered to stay where he was.

As the first boy stood in fear in the middle of Johnny's office, Johnny slowly walked to his desk, opened his drawer and removed the dreaded switch. He then flexed it between his hands. "Tell me which one of you is guilty or it will be you I'm switching." No reply. "Very well, bend over my desk."

Dutifully, the boy bent over Johnny's desk and then heard Johnny whisper into his ear, "Not a sound from you, boy." Johnny administered the cane not to the boy but to the top of his own desk. *Smack* and a horrifying scream, not from the boy but from Johnny. *Smack*, scream, *smack*, scream and a final *smack*, scream.

Leaving the boy bent over his desk, Johnny then opened his office door and hissed through clenched teeth to the boy waiting outside, "Well, are you next, or are you going to tell me who the thief is?"

"It was me, sir, it was me. I am sorry, I'm so sorry," followed by the pathetic sound of teenage whimpering.

Alan very much enjoyed telling me this story, and when he was finished gave me a big grin and proudly stated, "Johnny always got the truth out of these kids." I was happy never to have met Johnny, and I am sure that Johnny, even though he never knew it, was happy never to have met me.

The Cornish Pasty

One of the few interesting aspects of teaching in the school cafeteria was that it provided me with the opportunity to witness the importance that Brits placed on nutrition, especially nutrition for the student population. Nutritional awareness in schools was just beginning to be a topic of discussion in Vancouver, the year I taught in England. Coin-operated pop machines at school were on the way out, and school cafeterias were beginning to be scrutinized over the nutritional value of the food they served. At Helston School, the menu was not diverse. To be fair, there has been a massive improvement in the nutrition offered in schools in the UK since I was there. However, in 1986–87, there was not a salad to be seen, and student after student ordered the same thing. If I heard this order once in the year, I heard it a thousand times: "Pasty, chips and beans." This was the lunchtime meal staple of the Helston School student.

The Cornish pasty was originally designed for the convenience and nutrition of Cornish miners, who found it too difficult and time-consuming to return to the surface for their lunch break. The pasty is revered in Cornwall and has a 'protected geographical indication status' in Europe. I'm not sure what that is, but it sounds important. The traditional pasty has a thick pastry crust, which is crimped around the outside. Back in the day, the miners held the pasty by the crimping while eating, then threw the crimping away because their dirty hands would contaminate it. Inside one end of the traditional pasty is beef, potato, swede (turnip) and onion. The other end is filled with some variety of fruit. The student pasty served at Helston School had no fruit, just beef, potato, turnip and onion. And of course, lots of pastry, which the students readily consumed with hands slightly less dirty than those of a Cornish miner. 'Chips' are what we in North America call 'french fries', and 'beans' are what we refer to as 'baked beans', of the pork-and-beans variety. Every day, scores of growing adolescents ordered this combination of fat and salt in the school cafeteria. The county's Minister of State for Health at the time, Virginia Bottomley (now The Baroness Bottomley of Nettlestone), remarked on the poor nutritional habits of school-aged children in a speech the year after my year teaching in Cornwall and was promptly replaced by the prime minister of the day. The Brits, then and now, are very easily offended by criticism about their eating habits. Pasty, chips and beans was a sacred school dinner in the mid-eighties, and I dared not criticize it.

Shortly after the school year began, I was asked by one of the teachers if I would like to meet a retired teacher from the school and have a homemade pasty lunch at her home. Of course, I accepted and true to his word, Howard arranged for us to have lunch at Mary's. Mary was born and raised in Cornwall and was extremely proud of her heritage. Lunch was an hour and twenty minutes long at Helston School the year I taught there, so we had lots of time to get to Mary's, enjoy a traditional Cornish pasty and get back to school in time for the lesson after lunch.

Like everything else about her, Mary's pasty was authentically Cornish. I discovered this because Mary gave me not only a history lesson of the pasty but a detailed description of how she had prepared our pasties and made it clear that her way was the only way they should be made: beef, potato, swede, onion and of course, homemade pastry. She served it on a full-size dinner plate, and both its edges extended well past the rim of the plate. It was massive. It was also delicious and filled me until I thought I would explode. Teaching my 'after pasty' class was a challenge. All I wanted to do was sleep. The Cornish miners must have developed an immunity to the effects of the pasties they ate each day for their lunch. Setting and detonating explosives in a tin mine, a mile under the sea, while nodding off would not have led to a lengthy career.

The Slash

In the spring of each school year in England, students take a series of mock exams. These are practice exams that are meant to prepare the students for the real year-end final exams they write in July. At Helston School the exams were held in a large double classroom and were taken very seriously by both the staff and students. Teachers were assigned to supervise these mock exams, and one teacher was designated to lead the supervision team. I was flattered to be entrusted to be lead supervisor for the A-level mock history exam of 1987.

I diligently prepared for this great responsibility, hoping to prove to the entire school that assigning me only bottom-level groups to teach was a mistake, and the teacher from 'the colonies' could handle this noble task. I relished the opportunity to show off my talents and the talents of all Canadians.

The seating of the students and the distribution of the exams went very well. My staff of helpers looked on as I took charge of the room. The students respectfully waited for my instructions.

The first order of business was to have the students record the exam number onto their answer booklets. At the top of each answer booklet was a blank line. As exam boss, I was to call out the exam number and instruct the students to copy it onto the line.

"Please copy this exam number onto the blank line on the upper left corner of your answer sheet." Easy. My enunciation was powerful as I tried my best to minimize my Canadian accent. The exam number was printed in my supervisor's manual: 8763/42. So, in a clear and confident voice, I said, "eight, seven, six, three, slash, four, two." Masterful. Until the entire room, teachers and students, broke out in uproarious laughter.

I was the only one in the room who was not laughing. I was the only one in the room who did not know what was so funny. Ironically, I was the one in the room who was supposed to know best what was going on. I stood there in front of my tormentors for what felt like an eternity before sheepishly walking over to one of the supervisors who had become a close friend. I was not impressed that he, too, was laughing at me.

"What the hell is so funny?" I was desperate to quickly repair whatever damage I had caused and continue on with administering the exam.

"Well, Hugh, it's like this. The thing you called a slash is actually referred to here as an oblique. I believe your Canadian equivalent to our 'slash' is the word 'piss', like when you're in the pub and you say to your mates, 'I'll be back in a sec, I need to go to the loo and have a slash.'"

There it was again. Profound ineptitude. I had just told the A-level history students that their exam number was: eight, seven, six, three, piss, four, two. So much for showing off the Canadian way of doing things. Sorry, Canada.

The Leap

Another great Helston School memory for me is my participation in the Helston School charity parachute jump. During the winter and spring, our group collected donations. I concentrated my fundraising efforts on my friends and family at home. There was no need to compete with my 'jump mates', who were raising their funds locally. Many of the people I contacted at home thought I had lost my mind, including my parents. However, in response to my request, they donated generously.

To add to their sense of how crazy I had become during my time overseas, many of them had read an article that appeared in the local paper. The account detailed the misadventure of another charity jump group, also in the UK. Unfortunately, one of the readers of the article was my father. One of the participants of this ill-fated adventure had been blown away from the designated landing area by an unexpected gust of wind and had landed on the rotating blades of a helicopter that was waiting to take off. My father did not hold back in his description of how that worked out for the jumper when he shared the story with his friends and co-workers. Of course, to reinforce his opinion, my father, instead of keeping this piece of information to himself, showed the article to my mother. Thanks, Dad.

On July 12, 1987, after raising over £1,000 for the Guide Dogs for the Blind charity, twenty Helston School students and four teachers, myself included, jumped out of an airplane from a height of 2,500 feet. After our training was completed, I was designated as the first jumper. I asked our jump instructor, "Why me?" and the jump instructor explained, "When we have a group jump like this, I need to know the first person who walks out onto the wing will jump. If they freeze and come back into the plane, we have a problem with the rest of the jumpers. I have watched you in training, and I know there is no way you are not going to jump." A compliment or a comment on my sanity?

Our jump went without incident. My level of enjoyment from my parachute jump can be measured by how many jumps I did after the first one: none. But the level of enjoyment I derived from the team-building charity exercise could not be measured. In the realm of education, the best learning and the most enjoyment often come from the process, not the product.

That long drop raises £1,000 for charities

AFTER weeks of preparation, and at least one delay because of the weather, the parachute team known as the Helston Drop-Outs made their two-and-a-half minute descent from 25,000 feet at St. Merryn, near Wadebridge — and raised £1,000 for charity in the process.

In all, 24 people, including some teenagers, made the jump to raise money for Guide Dogs for the Blind and the Childline appeal.

Among them was 37-year-old Mr. Hugh Greer, a teacher on exchange from Canada. He is spending a year teaching in Helston and raised most of his money by post from friends in Vancouver.

He was joined by teaching colleagues Mrs. Ginny Wells and Mrs. Fran Wagstaff. Many of those who took part were so thrilled by the experience that they intend to do it again.

Meanwhile, pupils from Helston Middle School have added to the money raised by collecting £600 within their tutor groups at the school.

Newspaper article from the *Helston Packet* describing my charity parachute jump. Not the first time it was suggested I would be a 'drop out'.

The Cornish Colleagues

I met many interesting students at Helston School during my year on staff. Among the most notable was Petroc Trelawny, now a well-known radio and television presenter. Petroc's father, the imposing Major Trelawny, was the school's truancy officer. As it was described to me, his job was to monitor student attendance, and if a student missed too many classes, the major would conduct a home visit to inquire about the absences. At the time, many families of Helston School students received financial support from the government, but only as long as their children regularly attended school. This support also included a free school dinner of pasty, chips and beans, of course. The major had it in his power to have the funding cancelled if a child was not in regular attendance. I was told he had a remarkable rate of compliancy and was thought to be very effective in his job. He intimidated me, and I am sure he also intimidated the parents of the students who were not attending regularly.

In 2012, Petroc was arrested and jailed in Zimbabwe while hosting a charity music festival. Immigration officials claimed he was in the country without a work permit, but in fact he was presenting pro bono. His arrest caused widespread international condemnation in the media. On New Year's Day in both 2020 and 2021, he was the host of the BBC broadcast of the Vienna New Year's Concert. Today, Petroc is host of the BBC Radio 3 morning show *Breakfast*.

The best memories of my year teaching at Helston School, however, are of my teaching colleagues. There were many notable and unique characters teaching at the school during my year on staff.

Miss Batty often arrived at school with many fresh scratches on her face and arms. She owned several out-of-control monkeys and allowed them to run around loose in her home. This resulted in frequent confrontations between Miss Batty and her monkeys. Miss Batty (the irony being obvious) was no match for an angry monkey.

Mr. Curnow (the Cornish word for Cornwall), who was kind enough to arrange my visit to Mary's house for a Cornish pasty lunch, was a Cornish Bard and, in 1997, was designated the Tartan of Cornwall. Today, he is passionately involved in arranging meetings all over the world for people of Cornish ancestry. He has also penned numerous articles and books about his favourite topic, Cornwall and all things Cornish.

My good friend Mr. Thomas (Mickey T.) retired from Helston School and served for several years on the Helston Town Council before becoming the mayor.

Deputy Head Mr. Truscott, of the infamous 'Alan Show', received the prestigious national Rugby Football Union award for over fifty years of outstanding contribution to the game of rugby.

Mr. Rogers, PE department head at Helston School the year I was there, was also a Helston rugby player and coach and is a Cornish rugby legend.

Mr. Hanley is the published author of a historical fiction series detailing events on and around the Isle of Jersey during the Second World War.

Mr. Davies is a renowned geography teacher and author who has taught in many places in the world, including Kuwait, Kazakhstan and Sri Lanka. There is nothing he does not know about Cornish geography.

Mrs. Wells, head of year four at Helston School, welcomed me not only into her home, but into her family.

Today there is but one remaining member of staff at Helston school from my time. During that year, Mr. Martin was referred to as the 'repo man'. Not the traditional 'repossession' man we think of, but the 'reproduction' man who completed all the photocopying for the staff.

My year at Helston School was not my most professionally rewarding, but it was my most interesting and enjoyable. I became lifelong friends with several of my colleagues and continue today to value their friendships. Nonetheless, at the end of the school year (1986–87), it was time for me to go home and return to my career with the Vancouver School Board.

David Thompson Secondary

– 7 years –

Returning to the familiarity of the Vancouver School District after my year on exchange was more stressful than I had anticipated. The school board had been generous enough to allow me the opportunity to leave the district for a year and teach in another country, as well as guarantee me a job when I returned. However, they now were able, by contract, to place me at any school where they had to fill a vacancy and insist that I accept any load that was available. I had finished at John Oliver in June, had taught at Helston School for the following ten months and was going to begin at another school in September. Teaching at three different schools in fourteen months created a lot of change for me that caused several restless nights. Where I was going to teach and what I was going to teach were solely in the hands of the great wizard behind the curtain at the Vancouver School Board. That is, until my friend Dave came to my rescue.

I wish everyone throughout their career could have a guardian angel who would mentor them and save their ass when they needed help or when they screwed up. Dave was my guardian angel, and, after working for a number of years at Prince of Wales as vice-principal, he had been transferred to David Thompson Secondary (D.T.), in the same position. Fortuitously for me, one of the school's counsellors had just retired. Dave put in a good word for me with Lou, the principal, and convinced him to ask the school board to place me at D.T. as a full-time counsellor. For many years after, and on many occasions, Lou referred to Dave's recommendation as the biggest bunch of crap in history. Sometimes in jest, I think. Dave, Lou and I became very good friends. Many people at Thompson referred to us as Huey, Dewey and Louie. We played many games of golf together and told many lies at our monthly nickel-and-dime poker games.

David Thompson has many notable alumni, including Kayi Cheung, Miss Hong Kong 2007; Megan Wing, former Olympic figure skater; and Laurie Shong, former Olympic fencer and pen-tathlete and one of the nicest students I ever knew.

There were several reasons Lou thought Dave had 'sold him a bill of goods' about hiring me. Unfortunately, Lou's suspicions began soon after I arrived.

The Unimpressive Beginning

Shortly after I began working at Thompson, I was in Lou's office with Lou, one of my students and the student's mother. I have no idea what the issue was, but I remember thinking I had been involved in the discussion long enough, and knowing I had students waiting for me in my office who wanted to speak with me, I decided it was time for me to depart. The meeting had gone very well, but I was anxious to get back to my office. On my way out, as I passed through the doorway, I grabbed Lou's door in an attempt to close it behind me. I was not angry and did not intend to slam it, but I used a bit too much force. Unbeknownst to me, my student's mom was not ready to end the conversation with me and was following me out, hoping for a few minutes of private conversation. I knew there was a problem when, instead of hearing the normal sound of a door closing onto its frame, I heard the sickening thud of a door closing onto a person. My worries were confirmed when I heard Lou gasp, "Oh my God. I am so sorry. Are you all right?"

Mom was not angry but somewhat startled. I don't think she ever thought I had intended to slam the door into her, but I had done just that. I turned and faced my victim, while Lou, mom and student all stood frozen in disbelief. The receptionist, records clerk, accountant and secretary who were working in the office and had observed my faux pas stared in horror. My first thought was to say, "Why the hell did you just walk into that door?" but I had already done enough damage to my reputation, so in a rare moment of sanity I caught myself and sputtered out, "I am so, so sorry. Are you all right?"

She was, but the damage had been done, and for the rest of my time at Thompson, I would be constantly reminded of my first but not last screw-up at D.T.

The SLOs

A valuable member of any school's staff is the school liaison police officer, or SLO, an unfortunate and inaccurate acronym for their work. Most secondary schools have their own SLO; however, some smaller schools share a single officer. These Vancouver police constables have an office in the school and provide education to students and security for the school. If the school is lucky enough, the SLO assimilates as a member of the staff and participates in social activities.

The school liaison program began in 1972 and at the time of writing includes fifteen constables. It provides valuable safety and community needs as well as breaking down barriers between youth and police. Unfortunately, the future of the school liaison program is in jeopardy as school board trustees review the viability of the program.

During my time at D.T., the school was fortunate to have two extraordinary SLOs.

Terry Waterhouse loved his job as an SLO and was outstanding at it. When we worked together, Terry was not only an experienced police officer but had completed his bachelor of education degree at UBC. He later went on to complete his master of arts at Royal Roads University and his doctorate of education at Simon Fraser University.

He taught criminology at the University of the Fraser Valley and in November 2018 was hired by the City of Surrey as its first Director of Public Safety, with the responsibility to lead the city's transition from the RCMP to a municipal force.

The second SLO I had the privilege to work with during my tenure at Thompson was Don Kirkland. Don is a Canadian Armed Forces and United Nations tour veteran. Besides having been a school liaison officer, during his time with the Vancouver Police Department, he worked with the department's Emergency Response Team (a.k.a. SWAT) as a sniper and hostage negotiator. He also was a detective in vice and gambling, as well as an undercover operator. He is the recipient of the Attorney General's award for valour. He now works with his son, Glen, also a decorated Canadian soldier, with a service group called Law Enforcement Applicant Preparation, an organization that offers training to individuals who are considering a career in law enforcement.

Not only did Terry and Don help keep our school safe, but they were amazing role models for our students. It was a wonderful experience for me to work with them and get to know them as colleagues and friends.

One important service the SLO provides for the school is security. A significant number of the problems in schools during this time were caused by students who were not registered at the school but were skipping classes at their own school, or were not registered at any school and had nothing better to do than loiter around. These individuals were referred to as 'intruders' by our SLOs. I never could understand why a student who was skipping classes from their own school would choose to go to another school and hang out. My own thought about skipping school, if I had done such a thing during my time in high school, would be to avoid going anywhere near a school. Much better to hang out at a friend's home or at the mall, anywhere but at a school. However, at this time, it was not uncommon to find students from other schools wandering around the halls.

On one memorable and amusing afternoon, three such intruders were escorted to the office by one of our teachers. I was often amazed at how compliant most of these 'intruders/trespassers' were and how few of them 'fled the scene'. When I first came upon them, the three young men, approximately sixteen years of age so probably in grade ten, were sitting in chairs in the main office awaiting their interrogation by the vice-principal. Part of the routine strategy when dealing with more than one student was to sit them apart from each other and have them wait without speaking to each other until the VP was ready. The point of doing this is to prevent the students from coordinating their stories and to more easily uncover any lies and inconsistancies, which are usually plentiful, during interrogation. As they waited, these particular lads were indicating, through their body language, that they felt what was going on was all quite amusing and perhaps a bit of a joke. This irritated the hell out of Dave, so he decided to telephone the SLO and asked him to join the party.

School liaison officers often did not wear their uniform at school, but this particular day, Don was in full uniform as he entered the office and stood behind the counter. He invited his first visitor to stand in front of him on the other side of the counter and requested the student provide some form of identification. The mindset of the sixteen-year-old male is frequently difficult to understand. Difficult then and difficult today. Many of them suffer from what numerous educators refer to as 'the three *I*'s'. They think they are indestructible and confirm this by being shocked when they injure themselves performing some dangerous stunt. They think they are invisible and prove this by performing some outrageous behaviour right in front of you and look shocked when you actually deal with it. The third *I* stands for immature. They often prove this by behaving like they are six, not sixteen. On this particular day our visitors were firmly entrenched in the third *I*. The interrogation began with our constable asking, "Why are you here?"

"Visiting a friend."

"What school do you go to?"

"Killarney."

"Do you have your Go Card on you?"

"Nope."

"Do you have identification on you?"

Then, the mystery of a sixteen-year-old's thinking. "Am I under arrest?"

"No, I'm just asking you for some identification."

Then more evidence that sixteen-year-olds don't always think rationally. "I'm not going to show you any identification if I'm not under arrest."

In the thirty-five years I spent working in secondary schools and during the dozens of interactions I witnessed between students and the school liaison officers, I saw nothing but professionalism and patience from the officers—at times, too much patience, in my opinion—when dealing with disrespectful, foul-mouthed students. On this particular day, however, our constable made it clear he was not interested in any attitude from these boys, and he let them know it.

He calmly reached over the counter, grabbed the boy by his shirt collar and lifted him off the ground so that his torso was on top of the counter. He then pulled the boy forward so that the two of them were nose to nose. Killarney boy's legs were at least two feet off the floor and were kicking in the wind.

"Okay, asshole, you're under arrest," and he calmly placed him back in his previous location on the floor.

Watching the lad frantically search for his wallet was amusing but not nearly as entertaining as watching his two friends, who were still sitting on the office chairs, reach into their pockets with a clear sense of panic for any form of ID they could find. Both boys were shaking.

The boy who was now under arrest, unfortunately, suffered more because he was chosen first. He was taken away a short time later in a paddy wagon. His two friends, after politely showing some identification, were issued a warning, escorted off the property and sent on their way.

Everything that takes place at school should be about learning. Even though the three boys had very different learning experiences that day, I hope they all woke up the next morning wiser for their encounter with the D.T. SLO.

The Twin Confusion

Among the grads of 1994, I had a set of identical twin boys as students. In the five years they attended the school, the staff, including myself, never could identify one from the other. What is particularly unusual is that their friends and classmates never figured it out either. This led to several confusing incidents, some in error, some orchestrated by the boys, but none was more confusing than the mystery of the prank 911 calls.

One day during lunch, our switchboard received a call from the emergency communication centre (E-Comm) dispatcher informing us that the call centre had received a 911 call from our school and was inquiring to make sure everything was okay. Our switchboard operator informed the administration, who shared the information with the counselling department the next day.

We were told the call originated from the pay phone in the area by the entrance to the boys' gym. We were asked to keep an eye open, especially at lunch, for any suspicious 'pay phone behaviour'. None of us were sure what that was, but we all nodded in agreement.

Two days later, the switchboard received another call from E-Comm informing us the same phone had been used for another 911 call, again during the lunch break.

After school that day, I wandered down to the gym and took a look at the offending phone and devised a plan. James Bond I am not, but this plan turned out to be most effective.

The door leading to the men's PE office faced the pay phone of interest, and it occurred to me that if someone could peek through the window of the door, they would get an excellent view of the phone and anyone who used it. Unfortunately, the window in the door had a pull-down blind, and it was impossible to get a glimpse of the phone from inside the office. That is, until I took my pen and gouged a small hole in it. I decided it was not vandalism if a teacher did it.

The next day I assumed my stakeout position inside the gym office and waited for my prey. Nothing, not a single call from the phone. The next day, the same thing. The following day I was involved in a student counselling situation during the lunch break, and wouldn't you know it, another call to E-Comm from the same phone. My timing stunk. However, the very next day, I hit the jackpot.

I was in position and peeking through my little view hole, and bingo, a boy I did not recognize picked up the receiver, pushed three numbers, waited and hung up. I wanted to pounce but held back, waiting to see if there were any other calls made and if any other boys were involved. I knew I could identify the student, so I was in no hurry to talk to him.

At the conclusion of the lunch break I walked into the main office and confidently stated, "You got another call from E-Comm, didn't you?" The entire office went silent, and, from his office, I heard Dave.

"How the hell did you know that?"

Proudly, I announced, "Because I watched it happen."

For the next twenty minutes or so, I perused the student identification cards and found our prankster. He was in grade eight and one of the students whom I had not yet met. The SLO, Dave and I had a little strategy meeting and called for our suspect to come down to the office and have a chat (a.k.a. be interrogated).

The three of us had worked together long enough to know our roles very well. We spent the next thirty minutes doing our best to get a confession from our guy, but nothing we did or said broke him down. It was all deny, deny, deny. For a grade-eight student not to break down after this length of time was very unusual. It is much more common that, in his position, he would have given us the confession we were after.

Our SLO had enough and finally out of desperation announced, "You have been positively identified by a very credible witness. Mr. Greer saw you make this call. Stop lying and tell us the truth. We know it was you."

The three of us did our best to stare down the boy, until we saw his innocent little face tighten in thought and heard his soft, meek little voice ask, "Did you know I have a twin brother?"

Dave jumped up from his desk and sprinted into the main office to retrieve the student identification book. After feverishly searching the book, he had an aha moment.

Back to class went twin number one and into the office came twin number two. It took seconds for us to get our confession and months to get over our embarrassment.

The follow-up to this situation involved taking the twins and several of their friends to the E-Comm headquarters on East Hastings Street and having them meet the people who were working there. The E-Comm staff were terrific. Their explanation to our students about the seriousness of the work they do at E-Comm, I believe, left a lasting impression on the boys and provided them with a valuable learning experience; at least I hope it did.

The Fireworks Confession

One October day, a few days before Halloween, just as lunch was about to end, I received a phone call from Dave asking me if I would join him and the school nurse to deal with a situation. He asked me to meet him in the nurse's office. When I arrived, there were half a dozen of our male students, all receiving treatment for minor cuts and scrapes. A couple of them were holding ice packs on various parts of their bodies, a couple more had been bandaged and were sitting in stunned silence. One was lying on the medical bed and appeared to be unconscious. The nurse informed me there were no serious injuries, but she had been treating multiple grade-nine and -ten boys for the last twenty minutes and had been told by many of them that there had been some incident in the cafeteria during lunch. The stories the boys told were all quite consistent. It seemed that one of their classmates had been throwing money around the cafeteria, and their injuries had occurred as a result of them diving on the ground for the money and in the process being piled on by other 'money grabbers'. The story sounded too bizarre to be real, but the student they all identified as the 'money boy' was the same student. Dave and I walked across to his office and called for the boy in question to report to the office.

Dave began. "Adnan, where were you at lunch today?"

"I was in the caf, sir."

"Doing anything in particular?"

"Just throwing a bunch of money around."

Both Dave and I knew Adnan and had had a few minor dealings with him, but never anything major. He was a typical grade-nine boy. His behaviour was a little immature, but he was respectful and had not been in any serious trouble.

The story he gave us was so original, and he told it with such sincerity, that it was impossible not to believe him. It was a pattern at Thompson with the grade-nine boys. They were surprisingly truthful.

In great detail, he explained to us that in the morning, after breakfast, he had gone into his mother's purse and stolen a considerable amount of money. He was not exactly sure how much. He came up with the idea that it would be fun to throw money around the cafeteria and watch his friends scramble for it but decided that many of the bills were too large and the fun would not last as long as he wanted. So, on the way to school, he stopped in at several small stores and converted some of the larger bills into smaller bills. He also asked for and was given change from the cafeteria at the beginning of the lunch break. About halfway through lunch, he began his quest of mayhem.

To confirm his story, Dave phoned Adnan's mom, who substantiated that there was approximately $100 missing from her purse. Dave hung up the phone and stared into my eyes. I had seen this look before, and it terrified me. Dave was about to go on a mission. I had witnessed a couple of Dave's missions previously, and they were a sight to behold. When he put his mind to it, Dave was an unstoppable force. A heat-seeking missile of vice-principalage. I knew immediately that he was about to begin a journey to retrieve as much of the scrambled money as he could, and he would not be satisfied until he succeeded.

The next two hours saw a conveyer belt of students enter and depart from the vice-principal's office. As he interviewed one student, he would get the name of another student and would then shout the name to Mary, our school receptionist, who would look in the school locator to find the classroom the next victim was in, and call that room to have him come to the office. Dave got into a rhythm.

"Were you in the cafeteria today at lunch?"

"Yes, sir."

"Do you have any of the money that was thrown around?"

"Yes, sir."

"Where is it?"

"In my locker."

"Go get it." And on and on it went.

Dave hadn't bothered stopping for his lunch, and as the time passed, his blood sugar depleted and he became more and more abrupt with his questioning. Near the end of this two-hour on-slaught, this one confused lad arrived at Dave's door.

"Where is it?"

Without hesitation, "In my locker, sir." I guess word had spread.

"Go get it."

Off to his locker said student hurried and returned a short time later with his arms filled with fireworks. He entered Dave's office and gently placed them on the desk. It was one of the very few times I saw Dave speechless. Finally, after what seemed like a very long time, Dave managed to sputter out, "What's all this?"

"It's the fireworks you sent me to my locker to get. How did you know I had them, sir?"

After another silence, "I know everything that goes on in this school, and don't you ever forget it."

One of the delightful aspects of working in a school is that you never know where a situation is going to take you. What started out to be a bizarre incident involving the throwing of money around in the cafeteria resulted in busting a student for the possession of fireworks. Who'da guessed?

The Drunk

During my seven years at Thompson, there was one other time I was asked to come to the nurse's room. It was a couple of years after the mad money scramble. This incident involved only one of my students but turned out to be just as time-consuming and resulted in a ride for me in a BC ambulance.

I was in my office after having lunch in the staff cafeteria when my phone rang. It was the nurse requesting I join her in her room, which was directly across the hall from the school's counselling centre. When I arrived, I saw one of my female students lying prone on the floor. The room reeked of alcohol, and poor Christi Ann was out cold. Being the Sherlock that I was, I immediately recognized the issue.

In precise detail, the nurse relayed the story she had heard from Christi Ann's five friends, who had escorted her into the nurse's room.

Christi Ann had a reputation of being a bit on the aggressive side. She was a large young lady who was half Maori. Her claim to fame was that she was the first female high school student allowed to play competitively on a boys' inter-high rugby team. She was physically strong as well as tough in personality, and at lunch this particular day, she had consumed an entire twenty-sixer of vodka, according to her friends.

The nurse was concerned that she was suffering from alcohol poisoning and felt it would be a good idea to call an ambulance. I immediately performed two important tasks. I ran to the main office and asked the receptionist to call an ambulance, and I yelled for my friend and guardian angel to come and help.

For the next several minutes the three of us, the nurse, Dave and I, stood and stared at my grade-eleven student as she lay completely comatose on the floor.

The ambulance arrived in short order and two rather large young male paramedics lifted Christi Ann onto the stretcher with great effort. Much to our surprise, Christi Ann then came to life. She was not happy. She was angry, violent and completely irrational. She attempted to bite one of the paramedics and let out a spew of expletives that would have made a longshoreman blush. The paramedics then did something I had never seen before. One of them reached into his bag and took out two very wide, imposing-looking straps and buckled her hands to the stretcher. The second paramedic performed the same manoeuvre to her legs. She was really not happy about this and put in great effort in an attempt to escape her captivity. After a fairly short struggle, she stopped, raised herself up as much as she could, looked up at Dave and shouted, "I hate you. Why don't you suck my dick?" She then flopped down on to the stretcher, took a deep breath and let out a bit of a chuckle. She then looked back at Dave and in a calm and quiet voice inquired, "I don't have a dick, do I, sir?" followed by a loud and lengthy gale of laughter, after which she slipped back into her previous state of unconsciousness.

I decided to escort her in the ambulance, and Dave phoned her mom to let her know that her daughter was on the way to Mount Saint Joseph's Hospital.

On the ride to the hospital, Christi Ann remained unconscious but came back to life when we arrived. The doors of the ambulance opened, and she was removed from the back. I followed the entourage of paramedics and hospital personnel into the emergency room and into a cubicle surrounded by curtains.

Christi Ann fell back to sleep for the twenty or twenty-five minutes it took her mom to arrive. Her mom was not amused. Dave had told her that her daughter was drunk, and her mom had decided this was not the case and the school was out to get rid of her daughter because of all the furor her daughter had caused around playing on the boys' rugby team.

Although I had advocated for her daughter to play rugby, Mom decided to also take out her anger on me. Out spewed accusations of racism, derogatory conjectures and expletive-filled remarks. According to Mom, her daughter was not drunk, and this was somehow all my fault. Until, to my great relief and satisfaction, the evidence presented itself.

Like Old Faithful itself, out gushed the entire twenty-sixer of vodka right onto the hospital room floor. Christi Ann's mom looked down at the upchuck that had seconds before been in her daughter's stomach and was now on display at her feet. If the visual evidence was not enough to convince her that perhaps she had not got this quite right, the olfactory evidence certainly was.

I decided I had had enough and called a taxi to allow me to escape this chaos and transport me back to school, where I hoped the remainder of my day would make more sense.

For reasons never explained to me, Christi Ann was allowed to remain at the school and was a member of the David Thompson graduating class of 1992. For the remainder of her grade-eleven year and for all of her grade-twelve year, she was a model student. Perhaps the policy of transferring students who arrive at school under the influence of alcohol should be re-examined. Maybe it is sound educational policy to give these students a second chance.

The Computer Resistance

My time at David Thompson included what I call 'the computer transformation' era. Up until this time, all communication, including timetable changes, memos, etc., had been done in written form. Memos back and forth and multiple forms to fill in were the method of the day. Suddenly, counsellors were mandated to communicate and perform all timetable-related duties via computer. This was a massive change for those counsellors who, up to this point in their careers, had never been exposed to any form of work-related technology. In all fairness, the school district did provide ample education for us, but depending on how many years into the paper method one's career was, the transition for many of us proved to be very difficult. There was a definite correlation between how difficult the new method was to adapt to and the age of the learner. The younger counsellors just 'got it'. No effort. No hesitation. No frustration. My age group, the group I refer to as 'the group in the middle', got it after some serious effort and a lot of cursing. Then there was the group that decided they were close enough to retirement that they were not going to bother with this 'computer fad' and would simply carry on as in the past until they retired. During this time of change, our counselling department had five from the second group and one from the third group.

Ralph was in the third group. He had not declared a retirement date but had made it clear it was not far off. He dutifully attended all the required computer education classes and was most cooperative and pleasant throughout. Because of his religious beliefs, not once did a curse word pass his lips. In the David Thompson counselling department, it was all good. Until the day of our first department meeting after we had transitioned into the computer era.

Our department head had decided to take a one-year leave of absence, and as a result, the position became available. I applied for and was selected as the new counselling department head. Unlike my first 'promotion' as head teacher at the P.W. Mini School, this one actually happened. Typical of many of the promotions in the district, mine was not really based on what I knew or how good a counsellor and leader I was. It came about because I was very good friends with the principal and vice-principal at the school. They both were on the selection committee for the new department head. I may very well have been the best candidate; I'll never know. However, I am sure the selection was a done deal before the interviews began. I was actually told this by one of the unsuccessful candidates. Today, I am a little embarrassed looking back at the process leading to my promotion. However, in 1990, I was just happy to get promoted.

I had spent some time during the summer holidays learning as much as I could about the new computer way of doing business and was feeling quite smart about having emailed the members of the department our first meeting date, time and location. I also included an attachment of the agenda. No small feat for me and my scant amount of knowledge.

I assumed that all the new computers were unwrapped from their cocoons and were prominently displayed on the desks of all our department members. The David Thompson Counselling Department had entered the computer era, and I, as their leader, was proud of this achievement. But only for a very short period of time.

Five of the six members of the department assembled, as requested, at the appointed time for our first department meeting of the school year and my first as department head. Such excitement.

"Anybody seen Ralph? Where's Ralph?"

Accepting the mantle of my new-found leadership, I jumped up and began the search for our missing member. Down the hall and past two counselling offices I went, and then, there was Ralph, sitting comfortably at his desk with one of his students, busily writing out a paper copy of a student timetable change. I should have clued in then, but as usual, I missed it.

"Um, excuse me, Ralph, we are ready to start our meeting."

"What meeting?"

"Our department meeting."

"Oh, sure. I didn't know about it. I guess I didn't get the memo." Another missed clue.

"I sent you an email."

And then a soft, quiet, polite laugh, followed by "I will be there shortly."

Finally, I got it. I stood there staring at Ralph for a few seconds and noticed something was missing from his desk. There was lots of paper. Multiple pencils. Pictures of his family. But no computer.

It occurred to me he may have thrown it out the window, but after a quick perusal around his office, I located it. It was tidily, and as it turned out, permanently, located on the floor of his office, tucked away in the corner, all neatly secured in bubble wrap.

This was not the time nor the location to discuss this with Ralph. I knew he had a temper, and I knew he was very set in his ways. A computer conversation in front of a student was not going to go well.

Ralph did eventually join us for our meeting, and at the end of it, I had a conversation with him about the use of his computer. This was to be the first of many conversations I had with Ralph that lasted until he retired at the end of June, ten months later. On the last day of school and Ralph's last day working, his computer was still sitting on his office floor, still protected by bubble wrap. Sometimes in education, and for that matter in life, it is not worth trying to move an immovable object, and it is never a good idea to start a fight you know you can never win.

The Ultimate Field Trip

During the early 1990s, the Vancouver School Board initiated an international student exchange program. For several years, students from various Vancouver secondary schools were selected to travel to Atlanta; Georgia; Beijing; China; Bombay, India; and Odessa, Ukraine; and billet with students from a partnered school. Shortly after the Vancouver students returned from their trip, the students from the exchange school visited Vancouver. I was extremely fortunate to have been selected as one of the two teacher chaperones to accompany nine Vancouver students to Odessa.

This was like no other field trip I had ever participated in or even heard of. Rather than the usual model of all the participating students attending the same school, these nine fortunate young people were selected from nine different secondary schools in the district. None of them were students at David Thompson, so I was about to supervise nine grade-eleven students whom I had never met to Moscow and Odessa. This scenario was way outside my comfort zone, but I really wanted to go on this trip, so I put faith in the selection committee to have selected nine superstar kids. After all, they had selected me as a chaperone. Better not to think about that.

My chaperone partner and I met with the parents once and with the students twice. We laid out our expectations and departed from Vancouver International Airport at 3:50 p.m. on May 15, 1991. We arrived in Amsterdam the next morning and caught a connecting flight to Moscow.

We were met at the airport in Moscow by our Intourist (the old Soviet State Committee for Tourism) guide and Nina, a teacher from School 9, our exchange school in Odessa. Apparently, if we did not have an official Intourist guide, we would not be able to tour anywhere in Moscow. This was our introduction to the 'Soviet way'. This 'way' reared its mysterious head on many occasions during our visit and included daily encounters that required multiple permission documents and many rubber stamps and meant always being guided by someone wearing a very official-looking uniform.

We enjoyed three wonderful days in Moscow, where we visited the highlights of the city: Red Square, the Kremlin, St. Basil's, Lenin's Tomb and, of course, the famous Moscow underground. An amazing experience for all of us. We experienced a minor and somewhat nerve-racking glitch during our visit to Lenin's Tomb when we were approached by three armed, uniformed, military-looking gentleman who were not happy that two of our boys were playing hacky-sack in front of Lenin's Tomb. Sorry, Vlad.

The flight from Moscow to Odessa took about six hours. The airplane had several seats that were not totally secured to the floor of the aircraft and moved with any vibration from the plane. The flight also included a feral cat that spent the entire flight wandering around the cabin. Our in-flight beverage was soda water delivered in an old, chipped plastic bowl. At the Odessa airport we were met by a large delegation from School 9. All our greeters presented us with large bouquets of flowers and were overjoyed to see us. We were quickly whisked away to the homes of our billets. I then began my nine days' stay living with Victor, Ludmilla and their daughter, Lena, who was a student at School 9.

Our time in Odessa was amazing. We were treated like royalty. We watched a wonderful opera performed at the Odessa Opera House, were entertained several times by student dancers who attended School 9, met with the mayor of Odessa and generally had the experience of a lifetime. As great a time as we were all having, I was not without a certain amount of anxiety.

In my opinion, a successful field trip is one where the supervisors bring back the same number of students they left with, hopefully, all of whom are alive and undamaged. As I had left with nine, I was determined to return with nine. Early in our stay, I discovered a potential reason for us returning with fewer than the nine students we had departed with.

Like all other young people in Vancouver, our students expected cars to yield to them when they crossed the street. In Odessa, there was never a question of who was going to yield, and it was never going to be the car. To say that the drivers in Odessa were a little aggressive would massively understate how Odessa drivers drove. Drivers would drive up onto the sidewalk to get around other cars, and they never yielded to pedestrians. I was sure that if we returned with less than nine students it was going to be the result of one of them being run over by a car. It even occurred to me that we may arrive home with fewer than eight.

At no time during our trip did I really need to lecture this group about their behaviour. They were very respectful and cooperative, but at the end of our first day in Odessa, I called a meeting and emphasized as strongly as I could that if they thought a car was ever to stop for them in a crosswalk, at a corner, halfway across the street or even on the sidewalk, they were sadly mistaken and this mistake could quite possibly result in their demise. I was pleased to see them looking back at me with a recognition of complete understanding and agreement. I believe at some time during that first day, most, and perhaps all of them, had experienced at least one near miss or even multiple near misses. I am pleased to report that in spite of my feelings of absolute certainty that one or more of our students would be struck by a car or truck, we did indeed complete a successful field trip and bring back the same number of students that we left with, all of whom were undamaged.

During my nine days' stay at Victor and Ludmilla's, Victor spoke not a word of English. I assumed he had never learned the language. However, on the last morning of our stay I discovered that Victor's

English was actually quite good. I had joined him in his driveway as he was replacing the spark plugs in his car when he paused, lifted his head from the engine and stated in perfect English, "I think in my country we ask, 'Do you own a car?' and I think in your country you ask, 'How many cars do you own?'" I believe this was, and still is, symbolic of the perception many Ukrainians have of the difference in our two countries. Mikhail Gorbachev's perestroika movement of openness revealed to the Ukrainian people how little they had

Back in the
U.S.S.R.

KEIR PETERSON
Grade 12, University Hill
secondary school, Vancouver

I WAS ONE OF eight secondary students chosen by the Vancouver school board to travel in May to Odessa, one of Vancouver's sister cities.

We began by flying to Moscow, stopping off in Amsterdam on the way. Moscow was, for lack of a better word, interesting. We passed though various security check points, had our passports checked, our bags x-rayed more than once, and met many unsmiling security officers.

To get a rough idea of what we saw when we arrived, imagine Toronto. Get rid of all the skyscrapers, modern houses and anything made within the last few decades. Now add some dust, beautiful architecture, fill the streets with Soviet cars (Ladas) and add some people who don't look too happy but are really very kind. What you get is Moscow, capital of the Soviet Union.

We spent our first night in the Cosmos, a hotel built in 1980 for the Olympic Games. We left the next morning for Odessa, a port city on the Black Sea, where we would spend the remaining 10 days of our exchange.

To get from Moscow to Odessa, in Ukraine, we flew Aeroflot, the one and only airline in the Soviet Union.

The Aeroflot experience is difficult to describe: our flight involved seats that moved during the flight, strange noises from the plane's door, and a near miss with another airplane on the runway.

Odessa and Moscow are similar as far as buildings go, and the cars still speed up when pedestrians step on to the street, but there were significant differences.

The food lines that we see on television are typical in Moscow, but shortages don't seem to be as big a problem in Odessa.

The shelves in food stores are far from being full, but our hosts made sure that we always had plenty to eat. Shortages and refrigeration were not great, and we could only eat what was in season.

We enjoyed tomatoes, cucumbers and numerous desserts made with apricots at least twice a day.

The final, and most obvious, difference between Odessa and Moscow was the people themselves. While the people of Moscow always look slightly harassed, the people we met in Odessa were often smiling and frequently had a great sense of humor.

We were exposed to various aspects of life in Odessa. We spent much of our time at School Number 9 (their schools don't have names, only numbers), the school that all of the Soviet exchange students attended. Fortunately for us, it was an English immersion school.

Of the many things we did and saw, the families had the biggest impact on us. They were hospitable and generous, going out of their way to do things for us. Our hosts bought gifts for us when we could have afforded to buy them more easily. (Ten Canadian dollars converted to a teacher's salary for almost a month.)

The Odessa students are scheduled to arrive in Vancouver on Wednesday.

If their experiences here are half as interesting (and unusual) as ours were in their country, their excursion will be one they will never forget.

SPLENDOR: lucky Vancouver students gather before beautiful 19th-century opera house in Odessa, Ukraine

Newspaper article from the *Vancouver Sun* written by one of our exchange students compared to people in many other parts of the world. This was to be made embarrassingly obvious when the students from School 9 came to Vancouver and repeatedly were overwhelmed by the disparity between the two countries. I continue to hope that this left with our nine students an appreciation of how fortunate they were to live where and when they did. It certainly did for me.

The Unbearable Sorrow

There is no doubt that the seven years I spent at David Thompson were the happiest and most fun-filled years of my career. The staff got along well together. The students were, by and large, cooperative and the parent community supportive. Unfortunately, as in Dickens' *Tale of Two Cities*, "It was the best of times, it was the worst of times." In the spring of 1993 at David Thompson Secondary, it truly was the worst of times.

During spring break of 1993, a group of D.T. students travelled to a Howe Sound outdoor camp to work toward their Duke of Edinburgh awards. They were accompanied by one of our teachers. One evening, three of the senior students who were on the trip decided it was a good idea to sneak out of camp after dark. They thought it would be fun to go down to the wharf and take a late-night canoe ride. The canoe they chose for their ride had been put out of service because it had developed a leak in its ballast. The boys decided they did not need to wear life jackets, and none of the three could swim. As with most tragedies, there were many contributing factors and not one single cause.

It wasn't until morning that the boys were missed, and by then it was too late. The frigid waters of Howe Sound gave them no chance of survival. One of the boys was located shortly after the frantic search began, but it took several days of searching for the bodies of the other two to be recovered. Several days of unbearable misery.

I was watching the morning news when I learned what had happened. There was no doubt in my mind that the boys were 'our boys'. As when any of us loses a loved one, the time of grief is also the time that we must be practical and organize the dozens of things that need to be done. I knew from my previous training that one of the things that needed to be done was to get into the school and empty the boys' lockers before the students arrived. This was one of the recommendations in the sudden death protocol, and I knew it made sense. During the training we had been told that there had been several incidents where friends of deceased students had broken into their lockers to collect mementos. Dave and I agreed to meet at the school on Sunday afternoon and empty the contents of the three lockers. That way, we could return all the students' belongings to their families before any of the friends could break into the lockers and take them.

During the following week, a number of staff from the school visited the homes of the three boys and met with staff and students to give information about the families' wishes with regard to attending services. From the families, we discovered that the three boys were all of different religions and were to have different faith-based services. We invited all the students who thought they might attend one or more of the services to meet in the auditorium and gave them a summary of how the service would be conducted and what the various protocols would be for each. We wanted our students to know what to expect and feel confident if they decided to attend.

At the school, there was massive grief throughout the grade eleven and -twelve group of students. Members of the staff grieved as well. A shroud of sorrow draped over the entire building.

Dozens of students wandered the halls not knowing what to do or what to say. The school designated the cafeteria as a place where students could come and be together. None of the staff cared whether students attended their classes or not.

Many staff members attended all three services the week after the incident. I could not have been prouder of our students. They were respectful, supportive and provided the families an opportunity to understand how well-liked their sons had been. Our staff was magnificent as well. They supported our students and never judged the grief our students displayed.

It is difficult to look back on this week and find any positives, but when I hear adults criticize and belittle young people, I think back to this time and remember how so many young people behaved in such a remarkably compassionate and mature manner. This was the rule, not the exception, during my entire career working with adolescents.

In retrospect, I perhaps should have spent the remainder of my career as a counsellor. I was a supportive enough counsellor for my students and their parents, and I generally felt appreciated by the staff at Thompson. I was, however, being encouraged by several people to apply for a vice-principalship, so decided to throw my hat into the ring after eleven years of counselling.

The Mystery of Promotion

In many ways, my third promotion was like my second. I am still not sure I was the best candidate, but in its wisdom, the Vancouver School Board decided to promote me to the position of vice-principal. It took me three attempts, and I often wondered why I was acceptable for promotion the third time I applied and not the first or the second time. Nothing had changed. My resumé was the same, and I still had the same job. Maybe they just got sick of looking at my application and decided it would be easier for them to give me the job and avoid the hassle of dealing with me applying a fourth time. For whatever reason, I was about to leave David Thompson and begin a completely new career at one of Vancouver's oldest and most infamous schools.

Part 4

The Vice-Principal Years

Vancouver Technical Secondary

– 2 ½ years –

After seven years at David Thompson and the most fun I would have in my career, I was promoted to the position of vice-principal and assigned to Vancouver Technical Secondary School, often referred to as 'the jewel of the east'. 'Tech' is an east-side school that was opened in 1916 as a 'boys only' technical school. Former students include John Ferguson, five-time Stanley Cup winner with the Montreal Canadiens, and Sam Sullivan, former Vancouver mayor and provincial MLA. The school's first principal, James Sinclair, was the great-grandfather of Prime Minister Justin Trudeau. In 1940, Tech registered its first female students. In 1994, when I arrived, Tech was a wonderfully diverse school with students representing over twenty nationalities.

It also had an erroneous reputation as being a tough place to work. Erroneous because even though it was a building filled with loud, energetic young people, it was a wonderful place to work. Contrary to their reputation, Tech students were terrific, as I discovered.

The Tears of Joy

The day after I received the phone call informing me of my new job, I made arrangements to have dinner with my mom and dad and share my good news. I brought a small bottle of champagne so the three of us could toast my promotion. I was looking forward to seeing their reaction. I began by telling them that the Vancouver School District no longer wanted me to be one of their counsellors. Mom looked quite alarmed and my dad nodded his head as if to indicate he knew it was only a matter of time before I got fired. When I continued and informed them that my new job was going to be vice-principal and I had been assigned to Vancouver Tech, my dad froze in stunned disbelief and my mother began to cry. I understood my dad's reaction, as it was predictable, but my mom's tears confused me.

After composing herself and having a sip of champagne, she explained her tears were tears of redemption. I had no idea that as a little girl, my mom had lived a very short distance from Tech. In fact, she could see the school from her bedroom window. After completing grade seven she was, in her words, "forbidden" from attending Tech because of its 'boys only' requirement and was "forced" to take the bus each day from one side of town to the other in order to attend Kitsilano High School. This had irked her for fifty-eight years. Triumphantly, she raised her glass and proposed a toast: "Finally, after all these years, someone from this family gets to go to Van Tech."

The Bathroom Office

As a requirement of my new job, I was expected to start work two weeks before students began their classes. Part of this extra time was to help justify making, as I often heard during the next fifteen years, 'the big bucks', but it was also an opportunity to settle in, finalize the school's timetable and begin to learn the culture of the school. After twenty years of having the entire months of July and August to relax and dress like a slob, it was a bitter blow to don real pants, real shoes and a real shirt and go to work on the fifteenth of August.

In the morning of my second day on the job, I was in the main office talking to the head secretary and noticed a gentleman in his mid-thirties come into the office and request a copy of his high school transcript. After waiting a short period of time and having his request granted, he proceeded to walk down the office hall, turn right and walk into my office. I followed him down the hall and confronted him as he exited.

"May I help you, sir?"

"Where did the bathroom go?"

"I'm sorry, I don't understand."

I could see the wheels turning in his brain and his inner voice saying, *Typical, useless administrator.*

"Where did the bathroom go?"

"You just came out of my office."

"Well, when I was a student here, this was a bathroom. Ha, I guess nothing much has changed," and off he went.

As I discovered a few weeks later after asking some of the long-serving staff members about this, before a third vice-principal had been added to Tech, my tiny windowless office had been a bathroom. During my two and a half years at Tech, I lost count of how many references involving the word 'crap' and its many synonyms were directed at my office and my work in that office.

The vice-principal's office is never a happy place. Students end up in the office only if they are in trouble. Parents are either invited there because of an issue involving their son or daughter, or they invite themselves because they are unhappy with something going on at the school. Neighbours who visit the office are always angry about something. Occasionally they come to complain about the number of students hanging around their property but more frequently to express their displeasure about the amount of litter strewn in front of their home. You can guarantee that teachers who decide to drop by are unhappy about something. They don't like their teaching load, or they want a student removed from their class, or they want the school to purchase more technology resources. Very few of the visitors to my office left with a smile on their face. I hope this was issue-based and not personal.

The First but Not Last Poor Decision

The first school dance of the year is always the Halloween dance, the least favourite dance of the year for most school administrators. Security is a priority at all high school dances. Administrators and supervising teachers go to great lengths to ensure only registered students are allowed into the dances. There is great vigilance as students enter the gym or cafeteria, depending on where the dance is being held, to prevent any guests or non-students from entering. It is difficult enough at school dances to supervise the students who actually attend the school without adding to the mix students from other schools, or worse, students' boyfriends who are possibly nineteen or twenty years old. The Halloween dance is especially difficult to supervise because of the costumes and makeup most of the students wear, which hide their identity.

Administrators are required to supervise dances, while teachers supervise on a volunteer basis. The school always appreciates the time and support from teachers who choose to come out on their own time to supervise school activities. My first Tech dance was my first non-volunteer dance and resulted in two very unfortunate incidents.

Parents may rest assured that school dance supervisors diligently check all students as they enter the dance. Students are required to have a ticket, which they have purchased from members of the students' council, they must produce a student identification card, which includes their picture, and they are visually screened by the supervisors to ensure no one under the influence of drugs or alcohol comes in. What could go wrong? Lots, that's what.

Shortly after my first Tech dance began, someone pulled the fire alarm. This is a no-brainer for school staff. No ifs, ands or buts—everyone out.

We received nothing but cooperation from the students as they exited the dance; the problem arose after the 'all clear' bell rang and the students began to reenter. To prevent students from passing the tickets out windows or through doors to their friends waiting outside, we had very cleverly collected all the tickets from the students as they came in. As a result, none of them could produce a ticket. We now had no idea who had bought or not bought a ticket. To make matters worse, most of the students had left their coats and jackets inside the dance, with their ID in the pocket. Now we had no way of asking for proof that a person was registered at the school. Given the size of Tech's student enrolment, which at the time was nearly 1,800, it is impossible for every staff member to tell the difference between a registered and non-registered student, especially someone like me who had only been there two months. This confusion was compounded because of the makeup they were still wearing. In sum, after initially being as cautious as we could be vetting the students as they came in, we let anyone and everyone in the second time.

It may have just been my paranoia, but it seemed to me that we had at least twice as many students dancing after the fire alarm as we had before the fire alarm. In spite of this confusion and potential for disaster, the rest of the dance passed without incident, with the exception of my misguided adventure into unsafe territory.

One of the tasks taken on by school administrators during these school dances is to occasionally walk outside and make sure nothing untoward is taking place. I had been warned that this should never be a one-administrator undertaking. About halfway through my first school dance, I made a serious rookie mistake.

At the time, it seemed like a good idea to take a break from the thunderous volume and horrendous humidity that was pervasive in the school cafeteria and get out into the fresh air. A nice quiet walk around the outside of the building seemed like just the thing. I took a quick look around to see if I could locate any of my three fellow administrators, but after seeing none decided I could handle this simple task myself and ventured forth on my own.

Most of the exterior of the Tech site is well lit. However, as with all large secondary schools, there are areas that are poorly lit and somewhat isolated. As I came around the corner adjacent to the automotive shop, I noticed a small congregation of young males, none of whom I recognized. I approached the group with naive confidence and introduced myself. Because I was so new in the job, I thought adding 'vice-principal' after the 'Mr. Greer' would in some way give me credibility and keep me from harm's way. Wrong again.

"Good evening, boys. I'm Mr. Greer, the vice-principal. What's going on?"

"None of your fucking business," came the less than respectful reply. Clearly the vice-principal thing had not produced the hoped-for respect.

I am not exactly sure what I said after that, but I do remember that whatever it was, it did not improve my situation or my safety. All the boys were now giving me the major stare-down, and I was beginning to understand the 'two-administrator' recommendation.

I then reached for my new best friend, the school board–issued cellphone. One of the perks of my new job was to be issued my very first cell, and better yet, at no charge to me. The instrument was enormous by today's standards and so heavy I could barely lift it to my ear. Its nickname was 'the club'. Not only was my enormous friend a perk, but a status symbol that I knew would keep me safe in the precarious position I had placed myself in. I continued my dialogue in hope of convincing these young follows to heed my request to leave the property.

"Okay, boys, you need to leave now, or I will be forced to call 911 and ask the police to help me remove you from the property."

Not a movement. So, true to my threat, I pushed 911. I looked in disbelief as nothing on the phone lit up and there was not a sound. During my vice-principal training sessions I had been instructed about how to use this phone, and during the training it always lit up and made a noise when I pushed the buttons. Idiot, I thought, you didn't turn it on. So I pushed the on button and tried again. Still nothing. Dead as a doornail. In my excitement to learn all I needed to know about being a great vice-principal, I had not bothered to charge the battery on my fancy new device. My mind raced back in time to the wise words of my Hamber sponsor teacher, Bruce: "Bullshit baffles brains." This became the solution to how I was going to save my ass and get out of this mess. Thanks, Bruce.

I pushed the 911 buttons again and spoke confidently into my dead phone.

"Yes, hello, I need police for the City of Vancouver. I am the vice-principal at Vancouver Technical Secondary School. The address is 2600 East Broadway. I am surrounded by a group of teenaged males and need help. Please send some officers as soon as possible."

I turned to my adversaries and calmly announced, "The police will be here any minute, and if you've got a brain in your head, you'll get out of here before they arrive."

And then, literally seconds later, I experienced the first miracle of my entire life: the loud blaring of an emergency siren. The boys scurried like their lives depended on it, and I stood in disbelief watching them disappear from my view.

Broadway is one of Vancouver's busiest streets, and emergency vehicles with lights flashing and sirens blaring frequently pass by the school. But the odds of one of these vehicles passing by at that exact moment, completely unrelated to my phantom call, are astronomical. Yet, that very thing happened to me on this night. If only I had been that lucky during the rest of my administrative career.

The Penticton Street Entertainment

Penticton Street is the road that runs north–south and is the street that borders Tech to the west. Penticton Street, over the years, had become the 'entitlement' area for the grade twelves to hang out. After four years of attending the school and now being in the most senior grade, the members of the grade-twelve class felt the area belonged to them, and as a result the grades-eight to -eleven students did not dare infringe on their beloved territory. With a few exceptions, the Penticton Street area was quiet and uneventful. Occasionally, a car would drive by with students from another school and our grads would get 'egged', which, of course, led to the inevitable retaliation from our students, who would soon after perform a reciprocal egging at a different school that had nothing to do with who had performed the egging at Tech.

A Penticton Street legend goes back to the days when there was an empty lot on the other side of the street from Tech. Each June, the grads would choose a hot, sunny day and declare it Tech Beach Day. Upon arriving to school on this day, they would set up umbrellas, lounge chairs, blankets and other appropriate beach accessories and spend the day basking in the sun. One particular year, a student in the grad class was a member of a family that owned a large Vancouver construction company, and when the son described this tradition to his father, dad thought it would be a great idea to not only support the tradition, but take it to an entirely new level.

Rather than passively allowing another year of celebrating Beach Day on a vacant lot covered with weeds and debris, he arranged to have several dump trucks belonging to the company deposit and smooth out multiple yards of sand. The morning after the 'secret dump', the majority of the graduating class arrived with all the necessary materials to spend the day at the new and improved Tech Beach. Even though Tech Beach is today occupied by several dozen large condominiums, the tradition continues, albeit on a block-long sidewalk and stretch of boulevard. During my years at Tech, it appeared to me that the grads of 1994, '95 and '96 enjoyed Tech Beach Day every bit as much as the grads of previous years, even though the size of the beach was significantly diminished.

Another popular activity performed on Penticton Street was the closest-to-the-curb coin toss. This game may technically be labelled as gambling but involved very little exchange of money and was always good-natured. The goal was to stand in the middle of the street and toss a quarter toward the curb. The student whose quarter landed closest to the curb was allowed to retrieve their quarter as well as the quarter of their opponent.

The first time I came upon this activity, I was standing at the top of the stairs that lead down from the school to the street. I felt this presented itself as an opportunity to gain some credibility with the grade twelves, so I good-naturedly made several comments about how terrible they were at this and assured them I could do much better. "Put your quarter where your mouth is, new guy," came the challenging reply. For me this was not gambling, it was 'bonding with my students'.

It turned out that there was more skill involved in this contest than I had thought. I promptly lost the five quarters I had in my pocket, as 'new guy' provided gales of laughter for several members of the grade-twelve class.

Shortly after my bonding, not gambling, encounter on the Penticton side of the school, I witnessed in the same location another mystery of the adolescent mind, similar to what took place in the office at David Thompson, when one young man talked himself into being arrested and taken away in a paddy wagon.

On this particular day, the centre of attention was not eggs, quarters or sand. It was a black Toyota Corolla.

As our school police officer and I stood at the top of the stairs observing the friendly and peaceful interactions of our senior students, a Toyota came speeding up East 11th Avenue and screeched north onto Penticton Street. Identifying the dangerous manner in which this car was being operated, our constable ran down the stairs, jumped out into the street holding up both his hands and stood firmly in the path of the car. The driver appeared to make no attempt to stop but swerved around our startled SLO at the last second and coasted to a gradual stop a considerable distance up the street. Our SLO was now even less impressed.

The driver and his three passengers exited the vehicle in quick order as our school police officer marched toward the car and its passengers. I followed at my usual vice-principal crawl. What transpired next reminded me of the incident at David Thompson when the trespassing student used his mouth to dig a huge hole for himself and ended up getting arrested.

Our SLO began, "What the hell was that all about?"

"Sorry, constable, but my brakes failed. I couldn't stop."

"Your brakes failed?"

"Yes, sir. I wanted to slow down as I came around the corner, but when I pushed the brake pedal, it went straight down to the floor and I had nothing. I'm really sorry."

Our officer then asked the driver, whom I recognized as being one of our more pleasant and cooperative students, for his driver's licence, registration and insurance papers, all of which checked out to be satisfactory. I then observed a very short, discreet moment of eye contact between the driver and one of his passengers. During the moment, the driver gave the slightest head nod and a tiny little grin. I am pretty sure our SLO saw it as well, because he quickly pressed the send button on his police radio and sent his badge number to police dispatch. This certainly got the attention of our driver and his passengers.

Our police officer then gave his location and requested a tow truck. Our student had lost the smirk on his face and was now paying attention. "What did you just do?"

"I asked for a tow truck to come and tow your car away."

"What? Why did you do that?"

"You just told me the brakes don't work. I can't let you drive your car if it's unsafe."

A very short time later, our student stood in complete disbelief as his car disappeared around the corner and down Broadway on its way to the police impound lot.

Another day, another great learning experience for one of our students.

The Runaway Santa

Regardless of their religion, for most high school students, the Christmas season at school is a happy time and a time of celebration. I am not one who subscribes to the notion that at schools we should not call Christmas, Christmas. We call Ramadan, Ramadan. We call Hanukkah, Hanukkah. We call Diwali, Diwali. Why shouldn't we call Christmas, Christmas? Most of the non-Christian students seem to like this time of year as well. At most of the schools where I worked, it was the Sikh students who were the first to ask if they could help decorate the Christmas tree that was put on display in the main hall. Another school tradition that many students like to participate in at this time of year is the last-day-before-holidays sing-a-long in the gym, where, to the delight of the students, school staff, usually very badly, sing carols.

Another Christmas tradition at many schools is the 'picture with Santa' fundraiser. Usually the money that is raised goes to a local food bank. Santa sets up in the main hall during lunch break and, like the traditional department-store Santa, invites students to sit on his knee, ask him to deliver a gift and then have their picture taken. As I was the administrator sponsor for the students' council, I was informed that the Tech tradition dictated that I was to take on the awkward role of Santa. I say awkward because to me it seemed quite inappropriate that I would be inviting teenaged girls and teenaged boys to come and sit on my lap. This was not a comfort zone for me, but I was informed by my administrative colleagues and several members of the teaching staff that this was the Tech way and that I should be flattered to have been asked to don the red suit. "Have fun and relax about it," they said.

I agreed to be Santa on Monday, Wednesday and Friday of the week before the Christmas break. My Monday shift was surprisingly enjoyable. Students visited Santa, told him they had been good and asked for a gift. Dozens of other students looked on and took hundreds of photos. I was pleasantly surprised and even looked forward to my two remaining shifts. Another mistake.

The first half of the Wednesday shift passed without incident, but as the second half began, I heard screaming and shouting coming from down the hall. I stood up and peered over the mass of congregated students and could not see anything until three young ladies I did not recognize but guessed to be about grade-eleven age, raced past me and down the hall like they were fleeing for their lives. They then sprinted out the front door and down the sidewalk that leads to Broadway. In hot pursuit were several young people I did recognize as Tech students. I immediately entered the chase and soon realized my pursuit was going to be seriously hampered by the Santa paraphernalia I was wearing, in particular the white beard, red suit and the black boots that were three sizes too large for my feet. But off I went, out the front door, down the sidewalk and onto East Broadway, one of Vancouver's busiest streets.

My quest to capture the three intruders ended about half a block from the school. Many of our students were standing on the sidewalk and were anxious to enlighten me with details of the escapade. Apparently, the three intruders were from a Surrey school and had come to Tech to settle a score with some of our female students. Our girls had defended themselves admirably and the Surrey Three had fled before they could inflict any damage or have any damage inflicted on them. They had met up with some friends who drove them away in an unidentified getaway vehicle. They were long gone, presumably halfway back to Surrey.

While I was getting the details of the incident, the bell rang to end the lunch break, and I instructed the students to return to the building and make sure they got to class on time. Cooperatively, as always, they departed and I was left standing alone on the sidewalk regaining my breath and attempting to will my body into not sweating under the ridiculously hot Santa suit. It was only then that it dawned on me exactly where I was and what I was wearing. I was standing all alone on the sidewalk on East Broadway, wearing a Santa suit. I did not go unnoticed by the passing motorists who began to honk, laugh and point. I also did not go unnoticed by the passengers in the many buses that drove by the school on a regular basis. Of course, the multitude of honking horns drew the attention of the students, who were by this time in class and had now lined up along the windows of their classrooms, yelling best wishes to me and my family and making other comments one would expect students to make to their vice-principal in his time of need.

By the time I returned to the sanctity of the school office, word had spread about my frolicking up East Broadway, and as I entered, I was greeted with rousing applause and more than a few ho, ho, ho's from the office staff and my admin colleagues. From that day on, the people who worked in the office never looked at me the same, or at least it never felt to me like they did. How could they? I had just sprinted down one of Vancouver's busiest streets in a Santa suit and had made a public spectacle of myself. When I finally got back into my office, shut the door and stripped off the threads of my humiliation, it occurred to me how proud my mother would be that I had taken such efforts to keep my students safe and how my father would feel validated about my ability as a high school vice-principal.

The Trustee Travesty

Occasionally, people who never worked in a high school would comment to me about how unsafe they thought it must be to work in one. I seldom felt unsafe at work, and I believe that the students who attended the schools I worked in also felt safe. However, any time one brings together several hundred teenagers, bad things can occasionally happen. One such bad thing occurred at Tech on a sunny spring afternoon.

It was lunchtime, and I was supervising the grounds of the school. I was walking through the staff parking lot when I was met by several senior students who urgently requested that I follow them to the other side of the building. By the time I arrived at the scene of the incident, the school's first-aid attendant had arrived and was working with great skill to stop the prolific flow of blood that was gushing from one of our ESL students. He had been attacked with a machete and in the process of defending himself had sustained a deep gash to his wrist. In very quick order, he was given excellent first-aid treatment and taken to hospital in an ambulance. The police arrived a short time after and began their investigation.

Generally speaking, young adolescent males who engage in this type of violent behaviour are not of the gifted variety. The attacker had decided to perform his assault on a bright sunny day and in front of several dozen of our students. He then dropped the machete and ran off. Needless to say, the attacker was quickly identified and arrested. The events of the next couple of weeks provided me with one of the most troublesome experiences of my career.

One of the responsibilities assigned to me at Tech was health and safety. As a result, I was tasked to deal with all media communication surrounding this event. Fortunately, I was offered, and readily accepted, mentoring from the school district's media relations director. My crash course in how to answer questions from the media heavily emphasized repeating one or two key messages. It was suggested to me that if I was asked a difficult question or one I really did not have an answer for, I would simply state, "Vancouver Tech is a very safe school for all students. These types of events are very rare." I considered this to be very good advice and wrote the key message, word for word, on a piece of paper and placed it right in front of me as I began the first of many interviews with the local media.

My first interview was conducted over the telephone and was with CBC Radio. Thank goodness for my key message. It felt like I answered every question I was asked with the same scripted response. "Vancouver Tech is a safe school . . . blah, blah, blah." Today I do not remember one single question I was asked, but according to my media relations mentor I avoided saying anything really stupid, which given the history of my career to this date, was somewhat of a miracle. My mother, who listened to my interview, told me I was brilliant. Of course she did.

As if the media attention around this event was not stressful enough, the flood of phone calls from parents questioning their child's safety certainly was, as was appearing before the board of school trustees to debrief them on what had happened and what the school had done about it.

There are sixty public school districts in the province of British Columbia. Each district has a board of trustees that is elected by the citizens and mandated to assist in improving student achievement and to build and maintain a school system that reflects local priorities, values and expectations. Some members of the school board have a background in education, some do not. Some members are aware of educational issues and have great insight, some do not. In Vancouver there are nine trustees.

I had never attended a school board trustee meeting, much less been ordered to attend one. The closest I had ever come to talking to a trustee was during my interviews for the vice-principal job, where one trustee sat and observed but was not allowed to ask a question or even speak. I now was wondering why I had ever wanted this job.

I received no end of advice from no end of different people about how to talk to these trustees. One 'advisor' told me that each trustee had their own unique agenda and would be looking for an answer from me that reinforced that agenda. I was not sure what that meant. It did not escape me that this was the group of trustees that had supported my appointment as a vice-principal, and I wondered if there was an implied expectation that in some way I owed them for this. More likely, however, they had no memory of anything to do with my appointment. I was also told that I was not competent or experienced enough to attend this meeting on my own and that I would be accompanied by one of the district's assistant superintendents. I still didn't understand any of this, or who these people I was meeting with were, or for that matter why I had been invited to the boardroom for this meeting. But into the lion's den I went.

The meeting was to be held at the Vancouver School Board offices and was to begin at 7:00 p.m. sharp. I was advised that under no circumstances was I to be late, as it was poor form to keep these important people waiting. I was beginning to imagine these people as being similar to the mysterious wizard behind the curtain in *The Wizard of Oz*. Great and powerful and seldom seen. I was a mess.

At about 8:30 p.m., after waiting in the lobby for an hour and a half, I was beckoned into the inner chamber. There sat the nine wizards and one recording secretary.

The trustees were a potpourri of mystery. No dress code here. They were in a variety of garb that ranged from formal jacket and tie to less than casual T-shirt and jeans. They were a range of ages. Five were men and four were women. Two were persons of colour.

As I entered the room, I was startled to notice one of the trustees was asleep. I don't mean that he had his eyes closed in deep contemplation or that he was resting his eyes after working hard and reading detailed documents. He was out. I could tell from his breathing and the manner in which his head was slouched forward. I would not have been surprised to have seen drool escaping from his mouth. There were, however, yawning, looks of disinterest and a couple of one-to-one private conversations taking place from the other trustees as I nervously waited to be introduced. It occurred to me that I would not have tolerated this behaviour in any of the classrooms I had taught in during my career.

The chair of the board began by thanking me for attending, as if I had a choice, and explained that the board had several questions that had been generated by parents in the district regarding the machete attack at my school. I really wanted to say, "It's not my school, it's your school," but smart-ass was not going to work here. The first question literally left me speechless.

"Mr. Greer, what country was the attacker from?"

What the hell? I thought to myself. *What possible difference does it make where this kid was born?* I had been prepared to answer questions about how we at the school had responded to the event, or what first aid we provided for the victim, or what information we shared with our parents and what measures had been put in place to try to avoid this from happening again. All logical questions that had significant validity, in my opinion. But where did the kid come from? Again, and for the umpteenth time, I felt I was missing something.

Testing the waters, I said, "I believe the attacker was born in Vietnam."

As impossible as it may have seemed to me at the time, the trustee's response made me feel even worse than how I was already feeling.

"That figures."

I was stunned, appalled and catatonic. I must have appeared to the wizards to be the dumbest vice-principal in history.

I remember absolutely nothing about the remainder of the meeting. I have no recollection of leaving the school board building, getting into my car or any part of my drive home. I do, however, remember taking an inordinate amount of time to fall asleep that night and lying in bed wondering exactly what had just happened.

Mark Twain once famously said, "In the first place, God made idiots. This was for practice. Then he made school boards." This adage, I think, may not be a crock.

The Chrétien Magique

The most memorable event during my time at Tech was the day the Right Honorable Jean Chrétien, twentieth prime minister of Canada, came to visit. We were given very little notice of his visit, but during the short period of time we had to prepare, we were inundated with security personnel from his office and from the RCMP. I had no idea that what I had seen on American TV when a president visits somewhere was the same as what happens when our own prime minister was about to visit a school. We were swarmed with men and women wandering round our parking lots, looking under cars with mirrors attached to the end of long poles. Dozens of them performed the same inspections inside the building as well under tables and desks. I was astounded to see these men and women wearing long, dark trench coats and talking into the sleeves of these coats. It was a real-life *Men in Black* scene, and it was happening at Van Tech.

It was decided that M. Chrétien would address the entire student body, so we informed the staff that there was to be a special assembly in the gymnasium and all students and staff were to attend. That was all we were permitted to share with the staff, as the least number of people possible were to be informed.

The prime minister's entourage arrived right on time and stopped precisely at the designated location. A large, serious gentleman who happened to be dressed in black exited the limousine. He opened the rear door and out jumped the prime minister. The greeting party, which included the principal, the three vice-principals, the chair of the school's parent advisory committee and our student council president, were lined up, as directed, like little toy soldiers. To me it felt like meeting the Queen. It was all I could do not to bow. All of us were stiff, stressed and serious. Until the prime minister was introduced to our principal who, with great dignity said, "It is my honour, Mr. Prime Minister, to welcome you to Vancouver Technical Secondary School."

I had read that he often responded to such a greeting with, "So . . . you recognize the little guy from Shawinigan," but what I heard was a much more prime-ministerial "Thank you. It is wonderful to be here." He was led to our gymnasium, where he was to address our students then field questions from a few pre-selected students.

A very short time after he began to speak, it became obvious that he had every student eating out of the palm of his hand. It was remarkable. I had seen many presentations given to high school students and had given a few myself, but never had I seen a person captivate an audience like M. Chrétien did. The students hung on his every word. He spoke about the future, about hope and about being young in Canada. They ate it up. At one point I surveyed the gym and discovered that he had managed to captivate all the adults in the room as well. It was like he had some magical power.

His speaking style was informal, relaxed and natural and made people think they were having a one-on-one conversation with him.

He touched on the importance of education and addressed the concept of being proud to be Canadian.

It had been pre-arranged that after his formal remarks, which in reality were much more casual than formal, and after the students had asked their questions, he would be thanked by one of our grade-twelve students on behalf of the school. The boy who was selected was in our French immersion program and had been born in China. He spoke fluent English, French and Mandarin. He thanked the prime minister in all three languages, after which the prime minister paused, shook his head and smiled. To paraphrase what the PM then said: This young person is what Canada is all about. A young man who speaks his native language and can also flawlessly speak both of Canada's official languages. As a matter of fact, he can speak English better than his own prime minister.

The place erupted with laughter and applause, Chrétien walked out of the gym, got in his limo and drove away. It had been an extraordinary event. It left a lasting impression on me, and I hope it did the same for our students.

The 'Where Did This Kid Come From' Moment

One of the most enlightening responsibilities assigned to me during my time at Tech was being delegated as the liaison administrator to Tumanos, the school's First Nations program. In some Coast Salish languages, 'tumanos' means 'guardian spirit'. The program enrolled forty Indigenous grade-eight, -nine and -ten students and was mandated to provide education about Indigenous history, cultural beliefs and practices. It also taught the four basic subjects of English, social studies, science and math. The program was staffed with two teachers and two support workers. There was also an emphasis in the program on Indigenous arts and crafts.

Most of the students in the program had experienced limited success in regular school programs. One common theory about this lack of success was the generalized misconception that they had inherently poor attention spans and as a result had difficulty learning. On the contrary, many of the Tumanos students experienced great success in the program. One such student was Troy. Troy had experienced nothing but frustration and failure in regular programs and was doing great in the Tumanos program. He had arrived from his elementary school with the 'can't concentrate' designation. On one particular day, it took Troy exactly six minutes to render that assessment completely inaccurate.

The hoop dance is an Indigenous form of storytelling through dance. Each hoop is symbolic of an item, animal or design in Indigenous cultures. The dance itself represents the never-ending circle of life. Dancers are required to have an extraordinary amount of concentration and athleticism to perform this dance, as they use their hands, arms, legs and feet to shift the hoops into different positions. Up to as many as fifty hoops are used to perform this dance. Fourteen-year-old Troy, who had a reputation for inattention with any task, was a master performer of this dance.

I saw Troy perform the dance on three occasions, and every time he did it flawlessly and took my breath away. He was confident, focused and clearly loved performing. It transformed him from goofy child to mature adult. I believe every young person has their own 'hoop dance' potential somewhere in their life. As educators and as parents, our challenge is to help them find their own unique hoop dance. Thanks, Troy, for contributing to my education and reminding me how important it is for educators to promote the self-confidence of all students by respecting and promoting their cultural heritage.

The Totem Turmoil

When I arrived at Tech, the Tumanos program had decided to carve a totem pole (monumental pole) and to celebrate the raising of the pole with a large potlatch. This plan evolved into a major undertaking for the school and, at times, an overwhelming task for me.

The future pole, more aptly described as a log when I first saw it, had been delivered to the school during the spring of 1994. The goal was to have the carving completed by the spring of 1995 and, at that time, have the pole raised for display in the front of the school. The carver leading the project was an Indigenous woman named Billie, one of the staff assistants in the Tumanos program who had been hired several years earlier. She was the lead instructor for the students' Indigenous arts and crafts education. She had been trained by the famous Haida carver and recipient of the Order of British Columbia Bill Reid. What a wonderful way of highlighting our Indigenous students and their culture.

As someone who had limited experience working with Indigenous people, I had little understanding of their traditions and customs. This gap in my understanding caused some major problems during the process of carving the pole. On the upside, it gave me the opportunity to learn some valuable lessons.

The design of the pole was completed by the students in the program under the tutelage of Billie, the program's staff assistant. The carving itself was also to be done with the contribution of the students, some assistant carvers whom Billie knew and, of course, Billie herself.

It was not long into the carving process when I noticed some 'irregularities', the first of which was my receipt of an invoice for carving tools that totalled several hundred dollars. The correct procedure for submitting such invoices is explained to all members of staff at the beginning of each new school year. The person requesting the purchase of any materials submits a form to the appropriate administrator. The administrator either approves the request and returns it to the staff member or asks to meet with the member to discuss any issues. What had been submitted to me was not a request but an invoice for tools that had already been purchased. I phoned the carving site and asked for Billie to come to my office and discuss this with me.

"Hi, Billie. I have this invoice you left me, and I am wondering where the request to purchase these tools is."

"The what?"

"The request that has to be okayed by an administrator to give permission before actually buying anything."

"I don't need permission. I need tools. How the hell am I going to carve a pole without tools?"

"But everyone has to get permission to buy anything before they buy it."

"I didn't know that. Okay, whatever. Can I go now?" And off she went.

I authorized the payment and Billie got her money. I followed up with an informal written reminder of the school's request-for-purchase procedure. I did not hear from her, so I assumed she understood, and I left it at that.

A couple of weeks later I got another invoice for more tools. This one was not as large as the previous one, but it was still an invoice, not a request. I pulled out the first invoice and noticed that several of the newly purchased items were duplicates from the first purchase.

Another call for Billie to come and have a chat with me. This time she made me wait until the next day.

"Billie, I got another invoice from you but no request to buy these things. What happened?"

"I guess I forgot."

"I also noticed that several of the items on the second invoice are also on the first one."

"Right, a bunch of stuff got stolen."

"Did you report this to our school police officer?"

"Not yet."

"Billie, we can't keep replacing stolen items. I am going to ask you to report this to our school police officer, and I am going to have to make an insurance claim. Then we are going to have a discussion about security."

"Okay, whatever." And she was off again.

During the next several months I received more claims for stolen tools, and it was suggested to me by our school police officer that the tools may not have been stolen but 'relocated'. I really had no idea where the tools had gone, but I wonder now if I had put Billie in a tough spot questioning her about the tools. There were, after all, several other people involved in the carving process who had access to the tools, and as I learned some months later, Billie was training these individuals, who were considered part of the carving team.

Another 'irregularity' I observed during the carving had to do with the presence of other people in the school. One afternoon, I introduced myself to three visitors and asked them for their names. They told me who they were and informed me they were friends of Billie and that she was training them in the art of totem pole carving.

Another call to Billie and another request for a meeting.

"Hi, Billie. Did you know it is school policy that anyone entering the school must report to the office and sign in?"

"No, I didn't."

"Well, it is school board policy, so I am going to ask you to talk to the other carvers and make sure this happens."

"Sure. Whatever." And off she went.

I probably should have been more diligent checking that the visitors were signing in, but I had to choose my battles and this was one I let slide. Until I had a visit from our school police officer.

She had, at some point, chatted with our visitors and asked them for identification. She then ran their names and discovered some unsettling information. It turned out that more than a couple of them had a criminal record and in some cases had served time in jail. Even I, as a beginning vice-principal, knew this was not a good scenario. I knew that every person who would be in the presence of students at a school was required to complete a criminal record check. Yet here were several visitors to our school who had not only not undergone one, but who, according to our school liaison police officer, would not have passed one. Great, I thought to myself, another conversation with Billie.

"Hi, Billie. Thanks for coming to my office. I need to ask you what you know about the carvers you are training."

"They are really nice people and they are enjoying what I am teaching them."

"That's great. Did you know that a couple of them have a criminal record?"

"Yeah. Who cares?"

"Well, we can't have people with criminal records in the building interacting with our students."

"That's bullshit, and why are you always picking on me and my friends?"

Off she went.

The next morning, I received a phone call from a member of the human resources department at the Vancouver School Board informing me that there had been a complaint made against me by one of the staff members at the school. A meeting time and date had been arranged to discuss the complaint. Attending the meeting would be the complainant (no mystery who that was), her union rep, the head of human resources and myself. Two days later, with all my documentation in hand, I dutifully arrived at the human resources department. The meeting did not last long.

The four of us settled into our chairs and the head of HR began.

"We are here to discuss a complaint made against Mr. Greer by Billie. She has indicated that she believes Mr. Greer to be prejudiced against her. Billie, we will hear from you first."

"He keeps telling me what to do and telling me I can't buy the tools I need and I can't have my friends help me with the carving."

Next to speak was the HR boss. "Well, Billie, Mr. Greer is your supervisor."

"No, he's not. He's an asshole."

What immediately bolted into my mind was the words of one of my previous principals when he told me that a student had called his teacher a moron. "When you deal with this student," he advised me, "be sure to discipline him for being rude but not for lying."

Without delay, the union rep, not saying a word, got up from her chair, firmly gripped Billie by the arm and guided her from the room.

That, apparently, was the end of the meeting.

I never heard a thing after that about the complaint, and Billie and I coexisted in icy silence until I became convinced that the pole was not going to be finished even close to the arranged time. After contemplating this dilemma for several days, and with some desperation, I looked up Bill Reid's telephone number. His wife answered the phone, and I explained the situation. She told me her husband was not in good health, but she would have him call me back, which he did.

"Mr. Reid, thank you for your time. I am working with a carver who tells me she has been trained by you in the art of pole carving and jewellery making. I have some concerns that she may be in over her head with the pole she is presently carving for us here at the school." I then gave him her name.

"Well, Mr. Greer, let me say this. She is not too bad at making jewellery."

I had, of course, heard the expression 'It's not what a person says but what they don't say' several times. I had also heard stories and read articles about the great Bill Reid and had come to the conclusion that he was a wise and thoughtful individual. It occurred to me that I had been anything but wise and thoughtful in my handling of this project.

Mr. Reid was then gracious enough to take a few minutes to educate me in some of the cultural norms of Indigenous pole carving. Not surprisingly, I knew squat about such things.

He told me that very seldom is a pole carved from beginning to its completion by a single carver. I had unwittingly put Billie in a very difficult position by not allowing her friends to assist her. Mr. Reid also tactfully suggested that it may not be the ideal scenario for Billie to be supervised by an old white male.

Billie did find some carvers who helped her complete the project, and the pole was raised with great ceremony during a potlatch held at the school. During the potlatch, I was presented with a traditional Indigenous button blanket that had been designed and stitched by the students in the Tumanos program. I consider this one of my most prized possessions.

Billie spent several more years supporting the learning of the students in the program and has since been involved in the carving of eleven other totem poles. She remains the only woman to have been apprenticed by Bill Reid. As a result of her personal connection to the issue, Billie is today an active member of the organization investigating the cases of missing and murdered Indigenous women and girls in the province of British Columbia.

It is said that every totem pole tells its own unique story. This particular pole has two stories. The first recalls the struggle to complete its carving. The second story is captured in the symbolism of the images carved on the pole, which represent the traits of the students and staff members who toil inside the building every school day. The raven, symbolic of mischief and curiosity, and the eagle, symbolic of strength and wisdom, are two of these very appropriate images.

One morning in December during my third year at Tech, I received a call from my area assistant superintendent. I was exchanging positions with one of the vice-principals at Sir Winston Churchill Secondary. Two weeks later, I packed up my office—a.k.a. 'the bathroom'—and on the first day of school in January started my Churchill experience. All administrators realize that when they leave the teaching ranks and the union protection that goes along with it, they can get the dreaded 'You are being transferred' call at any time. While part of the job, it is also a shock when it happens. With some disappointment but without complaint, I packed up my belongings and headed west to begin my new adventure.

The totem pole proudly on display at the front entrance of Vancouver Tech

Sir Winston Churchill Secondary

– 3 ½ years –

Sir Winston Churchill Secondary is located on the west side of Vancouver. There is also a school named after Prime Minister Churchill in Winnipeg. That school is called Winston Churchill Secondary and was opened and named for him before the great British prime minister was knighted by Queen Elizabeth II. The Vancouver school was opened after he was knighted, hence the 'Sir' in its name.

Churchill was opened in 1956 and is the largest of the eighteen secondary schools in Vancouver. Its alumni include former British Columbia premier Mike Harcourt and Vancouver Canucks play-by-play announcer John Shorthouse. It is one of the two Vancouver secondary schools that offer an International Baccalaureate diploma. Churchill also offers a French immersion program. It is an academically driven school, which creates both a positive and negative element to its culture.

Generally speaking, the typical Churchill student is bright and motivated to learn. This creates a great learning environment for the classroom teacher. However, when bright kids decide to misbehave, they can be quite clever about it. When they get caught, it can create a more challenging situation for the school. Soon into my tenure at Churchill, one such challenge landed on my desk.

Le Verre de Vin

During my time at Churchill, one of the opportunities provided to the French immersion students was a trip to France. Every year, this trip took place during spring break and included popular tourist sites such as the Eiffel Tower, the Louvre, the Arc de Triomphe and the Notre-Dame Cathedral. Besides the obvious cultural enrichment for the students, the trip immersed them in the French language and gave them an opportunity to practise communicating the French language in France, as opposed to in Canada with the Québécois.

On the Monday morning after the French immersion students had returned from their trip, I received a note from one of the chaperones, who also happened to have been the teacher in charge of the French trip.

The note read, "Hi, Hugh. I need to talk to you about an incident that took place on the plane coming back from France." I knew this was not going to be a good news-talk, but I had no idea how complicated this situation would become.

I looked up the teaching schedule of the chaperone, and during his non-teaching block, or prep block as it is more correctly called, I telephoned his classroom to arrange a time for us to meet. He agreed to enlighten me about this situation at the beginning of period three, right after the lunch break.

As agreed, he appeared at my office and proceeded to clearly describe the events that concerned him. The airline served a meal on the flight to Vancouver, and when one of our students was asked by a flight attendant for his meal selection, he was also asked if he would like a drink. He asked for a glass of red wine. He was in grade ten and fifteen years old. Somehow, he got served this glass of wine. During the meal, the chaperone walked down the aisle and discovered our student enjoying his meal and his glass of wine. The glass was three-quarters empty.

The Vancouver School Board policy regarding the use of drugs and alcohol during any school event is very clear and had been explained to the participating students and their parents. Quite simply, there is to be no possession or consumption of drugs or alcohol during any school event. Clearly, this student had contravened the policy and there had to be consequences. The first question in my mind was, why would a flight attendant serve him? Of course, this was a separate issue, but the little voice inside my head told me that on the horizon was impending disaster.

The next day I met with the student and his father, and it was very clear in dad's mind that his son had no responsibility in this matter and the responsibility rested entirely with the flight attendant and the airline. In his opinion, there should not be any discipline imposed on his son, and this was his legal opinion as an experienced lawyer and full partner in his firm. Very few parents of my students ever shared with me what they did for a living. The exception to this was parents who were lawyers. They always told me what they did for a living.

I had a conundrum. Who actually was to blame here, the flight attendant or the student? The dad/lawyer made it very clear that he felt the attendant was to blame because the attendant was an adult and his son was only a child.

I had learned by this time that it was only worth starting a fight I could win and not to start something I was inevitably going to lose. Some people may say I chickened out, but the decision I rendered and shared with this dad/lawyer was what I thought to be reasonable and judicious. I would write a scathing letter to the airline expressing the school's outrage and summarize the problems it had caused for both the school and student's family. I decided I would administer a three-day 'in-school suspension' to the student. This means that our happy traveller would be officially suspended in accordance with the School Act but not miss any school time. He would sit in the office at break and lunch. He would also be required to leave the building immediately after school, and a letter would be placed in his student file summarizing the student's behaviour and the discipline resulting from his behaviour. I thought this was very reasonable, especially given that one of the options available to me was to transfer him to another school. I was certain that if I tried this, it would lead to an appeal and I would most likely lose it, so I decided on a path of less resistance. My decision was final and I shared it with the family in a serious and firm tone. That was it. I had decided. I was a rock. No changing my mind. Until Dad/lawyer asked about the suspension being recorded in his son's permanent record.

With great bravado I stated, "Because of the extenuating circumstances in this situation, and because I am a reasonable man, I have decided that this suspension will not be permanently recorded on your son's file." Dad was happy. He stood up, shook my hand and thanked me for my time. Little did Dad know that school suspensions never do get recorded on any permanent student record. The truth is, there is nowhere on the students' file to record any suspensions or for that matter any behaviour issues whatsoever. The only information contained on the permanent record of students is academic in nature. Just marks, nothing else. I like to think that I had out-lawyered the lawyer.

The Careful Car Thief

Unfortunately, during my time at Churchill, there was a discipline case that did result in me having to transfer a student to another school, and I was not happy about it. This had nothing to do with the fact that this student's father was not a lawyer, but similar to the 'glass of wine on the plane' issue, there was a conundrum in my mind about who was responsible for what took place.

One afternoon shortly before the end of the lunch break, one of Churchill's teachers came running into my office and was very upset. "Someone has stolen my car."

My first thought was to call for our school police officer. It seemed to me this situation was far more suited to him than to me. Unfortunately, he was downtown at a meeting and would not be coming back to the school for the rest of the day. I had no choice but to deal with this situation myself, so I put on my Columbo face and suggested we go out to where the car had been parked and take a look.

Looking back, this was not a brilliant idea. The teacher was quite clear her car was not where she had parked it that morning, and when we got to the spot, well, she was correct. There was no car, just an empty space.

"Lanora, are you sure this is where you parked your car?"

"Yes, Hugh, this is where I parked my car, and yes, Hugh, I am sure." The oozing of sarcasm was undeniable.

And then, to our common disbelief, she pointed out to the road and sputtered, "That's my car right there." Her car proceeded down the street and came to a stop beside the car in front of the empty space where Lanora had parked her car. It then completed a perfect parallel parking job. As if from a Laurel and Hardy movie, out clambered four of our students. Once again, I found myself in a state of speechlessness.

After I invited the four lads to join me in the office for a chat, Lanora went off to teach her next class. I set up my usual interview technique by separating the gang of four as they sat in the office waiting to be interviewed. This was definitely a 'one at a time' interview situation. After completing the four separate interviews, I discovered that their stories were identical.

Near the beginning of the lunch hour, the boys were walking down the sidewalk and happened to notice that the keys to a car parked on the street were sitting in the ashtray, in clear view. They had no idea who the owner of the car was. One of the boys tried the passenger door handle, and lo and behold the door opened. They now had the keys to an unlocked car and, combined with the fact that they were all quite hungry, thought it would be a good idea to drive to McDonald's for something to eat. They completed their mission without incident and hoped to return the car without anyone noticing. Luck and timing were not their friend on this day, since when they returned the car, there standing on the sidewalk were the car's owner and their vice-principal.

I had a flashback to the 'glass of wine on the airplane' situation. Who was to blame here? The students who borrowed the car (I use the word 'borrowed' loosely) or the teacher who left her keys in clear sight in her unlocked car?

I again made a firm and final decision. The boys would write a letter of apology to the teacher, be interviewed by the school police officer and perform school service. I would meet with their parents and discuss what had happened. My decision was irrevocable. Again, I was a rock. Until my principal came into my office to inquire about my investigation and the discipline I was going to administer.

I informed him of my findings and my decision regarding discipline. He then shared with me something that turned my decision completely on its head. The teacher had phoned her union, and the union expected total support for her and nothing less than a student transfer to another school. By now a firm believer in the principle of not taking on a fight I couldn't win, I transferred the driver of the borrowed car to another school.

My job often presented me with conundrums that made it impossible for me to make everyone happy all the time. I should have realized this and resolved it in my mind long before I did.

During my fifteen years as vice-principal, I transferred very few students to other schools for disciplinary reasons. Philosophically, this procedure made no sense to me. Why would a student behave better or improve academically because they were sent away to another school? This 'borrowed car' transfer was difficult for me to accept, and it bothers me to this day.

The 'Full of Himself' Student Teacher

Every year, most schools in the district welcome student teachers— university students enrolled in the Faculty of Education who are training to become teachers. These practicum students are assigned to a sponsor teacher and receive opportunities to teach the classes of their sponsors and receive helpful feedback. Most student teachers are well-trained and knowledgeable in their subject area. All student teachers I had ever known up to this point were nervous as hell when they began this nerve-racking part of their program. I certainly was. All except Kurt. He was pretty sure there was no reason for him to be nervous, as he was God's gift to the teaching profession.

Kurt was a Technical Studies (in my student days called Industrial Education) student teacher at Churchill. He was tall, good-looking and very fit. He was also extraordinarily arrogant.

One of my responsibilities at Churchill was to coordinate and supervise our student teachers. I was the go-to administrator for the university faculty advisors, the school sponsors and the university students. I paired up student teachers with their school sponsors and tried to be supportive if things did not go well. I met Kurt and the other student teachers the first day they arrived at Churchill and gave them a welcoming orientation. The next time I met with Kurt was a couple of months later when I called him to my office to discuss a field trip proposal form he had submitted. He had proposed taking ten of our senior 'tech ed' students to the Boundary Bay Airport on a Saturday morning to meet and speak with an aircraft mechanic and then go for a ride in a helicopter. The form had been neatly and fully completed. The only mistake on the form was the name of the supervising teacher. In that space he had filled in his own name.

There are many legal liabilities that must be considered when a teacher wants to take students off the school property for any field trip. All risks must be listed. Names of parents or guardians must be included, as well as all relevant medical information. All costs, the timing and location of the activity are also required to be included. Of course, there must be a supervising teacher who is willing to be responsible for the students' behaviour and safety. As Kurt was a student teacher, he did not qualify as a supervising teacher because he did not hold a valid British Columbia teaching certificate. Teachers receive this certification after they successfully complete their degree. Kurt was two years away from this milestone.

He was not happy when I informed him that he was not yet a teacher and that he would have to have one accompany him on the field trip.

"That's crazy. I am a better teacher than my sponsor teacher." I chose not to engage in the 'who's the better teacher' conversation and instead stuck to the legality issue and told him it was out of my control. A certified teacher had to accompany students on any field trip, and this included his field trip to the airport. He was not convinced and, as I discovered a few days later, checked my work with his sponsor teacher to make sure I knew what I was talking about. Several weeks later, I remember biting my tongue when his sponsor teacher laughingly said to me, "I don't think Kurt thinks much of you." Of course, what I wanted to say was, "That may be, but he thinks even less of you." Was it wrong to hold back my response? Not wrong at all, I think. As it turns out, Kurt's sponsor teacher was awarded the Prime Minister's Award for Teaching Excellence in 1993, which recognized him as being one of the finest teachers in the country.

Later in that same year, Kurt once again put me in the position of having to decide between what I wanted to say to Kurt personally versus what I was expected to say professionally.

Uninvited, and with great confidence, he walked into my office and sat down. He didn't bother to ask me if I was busy or if I had time for him, he just sat down and began asking me a series of questions. He was doing an assignment for his university advisor that required him to interview any member of staff and write a summary of the role that person had at the school. I was momentarily flattered that he had chosen to write about me and my role as vice-principal. It did not take me long to realize my feelings of flattery were severely miscalculated.

He began by asking me how a person becomes a secondary school administrator. I carefully explained to him how all administrators had successful teaching careers, had shown a level of leadership at the school and had a master's degree. As he doggedly made notes, he mumbled some comment about how he felt the job perfectly suited him and his talents. I then made a comment that included the word 'vice-principal', to which he responded with a very confused look.

"You don't think I'm interested in your job, do you? Your job looks like crap. I'm interested in his job," and he pointed across the office to where my principal was hard at work running the school.

Never during my career had I witnessed such arrogance. Imagine a student teacher thinking they were suited to be the school's principal. However, in fairness I must compliment Kurt on his insight about my job.

He was not entirely wrong. Sometimes my job was crap. Often, I was expected to support people who I felt did not deserve my support, and way too often I was asked to perform tasks that made no sense to me. Fortunately, along with the frustrations attached to my job, I was given many opportunities to help teachers be better at their job and support students to be more successful.

The Reunion

After I had completed six months working at Churchill, my oldest daughter, Sarah, transferred to the school. The preceding June she had completed grade nine, and neither she nor I was happy with the education she was getting at her local school. As her father, I applied to have her attend grade ten at Churchill. As the grade-ten administrator, I accepted the application.

Although being the vice-principal's daughter at the high school she was attending did not cause her any discomfort, there was one occasion where it caused great confusion for one of the school's custodians.

My daughter and I discussed what would be the most comfortable way for her to refer to me at school while in earshot of other students. I asked her if she would be more comfortable calling me Mr. Greer rather than Dad. She made it quite clear that she had no problem at all with 'Dad', as 'Mr. Greer' would, in her opinion, sound stupid.

Soon after arriving at Churchill, Sarah developed a group of friends who decided it would be fun to also call me Dad. As a result,

I had about a dozen grade-twelve girls calling me Dad. Most of the staff and students seemed to understand this joke and went about their business as if this was quite normal. However, one of the school's custodians was not in the know of this jest.

One day after school when he and I were deep in conversation, one of my daughter's friends walked by and politely said, "Hi, Dad."

I replied, "Hi, Michelle," and she continued down the hall.

I could see the confusion on his face and clearly understood it. My daughter's friend Michelle was one of the tallest female students in the school and I, well, let's just say I am 'vertically challenged'. My 'daughter' appeared to him to be about eight inches taller than me, and this made no sense to him.

It made even less sense when another of my daughter's friends walked by and pronounced the very same salutation.

"Hi, Dad."

To which I politely responded, "Hi, Karen."

The confusion on the custodian's face turned to complete bewilderment. His jaw dropped and he stood frozen in a catatonic stupor. I once again understood but said nothing. Unlike Michelle, who was significantly taller than me, Karen was of average height; however, she was of Chinese descent. Our custodian noticed I was not.

My daughter's first year at Churchill was a wake-up call for us both. In her grade-nine year at the local school she had received straight A's in enriched math. I use 'received', not 'earned', to make a point. The combination of courses she registered in for grade ten made it impossible for her to take enriched math, so as a result, she ended up in regular Math 10. Her first-term mark was C+. The take-away here is that not all schools are academically challenging.

Bob, my sponsor teacher and teaching colleague from Eric Hamber, was now a PE teacher at Churchill. I was now Bob's vice-principal and, in theory, his supervisor, although I did not consider it that way. This role reversal was not at all awkward or uncomfortable for either of us. He again made suggestions as to what I should be doing, and I again took them. No change there.

The only potential for a problem came when my daughter became a student in his PE 12 class in her grade-twelve year. I anticipated that there would be no issues with her being in his class, as my daughter was a polite and respectful student and a good athlete. At the end of term one, she received a mark for her PE 12 class of 100 percent. I will never know how much of this was due to my relationship with Bob and how much of it was granted to her on her own merit. My daughter received the same 100 percent for her term-two mark, and I decided I would write a letter to Bob. In the letter, I expressed my disappointment that there had been no improvement in her performance from term one to term two, nor had there been any suggestion from Bob as to how she could improve. I suggested in the letter that a good teacher would do this. I made the format of the letter quite formal and signed it, "Mr. H. W. Greer, concerned parent." I also made note at the bottom of the letter that a copy had been sent to the school's vice-principal, "Mr. H.W. Greer."

A very few days later, Bob appeared at my office door for the first time since I had arrived at the school. He had my letter in his hand. Very slowly he crumpled the letter up, threw it at me and became the only teacher during my fifteen-year tenure as vice-principal to tell me to 'eff off', at least to my face. I am certain there were many other teachers who had said this but did so out of my earshot. Bob not only did it to my face, but got away with it.

The Leader of the Pack

Churchill had an eclectic socio-economic mix of students during my time working there. There was a small group of students who were not at all wealthy and who lived in an area that was referred to as the Russian Ghetto. Most of these students were ESL learners and did not come from Russia but from several other Eastern European countries. Their parents rented older apartments and worked very hard to make a living and provide a good future for their children.

Generally speaking, they were a little more outspoken than the typical Churchill student, and many of them had a quick temper. They could also, on occasion, be edgy to deal with.

However, most of the Churchill students came from wealthy homes, drove better cars than their teachers and were very cooperative and respectful. Many of them had parents who had come to Canada with considerable wealth and ran successful businesses from their home country and/or Canada. One of our wealthy students was not at all cooperative and respectful and constantly frustrated me with his behaviour. I did everything I could to reciprocate and frustrate him. I called him Rootin' Tootin' Lewton. I called him this because his name was Lewton and he hated being called Rootin' Tootin' Lewton.

Lewton's family owned several successful businesses in Vancouver and Richmond, and he made no secret of the fact that he was stinking rich. He was arrogant, snobby, pompous and drove a brand new, fully loaded burgundy 5 series BMW. He was incredibly dislikable.

I had received several reports that he was into all sorts of mischief, but whenever I went to check it out, I never actually observed him doing anything untoward. He held court in the back alley of the school where he parked his car and was always surrounded by his little fan club of followers. I often saw him back there, leaning up against his car and using hand gestures to orchestrate his crew.

At the time, Churchill had a very good reputation as an excellent academic school, and families would lie about their address to get their children into the school. One way to remove a student from the school who was thought to be involved in unacceptable behaviour was to do an address check and hope to discover that they did not live in the school catchment area. I became convinced Lewton lived outside of the Churchill catchment area, so one morning at 7:30, on my way to work, I knocked on the front door of the address he had given the school as his residence. To my disappointment, a very polite lady answered the door, and after I requested an audience with Lewton, produced him for my inspection. Thwarted again.

During a Monday lunch break when I was supervising the area where Lewton usually hung out, I rounded the corner behind the gym and was shocked to see no Lewton and no Beemer. His boys were in their usual spots but not Lewton.

"Hi, boys. Where's Rootin' Tootin'?"

"He's home. He totalled his car on Saturday and spent the night in the hospital."

"That's a shame. I hope he will be all right."

I did not have any ill will toward Lewton, and I certainly never wished him any harm. To be completely honest, however, I was not saddened when I was informed that his injuries would prevent him from attending school for the entire week, that I was about to have five Lewton-free days.

After a very pleasant Lewtonless week, I was most disheartened the following Monday to find Lewton in his usual spot, leaning up against his BMW.

I sputtered out a lie, remarking, "Nice to see you again, Lewton. Missed you last week."

He was sneaky but not stupid. "Yeah, right. Missed you too."

"What happened?"

I really wanted to grind him into telling me all the details about how he screwed up and lost control of his car because he was driving too fast and how he felt stupid about it. No such luck.

"I totalled my car."

He said it with a tone that implied this was a badge of honour. It felt like I was never going to catch a break with this kid.

I was totally confused. His car couldn't have been totalled—he was leaning up against it. I was about to catch him in a lie. I couldn't wait. "If you totalled your car, what is this car you are leaning up against?"

"My dad felt sorry for me, so he bought me another one."

Speechless for the umpteenth time, all I could do was take a breath, turn around and walk away. I may have been paranoid, but I am certain I heard him chuckle and under his breath whisper, just loud enough for his friends to hear, "Keep walking, old man. I got you again."

I tried my best to understand and know what was going on with my students, but Lewton remains an enigma. I never did figure out what was really going on with him.

The Ice Cream War

On the Vancouver School Board's website, there is a page headed "Vice-Principal Selection Criteria." The page lists twenty-seven criteria that the school board uses to select their vice-principals. Included are "a thorough understanding of redesigned curriculum framework and assessment practices and supporting learning strategies" and "ability to break down complex concepts and orally present them in a consistent, engaging and understandable manner to a variety of partners." How did I ever get my job? I don't even know what these things are, much less how to do them.

Not surprisingly, nowhere listed in the criteria is "prevent one ice cream vendor from punching out another ice cream vendor," but on one sunny Friday afternoon in spring, that is exactly what I was called on to do.

Shortly after arriving at Churchill, I had noticed the Mr. Frosty ice cream truck that was frequently parked directly in front of the main entrance to the school and had introduced myself to Tony, the owner, operator, driver. Tony had driven his truck for over forty years and appeared to me to be personable and friendly. There was never any thought in my mind that he may be selling something other than ice cream products. I was confident Tony was not selling drugs. After all, this was South Vancouver, not an American TV drama, like Jack Webb's classic *Dragnet*.

On the day of the infamous Friday Ice Cream War, Tony was incensed. When he drove up in front of the school, parked in his space was another ice cream truck. What the hell was Mr. Freezie doing parked on his patch?

When I arrived on scene, the two drivers were nose to nose, screaming at each other. I was worried about Tony. He looked to me to be around seventy years of age, and I saw his face had turned crimson red. He had worked himself into a state. I feared, as Fred Sanford used to say on *Sanford and Son*, that he was about to have "the big one." On the other hand, the Mr. Freezie driver was a young, strapping specimen of about twenty-five, who had an obnoxious perma-grin on his face.

Soon after I arrived on scene, Tony informed me that in the ice cream truck world, there was an unwritten code of ethics. Once someone had established themselves in an area, it was very poor form for any other driver to encroach. This was just not done in the world of selling ice cream. New guy, it appeared, either had not learned the code or didn't care about it. Either way, new guy was adamant that he was going to stick around and sell ice cream this day and any other day he wanted. I had no idea how to help resolve this situation. Then, out of the blue, I got the craziest thought.

Just as I always separated students who were not getting along, I decided to separate my ice cream combatants. I instructed Tony to get back in his truck and continue selling. I then asked new guy to walk with me until we were out of earshot of Tony and the students. I knew it was a long shot, but I was going to give it a try.

I began with "You know, this is really none of my business, but have you ever been arrested or charged with a crime?" There was a long silence as the wheels in his head churned out not ice cream but a response.

"I don't have to tell you that." I was pretty sure I had just solved this dispute.

"You are absolutely right, you don't. However, if I ask our school police officer to check you out, and it turns out you have a record, then I am able to ban you from being anywhere near the school, and I will share this information with the owner of Mr. Freezie. You understand that we have to keep any bad guys away from our students."

Tony, Churchill's "famous" ice-cream man, makes his rounds.

From the 2000 Churchill yearbook: Tony, the ice cream war victor

Mr. Freezie froze. He stared at me with a blank look for several seconds, turned around, got in his truck and drove away. Tony and I never saw him again.

I instantly became Tony's hero. "Oh, thank you, sir. I can't thank you enough." Tony then jumped up into his truck, lifted the lid to one of his freezers and pulled out a Drumstick. I hadn't seen one in years, but there was no refusing. I was Tony's best friend, and my just reward was a Drumstick.

I was happy to accept his gift, and as I ate my reward and completed my daily supervision, I reminisced about a time long ago when my mom or dad would take me to the store and buy me a Drumstick, not as a reward or to thank me for preventing a war, just because it was a nice thing to do. Oh, how I longed for the good old days when life was so much easier to understand.

The Great Address Scam

Churchill has a great reputation in the district as being an excellent school. Some of this reputation is justified, some of it is not. This positive reputation is even prevalent in some countries overseas. I discovered this first-hand, several years before I had come to Churchill, when I sold my Vancouver home which was located within the school's catchment area. One of the offers I received through a realtor was from an overseas buyer who was not at all interested in viewing the home but had instructed the realtor to buy a home in the Churchill catchment.

As I mentioned, the perception of the school's academic excellence resulted in some parents lying about their address to enable their child to attend Churchill. When a student was registering at the school, the administrator insisted on meeting with a parent or guardian of the student. Producing a telephone bill or property tax notice was also necessary, as was a birth certificate or passport for the student. Parents were required to show some identification for themselves with the same last name as the student. Making sure the students lived in the catchment boundaries of the school with a parent or legal guardian, as in accordance with the School Act of British Columbia, is not a perfect science. Occasionally, a situation arises where the administrator feels the need to speak to a parent or legal guardian only to discover there isn't one around. Absentee parents were constant concerns at Churchill during this time. We referred to these students as 'parachute' students, because they seemed to have been dropped off by their parents and then left on their own.

This is very much a west-side school phenomenon.

One entrepreneurial resident who was living in the Churchill catchment discovered that the school was conducting random address checks and withdrawing students who did not live in the catchment. She posted an online advertisement offering to 'rent' her address to parents who lived outside the catchment but wanted their children to attend the school, for a substantial fee, of course.

Churchill administrators had for some time suspected some scam like this was going on; however, they found it impossible to prove. That is, until someone in the technology department at the school board created a program to identify students by address. This may sound somewhat technical, but the bottom line was that the school was now able to produce a printout that identified an address and listed the students who lived there. The first printout we ran at Churchill indicated that we had seventeen students living at a single address on Montcalm Street.

By the time we interviewed all of the seventeen Montcalm students and reassessed their proof of residence and legal guardianship, we discovered there was, in fact, not one legitimate Churchill student living at that address. All the families of these students were paying the owner a ridiculous amount of money to collect any mail sent from the school and provide a fake city tax notice. Educationally, it was not always clear what was best for the student when we discovered they didn't live in the catchment. We did not want to punish the students for their parents' dishonesty, especially if the student had attended the school for multiple years by the time we discovered the wrong address scenario.

One of the unofficial policies Churchill administrators used was based on compassion and common sense. This 'policy' was used by most of the secondary schools in the district. If a school discovered that a grade-twelve student was not living in the catchment, we would use the 'grandparent clause' and ignore this 'illegality'. It makes no sense, and is an unreasonable hardship on the student, to transfer a grade twelve to another school during their graduation year. Especially if they had been a student at the school for the previous four years. Another way we discovered how many of our students did not live in the catchment came each year in early April when the grade-twelve students were asked to check the accuracy of the Ministry of Education transcript verification reports (TVRs).

TVRs include personal student information such as correct legal name, date of birth, place of birth and so on and are used by the Ministry of Education to prepare the student's Dogwood Graduation Certificate. Final grades are listed on the Dogwood, which is the student's legal proof of graduation. Besides making sure the TVR lists the student's correct legal name, an important detail for the students is that their Dogwood be mailed to their correct address.

Every spring at Churchill, we called all the grade twelves down to the gym and requested they bring a red pen and hardcover book. The preprinted verification forms were distributed, and students were asked to check the accuracy and to use their red pen to cross out any errors and write above the errors the correct information. We always began with verifying the legal name. The grade-twelve counsellor was tasked with providing the instructions to the students.

"Please check the spelling of your name and make sure it is the same name that appears on your birth certificate." Every year there would be several students who needed to correct their name.

"Now check the date of birth is correct." I never saw anyone change this.

"If the address printed on your TVR is not the address where you want your Dogwood to be sent, cross it out and replace it with the correct address." Seldom did we see a red pen correction at this point in the procedure. Then another important instruction. "If you write down a new address and it is not in the Churchill catchment, we will ignore it. At this point, the school will not transfer you out because you do not live in the catchment." And then dozens of red pens frantically scratching out the preprinted address and replacing it with the real address.

Many of the red addresses were in another Vancouver school catchment, but what amazed us every year was how many of the new addresses were from another city, most commonly Richmond. One of the jokes in the Churchill staffroom was "If there is a vehicle accident in the morning on the Oak Street Bridge, 50 percent of the students will be late for first period."

The Pointless Policy

The Vancouver School Board has a policy that does not allow an administrator and a teacher to work at the same school if they are married or living together. Even though I don't agree with it, I do understand it philosophically. The administrator has a supervisory position and sometimes must act like a supervisor in regard to situations involving teachers. If this scenario were to take place between spouses at school, it might end up coming home and not going too well. The policy belittles the professionalism of both parties. I believe two mature people who work together and live together can come home and leave work at work. As for the perception that the administrator may favour their partner in work-related matters, again, let's give both parties some credit about their professionalism. Another reason this policy makes no sense has to do with how many towns in the province have only one school. For some reason, it is acceptable to have partners working at the same school in these one-school towns. I wonder why it works when an administrator and their spouse work together in the same school in a small town, but it can't work in Vancouver. But with the VSB, a rule is a rule, and because I was in a relationship and living with one of the teachers at the school (she is now my wife), one morning near the end of the year, I received a phone call from my assistant superintendent, who had been my principal at Vancouver Tech and whom I liked very much and got along with very well. He told me what I already knew, that I could not stay at Churchill because my partner was a teacher at the school, and as of September, my assignment would be as vice-principal at John Oliver Secondary School.

It had been fourteen years since I had left J.O. for my exchange year in England, and I was quite happy to return. I had very much enjoyed my four years there. However, as with many of the best laid plans of the VSB, things did not go as planned. Two weeks later, my partner was appointed department head of counselling at, of course, John Oliver. My replacement at Churchill had been announced, so I was not going to be able to stay even though she was not going to be on staff in September. Eighteen secondary schools in Vancouver, and she ends up transferring to the same school I had been transferred to so we could be separated. I thought it was hilarious, even if my assistant superintendent didn't. The day after my partner's appointment, my phone rang. "Greer, it's Mitchell."

I knew exactly why he was calling, and I was loving it. "Oh, hi. What's new?"

"You know bloody well what's knew. You can't go to J.O. now."

"Really? That's too bad. I was looking forward to it."

"Piss off. It's Windermere." And he hung up. I'm sure he could hear me laughing at the board office all the way downtown.

My replacement was a new appointment. She was a French teacher from Lord Byng Secondary and called me to set up an appointment to discuss the job. Her name was Nancy.

The 'Newbie'

Nancy and I met soon after she had been assigned to Churchill, and I discussed with her, in detail, what my duties were and a little about the staff and students at the school. She was very serious and confident during the meeting, and I had no doubt she would be successful in her new role and that she would do an excellent job.

When she left my office and I got back to work, the head secretary, now called the administrative assistant, poked her head in my door. The people who work in a school office are always very interested in new administrators who are coming to the school and will be sharing the office with them. The administrators and office staff work closely together, and for the office personnel, a difficult administrator always leads to a difficult work environment. Our head secretary was very keen to get the lowdown on the newbie.

"How did that go?"

"Fine. She seems quite nice."

"You know who she is, don't you?"

"Yes, her name's Nancy. She's coming from Byng."

"Oh, Hugh, you have to get out more." Yet another space-cadet moment. "She's the premier's wife."

I've never been 'gaga' about seeing or meeting well-known people. I liked Jean Chrétien when I met him but was not breathless when I did. I didn't pass out with excitement when the Queen waved at me from the *Britannia* when our paths crossed coincidently while visiting Melbourne in 1977. So I guess I was a little blasé when I discovered who I had just spent the last ninety minutes with.

Unfortunately, soon after Nancy moved into my office and began her new career, her office was firebombed. The arson was never solved, but media speculation was that the attack was not directed at her personally but rather at her husband. Pathetic, but it happened. There was a great deal of media attention, and I felt badly for her that this had happened. During the following weeks, she and I had no reason to communicate, so the incident was not discussed between us. However, at our next administrators' meeting I noticed that many of our colleagues were sharing their outrage and sadness with Nancy about the incident. I decided to change up the tone a little, and during a pause in her 'I'm so sorry' lineup, I decided to have a word.

"Nancy, so sorry to learn of the firebombing of our office."

"You mean my office."

"Well, even though the police have not been able to solve this, I have a theory."

"You do, do you?"

"I think whoever did this didn't know I had moved out and you had moved in, and this was directed at me. You know, Nancy, not everything is about you."

I think for one of the few times in my life, my timing was good and my humour appreciated. She burst out laughing, thanked me and returned to her group of well-wishers.

The Greatest Grad

At the end of June of the year 2000, my daughter graduated, my partner moved to J.O. and I left for Windermere. All high school graduation ceremonies, which of course have nothing at all to do with graduating but rather with leaving the school, are special for the students and their parents. Grad 2000 was especially thrilling for me, as I was given the responsibility of announcing my daughter's name as she crossed the stage.

One would assume that announcing the name of my daughter at her high school graduation would be my most memorable moment of the ceremony; however, there was another moment that sticks out in my memory even more.

When an administrator or counsellor is asked to announce the names of the graduating students in front of hundreds of their friends and members of their family, it becomes a priority to pronounce the names correctly. To ensure I did not screw this up, I read over the list of names I was going to read and highlighted the ones I was not absolutely certain I could correctly pronounce. During the days preceding the ceremony, I called these students to my office and asked them to give me a pronunciation lesson. I then rewrote the names phonetically so at the ceremony I would avoid embarrassing myself and the student. A great plan, or so I thought.

One of the students on my list had the last name Daroogheh-nokhodcheri. For her, just part of her name. For me, a potential twenty-letter trip into name-announcing hell. A virtual entanglement of potential tragedy. In my mind, there were an infinite number of ways I could mispronounce her name, and I knew there was only one way to pronounce it correctly. I made it my personal mission to prepare myself to smoothly and without hesitation pronounce it perfectly as this young lady walked across the stage at the Orpheum Theatre.

It was June 6, 2000, my fiftieth birthday and, coincidentally, the anniversary of the D-Day invasion. I had practiced the twenty-letter labyrinth of complexity a thousand times, and I was ready to triumph. Her name was the 103rd name I was going to read, and it was going to be perfect. As she appeared to my right, I nodded at her confidently. She nodded back. She had supreme faith in me, and then it all fell apart.

As I was concentrating on my pronunciation of her last name, I relaxed as I pronounced her first name and completely screwed it up. Her first name had four letters for goodness' sake. Her last name had twenty. After the disbelief of hearing myself bungle her first name, and hearing the pounding in my ears of the theme music from *Jaws*, I recovered and tried again. Victory. My second attempt at her four letter first name went off without a hitch. The question now was "Can I refocus and not screw up the last name?" Miracle of miracles, out came the sound of the twenty letters in perfect unison. Sometimes things just don't make any sense.

To my great relief, I announced my daughter without screwing up either her first or last name.

Windermere Secondary School

– 5 years –

During my fourth year at UBC, I had completed four weeks of student teaching at Windermere, and now I was looking forward to returning to the school twenty-eight years later. There was not a single teacher remaining from my student teaching days, but I had heard wonderful things about the school and its community.

Windermere Secondary School is located in a lovely, quiet neighbourhood a considerable distance from any busy street or shopping centre. A unique aspect of the student demographic is the significant number who have parents who also attended the school. At every meeting or parents' night, there were parents who wanted to share with us the fact they also had attended the school. Families generally loved the school and loved the neighbourhood. They were 'house proud' as well as 'school proud'. At the time, many of the homes in the school catchment were well maintained and had been owned by the same family for generations. Directly across the street from my office was a row of beautiful older homes, any of which I would have loved to own and live in. Of course, only if I hadn't worked at the school. No one I know who has ever taught at a school has wanted to live across the street from it. Given the tranquility of the neighbourhood,

I was surprised one summer morning during my first few days at the school, before classes had begun, when I looked out my window and saw a convoy of vehicles moving down the street and coming to rest in front of one of these magnificent homes.

The Bust

It was the BC Hydro truck I noticed first. Behind it, a BC Gas truck, and following closely behind, a City of Vancouver Bylaw Enforcement car, a hazardous materials fire truck and two Vancouver City Police cars. The first bit of business for this ensemble of enforcement was to have the BC Hydro crew disconnect the power and remove the meter. Then three burly VPD officers holding a battering ram, accompanied by two other officers, jogged up the stairs and proceeded to smash in the door. I could tell this was not this group's first rodeo, as shortly after, the haz-mat crew scurried up the stairs with great purpose and disappeared inside. A few minutes later, a large cargo truck arrived and parked on the sidewalk directly in front of the house. Everything went quiet for several minutes, until another group of police officers wearing masks and overalls climbed up the stairs and proceeded into the house.

Soon, the exodus began, as vast amounts of large, powerful electric lights, industrial-size fans and silver-coated venting were removed from the home and tossed into the cargo van. I was still naive about this kind of thing but knew grow-op materials when I saw them.

A short time later, our school liaison police officer walked into my office and introduced himself.

"You have the perfect view from your office. Interesting, isn't it? Want to go inside and take a closer look?" Of course I did.

We walked across the street, up the stairs and proceeded inside. It was an amazing sight. Within the house there was not a single stick of furniture. As was explained to me, the operators of the grow-op didn't want to waste any space that could be used to grow a plant. There were lights, fans and venting ducts everywhere. Every square inch of floor space was covered with a plastic pot containing a marijuana plant. The visual impact of this was overwhelming, but mild compared to the olfactory overload I was experiencing. The stench was overpowering, and I thanked my tour guide and made a hasty exit.

Sadly, because of the damage done and how many repairs would be necessary to enable the owner to be granted an occupancy permit, the house was demolished several weeks later and a new house twice the size and lacking character was constructed in its place.

The afternoon of the 'grow-bust', our SLO returned to my office and we had a pot chat. He enlightened me to the fact that because the rental prices of houses in the area were still quite reasonable, pot growers found it economically desirable to rent in the neighbourhood and set up shop. He told me that a high (no pun intended) number of houses in the area were grow-ops. He also mentioned that staff at the school had previously been asked to keep an eye out for students who had bites on their body and were prone to scratching themselves. Apparently, this was evidence that they may be living in a grow-op home where the plants had been infested with mites. My first thought was, How on earth could parents subject their children to this kind of thing? That night, as I often did, I lay in bed contemplating how lucky I was to have been raised in the conditions I was and to have been blessed with the parents I had. We struggled financially, but I never was forced to share my home with pot plant mites. That night I also contemplated how lucky my own kids were.

The One Who Stands Out

It is difficult to estimate how many students I met and interacted with during my years attending and working at schools. Most students I have no memory of, some I vaguely remember and a few are etched permanently in my bank of memories. One such 'permanent' student is Andrew from Windermere. Andrew was a great kid. He was funny, smart, popular, and his mom and dad were great people. Andrew had one serious disability that got him in no end of trouble, however. He suffered from a massive lack of impulse control. Today I am sure Andrew is all good. He is most likely successful, has a family and is making his parents proud. He probably doesn't remember how many times during his years at Windermere he was a visitor to my office or how constant a worry he was to his parents. He most assuredly doesn't share this with his own children.

Most of the time, I addressed the parents of my students with the formal Mr. and Mrs., and usually they referred to me as Mr. Greer. A bit old school, but it was comfortable for me because, well, I'm old school. As a result of getting to know each other so well and spending so much time together, Andrew's mom and I were on a first name basis. Of the many visits Andrew made to my office that necessitated his mom coming to see me, two stand out.

Mr. Usselman was Andrew's math teacher. I liked Mr. Usselman a lot. He was friendly, polite, worked hard and although he was new to his profession, was a solid teacher. Students and teachers liked him as well. I am sure Andrew liked him too, but one day, true to Andrew's form, his mouth got in the way of his feelings for his math teacher, and in the midst of a mild disagreement about the answer to a math question, Andrew blurted out, "This is not the right answer. Are you sure your name is Mr. Usselman and not Mr. Uselessman?"

As teachers are requested to do when they ask a student to leave their class, Mr. Usselman phoned down to my office from his classroom to tell me he had asked Andrew to leave and that Andrew was on his way. Mr. Usselman did not share with me why, but I knew this would not be a problem, as I was confident Andrew would tell me why and be truthful about it. This was just the kind of kid Andrew was.

"Do you know why you are here, Andrew?"

"Yes."

"Well, I don't, so why don't we start with you telling me."

"Mr. Usselman was explaining the answer to a question, and I thought he was wrong so I asked him if his name was Mr. Usselman or Mr. Uselessman."

I am not proud to say that at that moment I suffered a massive episode of regression and the class clown in me took over. I, too, suffered an episode of lack of impulse control in that moment. I flashed back forty years and was back in elementary school entertaining my classmates vicariously through this grade-ten student. I tried for a millisecond to control myself but failed miserably. I burst out laughing with a volume that was way too loud. I know the entire office staff heard me. I laughed so hard I had to leave my office and get a glass of water. After taking too long to compose myself, I returned to my office to face the dilemma I had created for myself. How was I going to discipline this student when he knew I thought what he had done was hilarious? I wondered if I was ever going to stop putting myself in positions that made me look stupid. I feared this was never going to happen.

This was now another one of the countless times I did not know what to say. Again, I sat there looking stunned and stupid. The best I could come up with was "That was rude."

I semi-composed myself and sputtered out something about Andrew writing a letter of apology. Not particularly original or clever, but in terms of best practice, acceptable.

I had a conversation with Mr. Usselman and vaguely hinted that I may not have been completely professional when Andrew disclosed his misdeed to me. True to his understanding nature, he was not at all bothered. Andrew did write his letter and everyone seemed satisfied. After my interview with him, Andrew returned to class, and I spent the next several weeks hoping for Andrew's discretion in not sharing with his teacher my reaction to learning why he had been sent out of class. I called Andrew's mom and shared the story with her. She insisted on coming to the school to discuss this further and ask me for my advice. She knew by this point in our relationship that I had been a counsellor for eleven years, and she was always open to any advice I could give her about raising this boy. Somehow in our discussion, the part about me bursting out laughing slipped my mind. She was another person I hoped Andrew would not share the story with. I believe Andrew kept the story to himself, as I heard nothing after the day of our meeting. Thank you, Andrew.

It wasn't always Andrew's mouth that got him into trouble. Occasionally, his hands and feet acted without impulse control. His second memorable misdeed did not involve his mouth.

Andrew also exhibited lack of impulse control by participating in several 'crimes of opportunity', perhaps more accurately described as 'stupidities of opportunity'. Whatever you want to call them, Andrew very seldom said no to one.

For many years, Vancouver secondary schools have had condom dispensing machines in the boys' washrooms. Many years ago, when the idea of these machines was first introduced, there was great outrage from parents who somehow believed that if their children had the opportunity to buy a condom, they would undoubtedly use them. The great condom controversy did not last long, and now these machines are accepted the same as the soap and toilet paper dispensers. The custodial staff is responsible for ensuring that the machines contain unexpired condoms and are expected to remove the coins used to purchase the condoms. One day, Andrew thought it would be a good idea to relieve several of the condom machines of their bounty—not their condoms, but their cash.

His *Ocean's Eleven*-type master plan was to 'borrow' a large screwdriver from his tech ed class and use it to pry open the dispenser. The custodian who was on duty during the day was not impressed when he entered the first-floor boys' washroom and discovered the mangled and moneyless machine. Nor was he impressed when he discovered three more dispensers in other washrooms in the same condition. He paid me a visit and invited me to one of the washrooms to observe this reckless destruction. For some reason, he found it more comfortable to ask me to view the 'great condom machine thefts' than my two admin colleagues. Surely his decision had nothing to do with the fact that they were both women. Upon seeing these distorted pieces of tin, I wondered, Who the hell would do this? It took a split second for the answer to appear in my mind. There was only one student in the building who would come up with this scheme. I couldn't imagine it being anyone but Andrew.

During the next couple of days, I managed to extract a confession from Andrew, meet once again with his beleaguered mother and track the flight of the missing money. It turned out that Andrew was not just a thief but a generous thief. He had invited several of his friends to join him at lunch and walk down to the neighbourhood 7-Eleven, where he generously treated them all to Slurpees. What a nice guy. Actually, he was.

The One Who Got under My Skin

There is another Windermere student I remember well. This one I did not care for at all. Bashir was obnoxious, annoying and worst of all, spoiled rotten. His mom looked after him way too well. At first, his issue with me was his attendance. I say at first because he developed another issue that was much more upsetting for me.

Bashir was in grade eleven and often did not make it to his first-period class. He was absent from his first-period class more often than he was in it. I went through the usual steps of trying to get him to improve this pattern, but he thwarted me on every attempt. He kept 'losing' his attendance card, he kept 'forgetting' to report to me in the morning and when he arrived late for first period (usually near the end of it) and was sent to my office to explain, he always got 'lost' on the way.

Whenever I discussed this issue with his mother, she always fabricated some lame excuse to justify his behaviour. She would tell me it was her fault because she had been late serving him his breakfast or because she couldn't find the car keys and was late leaving the house when she was driving him to school. Once it was her fault because she had not laid out the right clothes for him to wear in the morning.

Bashir happened to be the same grade as my niece, who was living with me and whom I drove to school each day. I was not made aware of it when it took place, but my niece had experienced an interaction with him shortly after she started attending the school. One day at lunch, just after she had paid for her school cafeteria meal and was walking to a table, Bashir bumped into her, causing her tray to tip over and spill its contents onto the floor. He apologized and began to walk away. My niece was having none of this and followed him to let him know he needed to replace the food. The discussion became rather heated, and Bashir told her that if she didn't leave him alone, he was going to report her to his vice-principal. To which my niece casually replied, "You mean Mr. Greer?"

"Yes, I mean Mr. Greer."

"You mean Mr. Greer, my uncle?" I guess the reason I didn't hear anything at the time about this incident was because my niece somehow managed to get Bashir to replace her lunch, and that was the end of that particular episode.

Although he was annoying, Bashir was not stupid. One morning, about halfway through period one, I received a telephone call from his teacher. Bashir was not in class. I asked the teacher to call me if he showed up and let him know that if I did not get a call, I would assume Bashir had not shown up at all. So after not hearing from the teacher, I called Bashir's period-two class, and as I expected, he was indeed there. I asked for him to be sent to my office.

Before he arrived, I called his mom in anticipation of hearing yet another weak excuse, but instead she asked me if I was sure he hadn't been in his first-period class, because she had given him his hot chocolate in the morning and he always got to school on time when she gave him his hot chocolate. She couldn't believe it. Well, I did, and when he arrived, I really started in on him.

"Why did you not get to period one today? There is no excuse. You had your hot chocolate, didn't you? Your mom says you always get to first period when you have your hot chocolate." My sarcasm was not lost on him.

I could tell he was not amused at me making fun of him. I could also tell he had something spinning around in his little mind that he wanted to tell me. And then he exposed his evil plan.

"Your niece is cute."

"What?"

"Your niece. She's in my grade, you know. Her locker is only two lockers away from mine."

"Yes, she is in your grade, but who cares where her locker is?"

"She's nice. I might ask her out sometime."

For a moment, I thought I would vomit. Then I contemplated grabbing this little jerk by the throat. Neither of these options were going to be good for me, so I did what I did best. I froze.

Then he broke the ice. "You know, sir, I am really tired of you harassing me about getting to period one. You might want to think about backing off." He was trying to blackmail me.

I actually experienced a rare moment of sanity and sent him back to class and walked down to the staff cafeteria and had a cup of tea and a scone. On British TV, no matter what the trauma, it is always better with a cup of tea. I was hoping this cuppa would work to ease my trauma.

After school, on the way home, I shared my interaction with Bashir with my niece. Even though I had not seen a morsel of humour in any of it, she thought it was hilarious. About a month previous to my near heart attack interview with Bashir, he had told her his plan. As she often did, she looked at me like I was some kind of alien fool and said, "You didn't think for a second that I would go out with that idiot, did you?" What enormous relief. For the remainder of our journey home, all I could think was, You moron. You have got to stop underestimating this girl.

The 'I Should Have Known Better' Moment

Most days, at the beginning of the lunch break, at least one administrator will go to the cafeteria and make sure all is well. They make sure no one is barging the line, will encourage students to throw their garbage in the bins and make sure all is safe and orderly. It was a cold and gloomy January afternoon, and I was the administrator in 'the caf'.

At Windermere, very few unpleasant things took place. It was a quiet, peaceful school full of respectful young people going about the business of getting an education and building a future. On this particular day, two grade-nine girls were not about to be quiet or peaceful and had something else on their mind besides getting an education and building a future. They decided they were going to have a serious brawl.

I didn't see it start, but soon after it began, I was made aware of it by the shouts and screams of the onlookers. I quickly made my way over to its location, separated the spectators and came first-hand upon the battle.

I had not forgotten my Cariboo Hill experience of watching my two female classmates fight each other. I knew the ferocity of the girl vs. girl fight, but this did not stop me from acting rather hastily. My first strategy was to give an almighty yell: "Stop now!" After seeing no response, another but louder: "I said, stop now!" I will never know how I thought yelling the same words a second time was going to produce a more desirable result. I believe there is some adage about the definition of insanity being doing the same thing over and over and expecting a different result, but this was all I had at the moment. Again, no response. I now believe that when students engage in this type of heated conflict, they go temporarily deaf. They were throwing some serious punches and in the process were doing each other some damage, and I had seen enough. I felt it was time to take my intervention to another level. I needed to separate them as soon as possible, before one of them got badly hurt.

What a time to experience a brain freeze. This can be the only explanation for what I did next. I stepped right in between the two of them and a split second later took a vicious left hook to the side of my head.

At first, I wasn't sure if the blow had rendered me deaf or if the cafeteria had gone stone quiet, but I couldn't hear a sound. I looked at the two girls and they were staring at me in disbelief. At least they had stopped throwing punches. I then gazed around the cafeteria and saw a frozen frame of humanity. No one was moving. I don't think a single student in the cafeteria was breathing. I then looked back at the girls, and they appeared to be in shock. I'm pretty sure they thought at any moment I was going to collapse in an unconscious heap.

I don't remember much about the next few minutes. I am relatively sure it wasn't me who escorted the girls to the office. I somehow ended up back in my office with an ice pack on my right temple. I regained what little senses I normally had and walked out into the main office. Both girls jumped to their feet and, with runny noses and tear-filled eyes, apologized multiple times.

I had no idea which one of them had administered the blow, and I really didn't care. My headache was my own fault. Clearly, I should have known better.

I gave them both some kind of discipline for fighting on school property, but during the meeting with their parents didn't mention the punch to the head. In my opinion, it was not necessary for the parents to think that perhaps their daughter had assaulted her vice-principal, when in truth it was the vice-principal's own fault.

The Custodian

During my career it wasn't always the students who tested my patience. Sometimes the teachers were a challenge to deal with, sometimes the parents and sometimes the people who lived in the neighbourhood. At Windermere, the person who most tested my patience was a custodian. My father spent the majority of his working career as a high school custodian, which gave me a first-hand understanding of the job and its responsibilities. This was both a curse and a blessing.

More than most of my colleagues, I understood the custodian's job. I knew what it took to properly maintain a school. My father took pride in his school. He wanted his school to be spotless and worked hard to make it that way. I watched him work himself into an ulcer with this dedication to his job. On the other hand, I often overreacted when I saw effort that was less than that of my father's, which led me to sometimes be overly critical of the custodial staff. The majority of the custodians at the schools where I worked were excellent. They worked hard, were respectful to me and got along well with the students. I tried my best to always be respectful to them, but it drove me crazy when I saw even a little bit of laziness or incompetence. At Windermere, we had a custodian who was great at his job. We socialized together, played poker together and he became my friend. We also had the custodian from hell, and it drove me around the bend.

Stan had many faults. The first indication I had that he was lazy was the morning of the first snowfall the December after I began at Windermere. I arrived to work at 7:30, after the city had a significant overnight snowfall, to find the sidewalks around and leading to the school completely covered in untouched snow. The snow was very beautiful but undisturbed by human-powered shovel. I made a quick stop to my office and proceeded downstairs to the custodian's lunchroom to find Stan and crew drinking coffee and lounging on their sofa. I damn well knew where my father would have been if he was the custodian, and it wouldn't be there.

"Um, good morning, guys. I'm hoping you get around to shovelling the snow soon."

"Sure, we will get to it soon."

"It's important that the sidewalks are clear when the staff and students arrive."

"Yup."

A short time later, I could hear the scraping of shovels on the sidewalks, and from my office window I could see the snow was being cleared. I was happy. It was all good. Until I saw from my window that Stan had deposited a large mound of snow from the sidewalk directly onto the path that led from the staff parking lot to the front stairs. Left where it was, the snow would create a small mountain for the teachers to climb over to get themselves into the building. So, boots, toque and winter coat on, I went out to have another snow chat with Stan.

"Um, Stan, you have piled the snow from the sidewalk onto the path that leads from the staff parking lot to the entrance."

"Really?"

"Yes, really. It is now almost impossible and very unsafe for the teachers to get into the building without climbing up a mountain of snow."

"Okay, I'll move it, I guess." However, after waiting for twenty minutes and seeing no evidence of this, and not being able to even think about another visit downstairs, I went to my car, opened the trunk and took out the shovel I carried on snowy days and began shovelling it myself. I became the highest paid snow-shoveller in the history of the Vancouver School Board. I was happy to get the exercise and make a safe path for the teachers. I was not happy, however, with how I smelled for the rest of the day. As everyone who has participated in this activity is aware, shovelling snow is hard work and causes vast amounts of sweating. I am not one who sweats without producing a pungent aroma. Sorry, everyone who got near me that day.

But it wasn't until the next day that I truly understood the dysfunction in Stan's mind. A day and a half after the snowfall, the front steps to the building still had only been cleared one shovel-width. The uncleared remainder had turned into a compacted, icy death trap, so down I went to ask Stan to clear the entire front steps. He politely obliged and got to the task right away. A short time later he stopped and disappeared.

Within minutes of Stan's disappearance, one of our science teachers appeared at my door.

"Have you seen what Stan is doing out there on the front steps?"

"Oh crap. What?"

"You have to see it to believe it."

She was not wrong. This was something I definitely needed to see myself. Stan had gone downstairs to the custodian's equipment room and taken a garden hose up to her science lab. He had connected the hose to one of the faucets and had turned on the hot water tap. He was now outside hosing the front steps with hot water.

"What are you doing, Stan?"

"It was really hard work chipping away the ice on the steps, so I thought this would be easier."

"Yes, Stan, maybe easier, but we'll end up with puddles of water all over the place that will freeze overnight. These steps will be like a skating rink in the morning."

"Oh, I guess maybe you're right. I'll get one of the night shift guys to finish clearing this." And with that, I was done with project snow removal.

Stan was not only lazy, but at times showed signs of a less-than-average understanding of some basic concepts. There was one particular time that this lack of understanding hampered the performance of his job and thoroughly bewildered me.

The first month I was at Windermere, former prime minister Pierre Elliot Trudeau passed away.

"Good morning, Stan. Former Prime Minister Trudeau died last night, and the school board has directed us to lower our flag to half-mast."

"Okay."

With great confidence I returned to my office, assured that all would be well.

Twenty minutes later, thirty minutes later, an hour later, our flag remained at the very top of the flagpole. I knew this because the flag was located directly in front of my office, and I had a full, unobstructed view from my office window. So downstairs I ventured.

"Stan, is there a problem with lowering the flag?"

"No."

"Well, why is it still flying at the top of the pole?"

"It's not, I lowered it right after you asked me to."

After all these years, I still questioned myself and my ability to know what was going on, so I asked Stan to come with me to my office and take a look. I pointed to the flag and let him have a clear look.

He was incredulous. "See, I told you. It's at half-mast."

I took another look and saw what I had seen all morning. Our flag, flying at the very top of the flagpole.

"No, it's not, it's flying right at the top, Stan."

"Hugh, I lowered it just like you asked. Are you okay?"

For a moment I contemplated that I was not okay. Maybe I had had a stroke. "And what exactly did I ask you to do?"

"You asked me to lower the flag to half-mast."

"And what exactly is that, Stan?"

"It's lowering the flag half its width." I was quite sure he was wrong, but to be sure, I sat down in front of my computer and googled "flag at half-mast."

"No, Stan, half-mast is half the length of the flagpole, not half the width of the flag. See, take a look." And in utter amazement he looked at my screen. There were even pictures.

"Are you sure?"

I wasn't sure of much, but I was sure about this.

"Yes, I'm sure. Please lower it halfway down the pole."

"Okay. If you're sure."

After waiting for way too long, our school was undoubtedly the last in the district to pay its respects to our former prime minister. I was pleased that after we received instructions from the school board to raise the flag to full mast, Stan knew how to do this and did not need direction from me.

I shared very few of my 'custodial situations' with my father, but this one was too good to pass up. I remember vividly sharing this tale of the half-mast flag with him after a couple of beers on a Sunday afternoon. To this day I remember his words: "You're making this up, aren't you?"

The Non-earthquake Earthquake

Earthquake preparedness is taken very seriously by the Vancouver School District. Everyone who works in the school system is aware of the high likelihood of experiencing an earthquake sometime while at work. Every school in the district is prepared for a quake. Each school is provided with a large container filled with water, dehydrated food, emergency blankets and what I referred to when I was the administrator responsible for health and safety as a "poop in a bag" container. Every year, schools practice the 'duck and cover' drill as well as the orderly evacuation of the school. For a period of time, part of the practice was to hide hand-picked students somewhere in the building to see if the teachers realized they were missing a student or two. However, no matter how many times you practise something, you can never be fully prepared for the real thing.

One afternoon shortly after the lunch break, I received a phone call from one of the teachers whose classroom overlooked the playing field.

"Hi, Hugh. I am looking out my window and it appears half the school is out there. What's going on?"

My usual answer to most of the questions I was asked: "I have no idea."

So out I went and discovered that yes indeed, about half the school was out there all nicely lined up in evacuation formation. There were teachers I preferred to avoid out on the field and teachers I enjoyed dealing with, typical of any staff I worked with. Jason was one of our English teachers and a really great young man, so I picked him to help me solve my confusion.

"Jason, what are you doing out here?"

"What do you mean what am I doing out here? I'm out here because of the earthquake."

For the millionth time, I was filled with that recurring feeling that I didn't know something I should.

"We had an earthquake?"

I knew immediately that I had picked the right teacher to deal with. Jason gave me a kind and generous look, as if to say, "You poor old 'out of it' man" but kept his feelings to himself.

"Yes, about fifteen minutes ago there was an earthquake. We did the 'duck and cover', and here we are wondering where everyone else is and where you are."

"I didn't feel it."

Another sad and pathetic look from Jason, but again, no words. Thank you, Jason.

I informed the classes lined up outside that the building was safe to reenter and instructed them to go back to their classrooms. After a couple of days of investigating, which included inviting the emergency protocol experts from the school board to help me, it was determined that, indeed, there had been an earthquake that approximately half the building had felt and the other half had not. A seismic engineer confirmed that this was quite possible because of the localized nature of many quakes. It was news to me that when there is an earthquake, the shaking can be so localized that only half a building may feel it. But there you go, one more thing I should have known but didn't.

At the next staff meeting, I did something I only did once in the fifteen years I was a VP. I thanked half the staff for doing something, and I thanked half the staff for doing nothing. It's good to be prepared, but delusional to think we are always going to be 100 percent prepared.

Upon reflection, I concluded that at the exact time of the earthquake I was in the men's staff washroom, standing in front of a urinal. It's a good thing I didn't feel the earth move while I was doing my business, or my business might have taken a much different course. I chose not to mention this to anyone at Windermere for fear of a repetition of the Van Tech bathroom jokes that haunted me during my time there.

The 007 Neighbour

I was the vice-principal at five different Vancouver secondary schools. I believe Windermere was the school where I was most liked and respected. Not that there was a high level of either of these at any of the schools, but of the five, Windermere, I think, would score the highest. One of the reasons for this was the staff's perception that I had an uncanny ability to prevent bad things from happening and to solve incidents that did happen. No one seemed to question how it was that I could do this at Windermere but not at Tech or Churchill. To this day, not a single person at the school knows how I did this. My secret at Windermere was that I had a spy.

My spy's name was Glen. His home was located directly behind the school, and his garage was located in the lane adjacent to the school. At Windermere, if anything bad was going on, it was happening in the lane. It is obvious to administrators where the 'hot spots' are around any school. Every school has them. Usually, they are in alleys close by; some are actually on school property in isolated corners around the building. These are the areas where drugs are sold and fights take place. Windermere's number one hot spot was the lane behind Glen's house.

Glen was a collector of used materials. He bought and sold anything that he thought he could get a dollar for. He spent most of his day in his garage stripping what he bought and separating the materials into piles he could sell. He sold a great deal of inventory from his garage and occasionally loaded up his ancient but trusty truck and drove to some mystery location where he could sell his wares.

I first met Glen during lunchtime shortly after I arrived at Windermere. I was wandering around the outside of the building, getting the lay of the land so I could discover where the Windermere hot spots were. Glen was covered in grease and greeted me with a broad smile and an offer to shake my hand, which I politely declined.

"Glad to meet you. I think you are the new VP at the school."

"Yes, I am. How do you know that?"

"I can see into your office from my kitchen window."

And to myself, Well, that's creepy.

Glen was happy to see me out in 'his' lane. He loved the neighbourhood, loved the school and was very complimentary of our students. He also was concerned about the increase in the "crap" he saw going on in his lane and hoped I would be keeping an eye on it.

It didn't happen often, but suddenly I got a brilliant idea. "Here, take my card and give me a call any time you see something going on out here. I'd really appreciate it."

Just like that, Glen and I began our mutually beneficial five-year relationship, him calling me when he saw anything going on and me pretending like I had some superpower. He would call from his garage, but he would also call from anywhere in the neighbourhood when he was driving to or from his home. I would arrive just as a fight was about to begin. I would show up just as someone was buying pot. I would swoop in during class time to confront a group of skippers.

I soon got a bit of a reputation from the students and the staff about my ability to be in the right place at the right time. Or in the eyes of the students, the wrong place at the wrong time. I was asked several times by students and members of staff how I knew suchand-such thing was going on and how I knew where it was going on. For five years, I gave the exact same answer, "It's a gift," and I would smile and walk away. It turns out that all those years ago, Bruce, my Hamber mentor, was correct. Bullshit does baffle brains.

After five very enjoyable years at Windermere, I realized I would probably be transferred one more time, so rather than wait for the powers that be to move me somewhere I didn't want to go, for the first time in my career, I requested a transfer. My good and longtime friend Randy Clark was principal at Britannia Secondary, and he had told me that one of his vice-principals was scheduled to be transferred, so I decided with four years left before I retired, it would be great to finish my career working with him.

Britannia Secondary

– 2 ½ years –

All eighteen secondary schools in Vancouver are unique. However, Britannia Secondary School is, in my opinion, the most unique in the district. It is the oldest remaining secondary school in the district and shares Canada's poorest postal code. Students at 'Brit' speak thirty-eight different languages. Approximately 28 percent of the students are of Indigenous descent. Thanks to the efforts of one of the school's previous principals, Britannia is a model of what a community school should be. On the Britannia site, there is an elementary school, a skating rink and a swimming pool. It is the only school in the district without its own library, as its students are able to use a branch of the Vancouver Public Library, which is also on site. The school boasts one of the two International Baccalaureate programs in the district. Notable alumni include Dave Barrett, former premier of BC; Tong Louie, founder of London Drugs; Angelo Branca, former justice of the Supreme Court of British Columbia; and Frank Iacobucci, former justice of the Supreme Court of Canada. Barbara Howard, internationally renowned sprinter and first person of colour to be hired by the Vancouver School Board, is also a Brit grad.

The majority of students are 'authentic' east-side kids. There is nothing phony about Brit kids. Most come from economically challenged homes and are honest to a fault. Most of them are terrific young people. Another great attribute of the school is the teaching staff. If you teach at Brit, you love Brit and Brit kids. Many teachers over the years have chosen to spend multiple years working at the school, and a significant number spend their entire career teaching at Brit. I was looking forward to learning 'the Brit way'. I was not, however, expecting the chaos and confusion that ensued during my first Brit dance.

The Old Friend, New Principal

Unlike most school dances, which are held in the school's gymnasium or cafeteria, Brit dances are held in the adjacent elementary school gym. The elementary gym is much easier to supervise than the secondary school gym. There is direct access from outside, and only one door leads to the main part of the school. There are never requests from students asking to go to their locker. Their locker is in another building. I had been told that supervising Brit dances was a dream.

About thirty minutes into the first dance of the school year, the dreaded Halloween dance, I was confronted by a panic-stricken grade-nine girl. "Sir, you need to come with us to the girls' locker room. Mandy can't breathe!"

Being told that one of your students can't breathe is rather alarming, so I followed her into the locker room and discovered Mandy lying on her back on top of one of the benches. She was having a difficult time breathing. I knelt down and took a close look at her.

"Hi, Mandy. My name is Mr. Greer. Not feeling well?" A stupid question, but I wasn't sure where else to start.

She drooled out a monosyllabic grunt, and I immediately noticed the smell of alcohol mixed with vomit. She was very pale and her breathing was laboured. I turned to one of the girls in the locker room and ordered, "Go get Mr. Clark and tell him Mr. Greer needs him right away. Then bring him here."

Randy arrived an instant later, and we decided there existed the possibility of alcohol poisoning and the situation warranted calling an ambulance. I ran out of the locker room, sprinted out the door and made the call from outside, where I could actually hear something over the deafening roar of the dance music. I have always maintained that the volume of the music at school dances is dangerous, and as a school community responsible for student well-being, we should not have allowed it. But on the multiple times I brought it up, no one paid any attention. I made the call and headed back into the locker room to let Randy know the ambulance was on its way and that I was going to wait outside for its arrival and would lead the paramedics to the locker room. Actually, the locker room was so hot, humid, loud and stench-filled from puke, I knew a few minutes of fresh air and quiet would be a wonderful respite.

Whatever I had said to the 911 dispatcher must have made an impact, because a very short time later, with lights flashing and sirens blaring, the ambulance arrived. I introduced myself to the paramedics, one of whom was a young Asian woman and the other a Caucasian man who had very white hair and a very pale complexion. (Although these physical descriptions may not seem relevant, they actually are.)

I led them into the looker room, which by this time contained only Randy and the semi-conscious Mandy. Upon entering the locker room, the male paramedic and my principal greeted each other with a friendly hug. It was obvious they knew each other quite well. The paramedics did what I had seen many paramedics do in the past. They asked questions, looked closely at Mandy, took her blood pressure and gave her oxygen. They placed her onto a stretcher and wheeled her out of the gym, into the awaiting ambulance.

I then walked over to the secondary school, to my office, looked up Mandy's home phone number and called her parents. I knew from past history that when making these kinds of calls I should never speculate as to what was wrong with a parent's child. I kept my description of the incident vague. Even though I knew she was, there was no way I was going to tell them their grade-nine daughter was stinking drunk.

The remainder of the dance went by without incident. At the conclusion of the dance, Randy and I stood at the door as the teachers were leaving and thanked them for volunteering to supervise. We said good night to the students and told them we hoped they had had a good time. Lastly, we thanked the student council members who had helped organize the dance. The other vice had left, so it was just Randy and me.

"I take it you know one of the paramedics who came tonight," I began.

"Yes, sorry, I should have introduced you to him. He's my brother." And for the millionth time in my life, I was without words.

"Your brother?"

"Yeah, my brother. His name's Sonny."

"Sonny, the pale white dude, is your brother?"

And as casually as possible, Randy replied, "Yup," and then walked away.

I was so flummoxed that I did not utter another word to Randy until we were in the parking lot getting into our cars and I managed to sputter out, "Good night."

As I drove home, my mind was working at warp speed to make sense of this, and as usual not getting anywhere. The pale white dude is Randy's brother. My good and long-time friend and now principal, Randy, is Black. Little wonder I was confused, until about halfway home when it hit me and I finally figured it out.

Several years prior to this night, at his mom's memorial service, Randy had spoken about how great it had been growing up in a large family. He also mentioned that the last child to join the family had been adopted, and his mom decided not to refer to him by the name he had been given but to call him Sonny. Her explanation for this was truly kind-hearted and loving. She had told him, and the entire family, that although Sonny didn't look like the rest of the family, he belonged in the family and was loved as much as any of the sons she had given birth to. She wanted him to remember that each and every time she called him Sonny. I wish I had met her. I think she must have been a remarkable woman. Her son, my good friend, is remarkable as well but in a different kind of way.

Randy is a very private man. For many years he lived on his own and was a devout bachelor. One Friday night, several years before Randy and I would work together at Brit, he and I and our mutual friends Bob of the Churchill letter and Bruce the Hamber philosopher met for dinner at The Keg. We had done this a few times before, and typical of previous dinners, we all ordered a steak and laughed about the silly things that only we found funny. We said good night and all went home. Four days later, I called Randy to let him know how much I had enjoyed the previous Friday and to tell him I hoped we could get together again soon. As casually as discussing the weather, Randy dropped a bombshell.

"Yeah, it was great. I enjoyed it too. It was a perfect stag."

"It was a what?"

"Stag."

"Whose stag?"

"Mine," followed by my usual stunned silence. "You still there?"

"What the hell are you talking about?"

"Oh, I guess I forgot to tell you. Elinor and I got married on Saturday."

A quick calculation determined that that Saturday was the day after our dinner.

"You got married the day after our dinner at The Keg, and you forgot to mention it?"

"It didn't matter."

"What a fool. If you had said something, you may have ended up with a free meal." For Randy it was a trade-off. A free meal or his privacy. No contest. He was happy to pay for his meal.

The Mistaken Identity

As their vice-principal, no matter how respectfully you treat students, no matter how polite, helpful and friendly you are, at every school there are going to be a handful of students who hate your guts. I don't think this has anything do with who you are but rather what you are. Some students have a preconceived notion that the vice-principal is someone to be hated, their enemy. One such student at Brit was Gabe.

Gabe hated the sight of me. We didn't have any negative history, he just decided I was crap and he was going to do everything he could to antagonize me and try to make my life miserable. I have to admit, I didn't much like Gabe either, but as the only adult in the relationship, I was respectful and as pleasant as I could manage to be. To make matters worse, Gabe's girlfriend was one of the nicest girls in grade nine. Mae was a wonderful girl. She was smart, respectful and beautiful. It is one of life's mysteries why good girls like bad boys. Another of life's mysteries is why Mae would have anything to do with this particular pain in my backside. The 'good girls liking bad boys' thing is very confusing, but it really does exist. During the time Gabe was a student at Brit, I treated him with respect, but it was a challenge for me every day. Mae doted on him. I never saw Gabe without Mae draped on his arm looking up at him with adoration. It was unbelievable. I remember thinking to myself, It could have been worse; at least she is not my daughter.

Gabe was a frequent visitor to my office. He was not only rude to me but to most of his teachers, which resulted in him being sent to the office on many occasions for an 'attitude adjustment'. He was a lost cause. Nothing I said or did had any impact on him. He also spent time with me because of his attendance. He was a constant skipper. Oh, Mae, what were you thinking?

I don't recall the issue, but one afternoon, Gabe and I really got into it. He said some things to me that he should not have said, and finally I had had enough. I directed him to sit in the outer office until I could figure out what to do with him. I knew what I wanted to do with him, but I planned to retire in the next couple of years and before that did not want to spend time in jail. I had already spoken to both of his parents on the phone many times. On one occasion, I had sent him home during the day, and before that, I had met with his parents twice. I decided I needed to up the ante, so I telephoned his mom and asked if she and Gabe's dad could come to the school and talk with me and then take Gabe home. When he saw them walk into the office, he was livid. We all went into my office and had a chat, and a few minutes later, Mom and Dad walked out with Gabe in tow. I was sure I had made my point. I was hoping they were going to have a heart-to-heart with Gabe, and he would finally get the message. Oh, how wrong I was.

About two hours after Gabe and his parents left, I looked up from my desk to find one of the school's longest serving and most respected teachers standing at my door. Mike had been a counsellor at Brit for many years and was now the community schools coordinator. For many years, he had also coached the senior girls' basketball team at the school. He was my friend and my neighbour. The Britannia School gymnasium is dedicated to him and carries his name today. It would not be an exaggeration to say that Mike is an icon at the school. On this particular afternoon, he also had a car with four slashed tires. "Hi, Hugh. Who did you piss off this afternoon?"

"What do you mean?"

"Well, whoever it was, they slashed all the tires on my car."

This was not rocket science for either of us to figure out. Mike and I drove the same car. Same make and same colour. Everyone at school loved Mike, and not a person in the building would consider slashing his tires. I, on the other hand, was never referred to as Mr. Popular and in some peoples' minds, was public enemy number one. Clearly this had been a case of mistaken identity. There was only one suspect.

Mike was remarkably calm. He told me he knew he needed new tires and maybe it was not the worst thing to let the insurance company buy him a new set. I, on the other hand, was furious. That little turd thought he was slashing my tires and was so careless and so stupid, he picked the wrong car. What a moron.

I had no evidence it was Gabe, but I didn't need evidence. My gut told me it had been Gabe. The next day, after sharing the events of the previous day and my suspicions about who was responsible, our school police officer informed me that my gut was not legally classified as evidence. Basically, without a witness, I was screwed. I knew Mae would have been at the scene of the crime, and I also knew she would never rat him out. What to do. What to do.

I pondered my options for a long time. I considered confronting him. I considered asking our police officer to deal with him. I considered a whole host of things, and then I came up with my best strategy. I would do nothing. I would let the school take care of it. I would let nature take its course. For one of the few times in my life, I made the right call.

Of course, I have no idea how it happened—this is my story and I am sticking to it—but word quickly spread throughout the building that one of our students had slashed the tires of the nicest teacher at Brit. Who would do such a thing? What an idiot they were. This was not right. This was not the Brit way. The Britannia student moral compass was outraged. People were pissed.

It is not only the teaching staff and administrators at schools who have the ability to solve student misbehaviour incidents, but students can also be effective at resolving these issues as well.

I was not unhappy to discover a short time later that the heat became just too great for Gabe and that he moved from living with one of his parents to living with the other and was going to be attending a school in another district.

The majority of the time, being proactive is the best strategy. Once in a while, being inactive is very effective, though, and leads to the best result.

The Plan B

Although it was my master plan to retire from Brit, working with Randy, it was not to be. For reasons that I never fully understood, the school board decided to do a switch of schools with Randy and another principal. So at Christmas, Randy went off to another school and my plan went up in smoke, in more ways than one. As fate would have it, not only was I not going to finish my career working with Randy, but I was also not going to finish my career at Brit.

My new principal and I had a difficult time seeing eye to eye on a few situations. I liked her as a person but often did not share her point of view about issues at the school. An example of this was how to deal with the profoundly important issue of the mouse turds under the drying kiln in the art room.

It is common practice for administrators, along with the administrative assistant, to meet every Monday morning and discuss the week's calendar. The admin assistant usually stays only for the beginning of the meeting. That leaves the principal and vice-principals to discuss current issues, problems and priorities. It was my practice to only bring topics to these meetings that I felt I needed help or support with. Not all my colleagues felt this way, and they brought up for discussion many items that I perceived as rather unimportant and not worthy of a time-consuming discussion.

One particular Monday morning, my vice-principal colleague informed us that she had received a note from our art teacher, who was unhappy about the mouse droppings she discovered under one of the kilns in her room. She wanted to discuss what to do about this situation. This in itself was a little confusing to me, as I was not sure the educational leaders in the school should necessarily be spending their time on such matters, but after forty-five minutes of turd talk, I had had enough and, without solicitation, expressed my frustration. My opinion was not appreciated by my principal, who, shortly after this meeting, was presented with an opportunity of ridding herself of my annoyance.

My transfer was not a disciplinary transfer but rather the result of some brainiac in senior management at the school board coming up with an idea to save the district a few dollars. One of the principals in the district was retiring at Christmas, and one of the vice-principals was being promoted to fill the position. The plan was to transfer one of the two Brit vice-principals or one of the two vice-principals at another high school to the school that was going to have the vacancy. This would leave a combined total of three vice-principals at the two schools. One VP at each school would be at the school full-time, and the third would work alternate days at each school. I was anointed to be the VP who was transferred to fill the vacancy left by the promoted vice-principal. As many of us suspected, this little experiment that cost me my position only lasted six months. I believe it turned out better for me than the 'floater' vice-principal, who worked at Brit one day and then Tupper the next, and so on. This 'save a few bucks' experiment created an impossible position for any one vice-principal to fill.

It was never officially announced, but I am sure that when the two principals who were at the schools affected by the reduction were meeting to discuss the situation, my principal stepped up and offered to 'sacrifice' me and keep the other vice-principal, who was a lot happier than I was about discussing mouse droppings.

Serendipitously, the vacancy was at Eric Hamber. Talk about things going around and coming around—I was to finish my career at the school where it had all begun.

Eric Hamber Secondary, Part 2

– 1 ½ years –

Thirty-two-and-a-half years had passed since I left Hamber. To my amazement, there were ten teachers on staff when I returned, all of them there when I had left, one of them my older daughter's godfather. There were also two of my former students on staff and a former classmate of my older daughter. I didn't know whether to view this as a positive thing or something to be worried about. It did not concern me that two of my former students were at Hamber. I remembered them both and had memories of positive relationships. I had been the vice-principal for my daughter's classmate and had never had any negative dealings with her. On the other hand, I was concerned about how my ten former Hamber colleagues were going to react to my return. When I left Hamber in 1976 at the age of twenty-six, I was not the most mature, gifted or 'most likely to succeed' candidate to become a vice-principal. I really hoped that during my thirty-two-year absence they all had experienced some significant memory loss about me.

When I returned, Hamber was a much different place from when I had left. I was also a different person. I was a year and a half from retiring and could hardly wait. I had never been a superstar

259

vice-principal and at this point was neither enjoying the job nor very good at it. My health was not great, and my mouth, which often had not served me well, was becoming a serious liability.

Some notable alumni had passed through during my absence, including actors Katie Findlay and Kristin Kreuk. Two other Hamber grads had been MLA Jenny Kwan and Jessica Trisko, who is evidence that beauty and brains are not mutually exclusive, as she is both a former Miss Earth 2007 and a McGill PhD graduate. The place still had a strong academic culture. Seventy percent of the grade-twelve class of 2008 graduated with honours. At the same time, Hamber supported an outstanding fine- and performing-arts program that was the envy of the district. Hamber enrolled 1,250 students, down from the 1,800 that were there when I first arrived in 1973. Another significant difference between 1973 and 2007 was the addition of a number of district special-education programs. One such program was called the Learning Assistance Class (LAC). Students were placed in the class as a result of testing that indicated they were delayed socially, emotionally and academically. Alexander was one of the more 'entertaining' students in the class. During my short stay at Hamber, we got to know each other very well.

The Costume Boy

When I arrived, Alexander was known throughout the building as 'costume boy'. In every school there are many students who choose to dress nicely to come to school, and there are many who choose to dress casually. Never had I met a student who chose to dress each day in a different costume. One day, he would be a football player and arrive dressed in full uniform, which included helmet, pads, mouthguard, tight pants and all the other necessary items to be a fully equipped football player. Another day, he would be a cowboy: cowboy boots, hat, holster and toy gun. It is never a good idea to bring a toy gun to school, but this did not dissuade him. The next day, he would be a bus driver. Hat, jacket and copies of the local bus schedules.

I have been told this is not a unique situation and there is history in other schools of students dressing in costumes. Before Alexander, at another Vancouver high school, a grade-eight boy was in the principal's office wearing army fatigues. The principal asked him what he was wearing and received a very clear reply: "It's my Rambo outfit."

"You like Rambo?" the principal inquired.

"Yep," came the reply.

"Well, I like Superman," the principal calmly retorted, "but you don't see me running around the office in a red cape and blue tights."

In itself, there is nothing wrong with dressing in a costume for school. However, when a student dresses in costume, it is guaranteed to draw attention, and it is always negative attention. Alexander was a constant visitor to my office, complaining about being bullied, harassed, picked on, pushed or some such other atrocity. He often complained that he was being laughed at. Snide comments were thrown his way. Occasionally, it was more physical, like when he wore his football uniform and for some reason that he could not understand, he kept getting tackled in the hall. Surprise, surprise.

At this point in my career, I was running low on empathy and advised Alexander that if he didn't want to get tackled, he shouldn't wear a football uniform to school. He was not impressed and informed me he was leaving my office to go to his counsellor's office and complain to her about me.

Soon after Alexander left my office, my phone rang. It was his counsellor requesting she come and discuss Alexander's situation with me. We had a brief chat and agreed to invite Alexander to join us. The counsellor more or less agreed with me and gave Alexander a similar message, except with many more empathic words. On this particular day, Alexander was dressed as a soccer player and was carrying a regulation FIFA Adidas soccer ball under his arm. The meeting did not last long, and Alexander left my office and dribbled off to class.

The next morning, I got a phone call from Alexander's grandmother, with whom he had lived for most of his life. We arranged to meet the next day, and grandma requested the counsellor also be present. I assume Alexander had convinced her that I was some kind of ogre from whom she needed to be protected. The next day, the four of us met. Grandma was dressed in a black dress that would have been suitable to greet the Queen; the counsellor in appropriate, professional garb; me in my usual jacket and tie; and Alexander dressed like a typical grade-nine boy in a T-shirt and jeans.

We had a wonderful discussion about how I felt it would be in Alexander's best interests to no longer dress in costume while at school but arrive each day in similar attire to what he was wearing on this day. He was a bit argumentative at first, but after I explained to grandma what the consequences had been for him when he dressed up, she decided that continuing this practice would not be in her grandson's best interests. Alexander began to cry when I informed him that if he ever again arrived to school dressed in a costume, he would be sent home. Blubbering through his tears he asked, "Can't I even dress up once in a while?"

And then the empathy from my counselling days kicked in. "Yes, you can. Every October thirty-first, you can come to school dressed in any costume you like." And with that he shrugged and walked off to class.

The Sponsor Teacher Returns

After a very quiet morning, which was not unusual at Hamber, I was standing in the doorway of my office perusing the main office and daydreaming about retirement when I noticed a visitor chatting with our head secretary. They were engaged in a friendly, relaxed conversation. The gentleman had his back to me, and as a result, I did not have a clear view of his face. I was able to identify that he was not a member of the staff, and because the conversation seemed to be pleasant, I had no concerns and returned to my office.

As I sat in my office contemplating what monumentally important task to next begin, my mind began to search its archives and came to the conclusion that I recognized the man in the office. My curiosity prompted me to return to my lookout and again observe the conversation between our guest and our secretary.

Eventually, our visitor turned around and saw me staring at him. His eyes met mine for only a split second before they darted up and read the name above the office door. They then returned to gaze in utter astonishment at my face.

Eventually, the penny dropped and I recognized him. I had been his student teacher at Hamber in 1972. Thirty-six years later, he was staring at the student teacher who had slagged off his best man, and he was now having a difficult time reconciling that this same idiot was working in the office of the school's vice-principal. I had never seen such a look of total confusion. I could read his mind: "This is Mr. O'Brien's office, and many other competent vice-principals, not my student teacher's office. This office belongs to educators who know what they are doing, not some arrogant know-nothing kid."

In 1972 and still in 2008, Bill was a classy guy. He composed himself and walked over to greet me. We had a brief conversation, and he left the office.

During my career, I only had three student teachers. I failed two of them. Eventually, they both became teachers. If I ever walked into a school and saw that one of them was now a vice-principal, I would not have been able to walk out, because I am certain I would have had to be carried out. I know he didn't fail me on my practicum, but the experience of discovering that I was now the vice-principal at his beloved school must have been surreal for him. Thanks, Bill, for being able to walk out and not be carried out.

The Grandpa

Every parent of an ESL student I ever met wanted their child to leave ESL (English as a second language) and be transferred into regular classes. This is one of the few constants that remained for my thirty-five years. Sometimes requests from parents to move their child out of ESL and into regular classes were based on a belief that the student had learned enough English to move 'up' to regular. These requests almost always came from non-English-speaking parents, and it always confused me how this group of parents could possibly know when their child was ready for regular classes, especially when their child's teachers felt otherwise. In spite of the recommendations from ESL teacher specialists and the data collected from testing, many parents of ESL students demanded the child be placed in regular classes. Eventually, I came to the conclusion that these parental requests often had little to do with their belief that their child would be successful but rather was based on a desire for status. It was not a good thing when your child was in ESL, especially if they had been there for a number of years. It was even harder for parents to accept this if their friend's child or a family member's child was enrolled in a regular program. It was a real fight sometimes to convince parents that their child needed more time in ESL.

One afternoon, I received a phone call from an 'advocate' who informed me they were representing the family of one of our ESL students. The family was requesting to meet with me about their child and discuss the courses he was registered in. I arranged to meet with the advocate and the parents, or rather that is what I thought I arranged. The next day, I was inundated with what I referred to at the time as a cast of thousands. I had asked our ESL department head to attend, as well as our Mandarin-speaking home–school support worker, who was responsible for translating and helping to explain any cultural differences. The family brought their own advocate and entourage, which included the mom and dad, two older sisters and two grandparents. It was a struggle, but eventually I managed to convince everyone that there were far too many people to have any kind of reasonable discussion and limited the attendees to the department head, the home–school worker, the advocate, mom and dad. Besides the 'too many opinions' aspect of such a meeting, my office was nowhere near large enough to comfortably accommodate all the participants.

The conversation did not go well. The older sisters had done very well at Hamber and had progressed through the ESL program quickly and with great success. Terrance, their younger brother, was now in his sixth year of ESL. I had seen this scenario many, many times.

I think it's great when families advocate for their children. I did the same thing for my kids, but parents need to be realistic. During the meeting, I did my very best to convince the parents that the criteria for Terrance to move into regular classes was based on results from testing and teacher assessment, not on the fact that his sisters had been able to do it.

Through the translator, Dad expressed what I had heard many times before: "My daughters were in ESL classes for only two years before they moved into regular classes. Terrance is in his sixth year in ESL. Explain this to me."

Unfortunately, my mouth, once again, engaged before my brain. "Yes, sir, I will. When your daughters attended Hamber, they were serious students and worked very hard. Terrance is lazy."

I could tell by the look she gave me that Amy, our home–school worker who was translating for me, did not want to translate what I had said. Over the years, Amy and I had participated in many family meetings and had come to know each other well. Not for the first time, Amy paused and stared at me. There was no need for her to speak; her look clearly communicated, "Please don't make me say this. It will not go well."

"Go ahead, Amy, and please translate exactly what I said." I'm pretty sure that before she began translating my words, she made a long and profound apology and maybe even mentioned the fact that I would be retiring soon.

There was deafening silence after Amy finished, and we all engaged in a short staring contest before Mom and Dad got up and exited my office. I recognized that this had not been my classiest response, but it was honest, and I think I delivered it respectfully. Fortunately, I kept my mouth shut when I contemplated saying, "You think your son should advance to regular classes in two years because your daughters did?"

Mom, Dad and the advocate left the meeting and reconvened with the rest of the family in the hall outside the office. I could hear much animated dialogue, which included a great deal of volume. Then grandpa reentered the office, grabbed a file folder from the counter and returned to the hall. A short time later, the family, led by grandpa, paraded in single file back into the office. They stood shoulder to shoulder in front of the office counter. We had a second staring contest, and then grandpa held up the file folder and exposed, for all to see, what he had printed. In large black block-capital letters he had scribed: "Eric Hamber is a murderer."

At this point in my career, I had little fight left in me, so I just stood there staring at him, shook my head, turned around and returned to my office. I had no appetite to argue with some crazy old man.

The Less-Than-Impressed Principal

This particular family was obviously not impressed with me. Neither was my current principal. My predecessor had been promoted to the position of principal and during his time at Hamber had prepared himself for his new position by assuming many of the roles of the principal. During one conversation with my principal, when we were discussing what she would do, what the other vice-principal would do and what I would do, I expressed my disagreement with being asked to do something I believed was the responsibility of the principal. With great frustration in her voice, she sputtered out to me, "But Jack always took care of that."

To which, yet again, my mouth replied before my brain engaged. "Yes, I know, but Jack was preparing to become a principal, I'm preparing to retire." Yet another moment when I knew it was time to go.

Fortunately for us both, shortly after my 'poor judgment' comment, my principal moved to the position of assistant superintendent in another district, and I was reunited with the principal I had worked with during my five years at Windermere. I knew she would be much more tolerant of me. She would be the last, and one of the best, of the seventeen principals I worked with during my career.

The Last Dance and Last Team

During my last year, I had the misfortune of supervising another dance from hell. In spite of our diligent inspection of the students as they entered the dance, several of them had snuck in quantities of alcohol and had consumed it during the dance. As the evening progressed, about a dozen of our students became very, very intoxicated, owing to a lack of oxygen in the gym, fluid loss from dancing and a total lack of experience regarding alcohol consumption. The situation got so bad that we decided to pull the plug on the dance, figuratively and literally, at nine o'clock, an hour early. We called several parents to come and collect their children because we felt our students were so drunk they were not safe to return home on their own. At ten o'clock, the last parent arrived. His grade-ten daughter was so intoxicated that she couldn't walk, so he lifted her over his shoulder to carry her to the car and she promptly vomited down his back. For me, this was a great thing. I knew when I interviewed Dad the next day, he was not going to argue with me about whether his daughter was drunk or not.

For my own self-preservation, I decided to coach the grade-eight girls' basketball team. This was one of my better decisions, as it enabled me to get out of my office by 3:30 and allowed me to interact with respectful, happy and well-behaved young people in an environment I understood but had spent very little time in during what I thought was going to be a career teaching PE. The team did not do all that well, and as a result, did not make the playoffs, but I really didn't care. It was a much-needed positive experience that reminded me how wonderful the majority of high school students really are.

Just before Christmas of 2008, I needed to renew my medication, so I made an appointment to see my family doctor. I shared with him that I had not been feeling well for several months and often felt dizzy when I stood up from my desk. I also informed him that my energy level had not been the same for some time.

He sent me to the lab for some tests and invited me to come back to his office to discuss the results. He informed me that he was concerned about my blood pressure and recommended that I not return to school after the Christmas break but take an extended period of time off. Apparently a blood pressure reading of 172/118 is not so good.

My extended Christmas break lasted until June of 2009, and that was that. After being a student at six different schools for twenty years and working at nine different schools for thirty-five years, my time in school was over. After over eleven thousand, I was out of days.

The Final Bell

The first day I walked into the Tinkerbell Cooperative Kindergarten, I was five years old and knew absolutely nothing about anything. Fifty-five years later, after almost eleven thousand days in school, I walked out of my last school and knew a little bit about a few things.

During my more than eleven thousand days, I was fortunate far beyond what I ever could have imagined and far beyond what I ever deserved. I was blessed to have been taught by dedicated teachers who not only tolerated me but inspired me. I was honoured to work with colleagues who supported me and made me a better educator. Best of all, I was entertained and amused and always kept on my toes by hundreds of wonderful young men and women.

Today, it is unusual for a person to work their entire career with one company. During their working careers, today's workers are more likely to be employed in several different jobs and with multiple organizations. I never regretted working my entire thirty-five-year career with the Vancouver School District. In reality, I had three very different careers that had little in common. Although all of them valuable to a student's education, they are entirely different in scope and challenge.

Classroom teaching is exhausting. The lesson preparation and the marking are relentless. Managing a classroom of twenty-eight to thirty teenagers is no easy task.

High school counselling is just as exhausting but in an entirely different way. The support and comfort that many students require is also relentless and demands an enormous amount of skill and empathy.

High school administration requires a skill set that few people possess. An effective administrator needs to have vast skills in understanding people, data and things. They also require a very thick skin.

I have been retired now for twelve years. I look at the Vancouver School District's list of high school administrators and recognize less than one-third of the names. The youngsters are now running the school system. This is not a bad thing. My peers and I had our time and did our best. It is now time for us to step back.

As Socrates said, "The secret of change is to focus all of your energy not on fighting the old, but on building the new."

Writing this book as part of my 'new' has been a joy for me. I began with the intention of writing a short memoir for my two (now three) grandsons. I never met my paternal grandfather, and by the time I was fifteen had lost my remaining three grandparents. I hoped to leave a small reminder to 'the boys' of what kind of a person their grandfather was and what he had done during his life.

Each time I finished a draft, I thought of a few more stories I could share with them. So I wrote another draft and then another and another.

The first draft was 6,000 words, the final draft over 90,000 words. I have clear memories of struggling to find the 250 words required to write my high school essays. Talk about being a late bloomer.

Today's students are fortunate to have the teachers they have. Educators have teaching skills and subject knowledge far beyond what my teachers had when I was a student and what I possessed when I was a teacher. They are highly trained in methodology and classroom management. Congratulations to you, educators of today, and my profound best wishes for a long and rewarding career. Thank you for your dedication and contribution.

Acknowledgements

I had contemplated writing a book for sometime. It seemed a logical extension of what I enjoyed doing during my days at school. Instead of entertaining people by telling stories and behaving foolishly, I became interested in doing the same thing through the written word. What I soon discovered was that it takes much more support from others to write a book than to publicly ad lib your own material. This project would not have been possible without the help of others, and to them I am forever grateful.

To Dianne Carr, principal; Pasqua Rubino and Nancy Wong, office support clerks at Burnaby Central; and to Dala Kawas, teacher librarian at Cariboo Hill, for their time and willingness to provide me with archived school yearbooks.

To my friends and former colleagues Iona Whishaw, author of *The Lane Winslow Mysteries*, and Gary Little, author of *To Hell and Back*, for their advice and encouragement.

To Kevan Moore, Diane Paterson, Mike Roberts and Sharon Vipond for agreeing to be my beta readers and taking the time to provide me with honest feedback.

To Linda Jones, for taking my vague notion of a cover design and creating exactly what was in my mind.

To the Granville Island Publishing team, under the leadership of Jo Blackmore, for enabling me to turn my manuscript into a book.

To Edward Zegarra and Marianne Ward, my editors, for proving that indeed "A good editor is a writer's best friend" (Heike Phelan).

To Paul DuVernet, founder and design director of Mica Design, for his creativity in preparing the layout of the book.

To my wife, Wendy, for her patience, perspective and kindness throughout this project.

Hugh Greer was born and raised in Burnaby, British Columbia. He worked thirty-five years for the Vancouver School District as a secondary school teacher, counsellor and vice-principal.

After retiring in 2009, he and his wife, Wendy, travelled extensively and have great plans to continue their adventures when possible. He is the father of two adult daughters and is blessed with the gift of three energetic and intelligent grandsons.

His reputation of being a 'late bloomer' continues. He completed *11,000 Days at School* at age seventy-one.